By the same authors

AN INTRODUCTION TO PRODUCTION AND INVENTORY CONTROL

Philips Technical Library

PRODUCTION AND INVENTORY CONTROL: THEORY AND PRACTICE

R. N. VAN HEES

and

W. MONHEMIUS

with major contributions by

A. R. W. MUYEN

BOOKS
10 East 53d St., New York 10022
(a division of Harper & Row Publishers, Inc.)

658.787
H 459

Original Dutch edition © N. V. Philips.' Gloeilampenfabrieken, Eindhoven, 1969
English edition © N. V. Philips' Gloeilampenfabrieken, Eindhoven, 1972

Published in the U.S.A. 1972 by:
HARPER & ROW PUBLISHERS, INC.
BARNES & NOBLE IMPORT DIVISION

ISBN 06 497161 9

PHILIPS

Trademarks of N. V. Philips' Gloeilampenfabrieken

Text set in 10/12 pt. IBM Press Roman, printed by photolithography, and bound in Great Britain at The Pitman Press, Bath

Preface

This book may be regarded as a continuation of 'An Introduction to Production and Inventory Control'. It gives the theoretical background of the topics discussed there. It is intended for specialists in production management and stock control, who should find the discussion given here of use in the development of methods or techniques, in the supervision or execution of practical investigations, or as a basis for courses of instruction for groups of consumers or workers in this field.

The reader will be well aware that, while the subjects dealt with in this book are not simple, the treatment given here is often simpler than the problems encountered in practice. In reality, the following complications are often found, alone or in combination: cascade effects (parallel or series); non-stationary demand; production capacity limitations. These topics are touched on in this book, but not dealt with in depth for the simple reason that the problems involved are still far from being solved. One might ask why, if this is the case, so much space has been devoted to such subjects as the (B, Q) system, the re-order level, Camp's equations and its variants.

The answer is two-fold:

— before dealing with the most difficult problems, we should master the simpler ones. Moreover, we still find that even the simpler approaches are less well known than they deserve to be, and could well be introduced for the solution of many practical problems;
— moreover, formulae for the simplified situations must be regarded as extremely valuable as a reasonable and above all understandable *approximation* to the solution for more complex problems. This point is so vital that we should like to illustrate it by a number of quotations from the literature.

Ackoff and Sasieni state:

Our experience indicates, that the results obtained from the more elaborate mathematical models seldom justify the additional computational effort that they require.
What is usually wanted in a practical problem is a good approximation that has the merit of simplicity of computation and implementation and which is easy to explain to those who must accept and use it. One must remember that the tacit assumption of fixed and known parameters is often far from realistic and the assumption of a known distribution for demand (let alone deterministic demand) is seldom justified.

In many situations the critical problem is to forecast demand over the lead time. Mélèsé writes:
' . . . seules les méthodes simples fonctionnent bien . . . '
Toute la question est justement de doser habilement la complexité des études et la simplicité des résultats.

Finally, Ackoff and Stafford Beer mention (in the last chapter of No. 16 of the ORSA series, 'The relation between OR and the computer') that their simulation showed that:

... the performance of a model depended as much on the accuracy and reliability of estimated values of its parameters as it did on its form. Consequently, in many complex stochastic situations, simple deterministic models performed as well as more complex probabilistic models or even better.

Apart from a correct insight into the desired degree of complexity of the models and methods used, it is of equal importance to consider the training and working pattern of all those who will eventually be involved in the realization and use of the new insights gained by the study of production management and stock control. This means that in each investigation where the investigator and the operator or supervisor are not the same person, training programmes form a very important part of the operational whole.

When new methods or techniques are introduced, a need is often felt for more information; or more information may be produced by the introduction. Further, other aids (for example, computers) may be involved. All these factors mean that the working pattern may be replaced by a new one, or its content may change. Since the 'working pattern' is really the same thing as the 'organization', it is important to include in each investigation a study of how the organization, the functions, the associated responsibilities and competances need to be modified to meet the new conditions.

It goes without saying that it is impossible to deal with all these topics in a single book. In fact, a number of very important aspects of this subject have not been dealt with at all, namely:

— forecasting. Forecasting may be regarded as the foundation of all work in this field, and sensitivity analysis has shown that the total variable costs are very sensitive to the quality of the forecasting;
— simulation. This method is coming to be used more and more widely; we expect that combined use of analytical methods and well-chosen simulation will bear rich fruits in the near future;
— the role of the computer. A great deal of literature exists on this subject; however, it remains true that one should always have a clear concept of one's aims and have worked out the method to be followed before using a computer. No mention has been made of the available software packages in this book. However,

the interested reader may be referred to excellent textbooks on the above subjects.

The use of statistical terms in this book may perhaps be judged to be rather careless by mathematicians. However, the fact that this book is largely based on reports and articles from many different sources means that the notation used may differ somewhat from place to place. Some symbols mean different things in different parts of the book. For example, d_t generally means the demand during a period of t units of time, while in some sections it is used to mean the demand in period no. t; further, in one particular section d_i is used to mean the demand for product i during a given period.

We should like to take this opportunity of thanking a number of people who have been associated with the writing of this book:

— Mr Schaafsma: he stimulated us to start writing this book when we worked under him; and later, when we have moved elsewhere, he constantly encouraged us to keep up the good work;
— Professor Goudriaan, from whom we have learnt much in public discussions and private correspondence;
— the many workers in planning and production control with whom we have co-operated and discussed problems.

We have learnt a great deal from all of them, maybe in particular that an existing system can seldom be called 'wrong'; the most that can be said is that it may be possible to improve it with the aid of modern tools and insights, and a great deal of effort;

— our co-authors Van Ham, Van Houten and Muyen for their friendly co-operation;
— Mr Schrakamp, a works economist who wrote a number of the internal reports used in the preparation of this book. Most of the works-economic concepts which we use in this book were worked out by discussion with him; however, any shortcomings in this connection naturally are our responsibility;
— Professor Hulshof who brought to our notice the lecture by Marx.

Finally, we should like to express the hope that this book will help to bridge what R. A. Howard called the 'practicality gap'.

Waalre, R. N. van Hees
Geldrop, W. Monhemius

Contents

SECTION III: FORECASTING (PLANS AND PREDICTIONS)

SECTION IV: CALCULATIONS ASSOCIATED WITH RE-ORDER SYSTEMS AND PRODUCTION BATCHES; INTERMITTENT SUPPLY

SECTION V: CALCULATION OF PRODUCTION LEVEL (CONTINUOUS SUPPLY)

SECTION VI: CALCULATION OF CAPACITY

SECTION VII: SOME EXAMPLES

SECTION VIII: APPROACH TO A PROBLEM

Section I: Background

1 Introduction

Any system of production and inventory control must be based upon a preliminary study of the relationship between the factors: DEMAND–INVENTORY–PRODUCTION. Each of these factors has certain characteristic features.

Demand is characterized by trend, cyclic movements and random variations. Furthermore, it is in principle impossible to forecast the demand exactly, since in the event such forecasts are invariably found to contain some element of error. There will also be differences between the real and the planned supply, which have a cumulative effect upon the stock. For this reason some form of feedback, enabling the real value of the quantity to be controlled (e.g., the inventory) to be compared with the desired value, is indispensable. Following this comparison, the production is adjusted on the basis of the difference between the two.

The inventory has two important aspects.It can be used effectively as a buffer to reduce the overall costs of stock holding and production. A properly controlled inventory is an asset which, like any other, can be made to show a profit. Moreover, articles produced for stock are available for quick delivery, which means that the inventory shortens the delivery time. This is borne out by the statement that stock is equivalent to productive capacity transferred in time. It is therefore important *for every product*, to ascertain whether this can, or cannot, be put into stock.

The production (or supply) process is characterized by the rate of production, the speed with which the production level can be varied and the manner in which this is done, and by the costs associated with such variation.

These characteristics are important in that they may have a great deal of influence upon the stock build-up and the service on delivery. A process in which it costs a great deal of time and money to vary the production level will necessitate maintaining the stock at a high level in order to ensure a reasonable standard of service. Unreliable forecasts have the same effect. It follows that the elements: demand — stock — production are of great importance and that the relationship between them is an essential factor in the study of control and stock problems. Such studies should ultimately result in the establishment of useful 'decision rules'.

The merit of decision rules, handled systematically, is on the one hand that they enable certain decisions to be delegated and on the other hand that they nevertheless give full scope for controlling the situation by changing the parameters in the decision rules. Computerization of production and inventory control would be impossible without such rules. In principle, it appears, all the rules governing inventory control can be presented in a chart, with the stock level plotted on the horizontal, and the production level on the vertical axis. The decision rules and the changing state of the system can be displayed in this chart, which is based upon a constant distribution of demand.

The relationship between production level and stock level in Fig. 1 is derived from a proposition in control theory, where the term proportional control is used for cases of this kind.

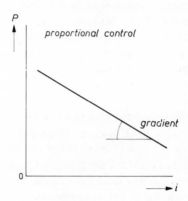

Fig. 1 Relationship between production level *P* and stock level *i* for various situations.

This means that any rise in the stock level (say, owing to a drop in sales) will have to be followed by a proportional lowering of the production level. However, the production level can often be adapted step-by-step, or the situation may only allow 'on–off' control (that is, decision as to whether or not to place an order). In some other cases the proportional control chart is superseded by an intermittent or two-step control system.

To complete the study, however, it is essential to take the stochastic behaviour of demand and production into account, together with the associated cost factors. Although this complicates the chart, the principles remain unchanged. Two aspects of intermittent production which have to be considered separately are production to order and production for stock.

Systems whereby parts for use on the assembly line are made for stock but are not, in principle, supplied from stock have been described by Burbridge [Bu 1] under the heading of 'programme controlled systems'. The particulars of his cyclic system are described in 'An Introduction to Production and Inventory Control'.

Inventory control decision rules governing delivery from stock fall into four categories, based upon two criteria:

a. Can orders be placed at any time or only periodically?
b. Does the order quantity for a given article depend partly upon the economic stock on hand at the time the order is placed?

TABLE 1

	Order quantity independent of stock at time of ordering	Order quantity dependent on stock at time of ordering
Continual possibility of ordering	(B, Q)-method	(B, S)-method
Periodic possibility of ordering	(s, Q)-method where the quantity covers consumption for more than one interval	(s, S)-method and various variants thereof
	The 'run-out list' method	'Periodic replenishment' as a special case of the (s, S)-method

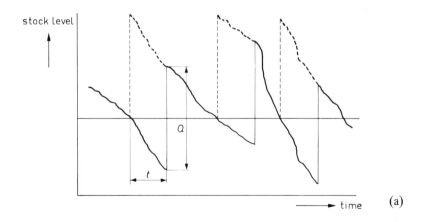

(a)

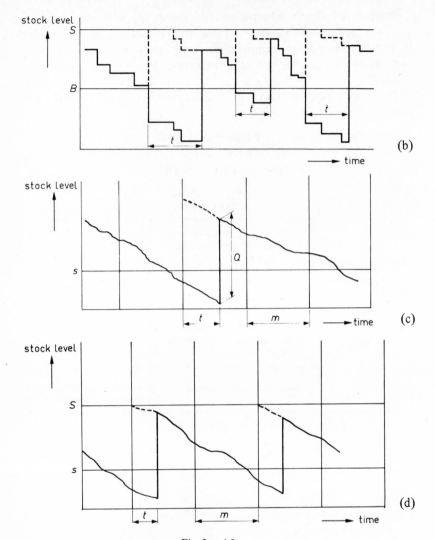

Fig. 2 and 3

Four basic forms of ordering rules
  (a) $(B\ Q)$ rule;
  (b) $(B\ S)$ rule;
  (c) $(S\ Q)$ rule;
  (d) $(s\ S)$ rule.
  ———— technical stock; t lead time;
  – – – – – economical stock; M ordering interval.

The economic stock is: the stock in stores (technical stock) plus what is on order from the supplier, but not yet received, and minus what has already been reserved by customers for a time ahead equal to the supplier's lead time. The re-order level and the buffer (or safety) stock level are indicated in Fig. 4.

The re-order level B may be defined as the maximum stock reduction which may reasonably be expected during the lead time. The buffer stock is that required to cover most discrepancies between predicted and actual demand (during the lead time).

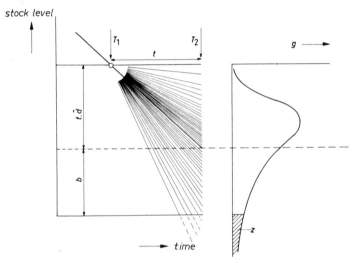

Fig. 4 Relationship between re-order level and buffer (or safety) stock level. At T_1: re-order; at T_2: ordered quantity arrives; g the distribution density for the demand.

To establish the re-order level it is necessary to know:

— the forecast average demand;
— the acceptable risk of being out of stock;
— the frequency distribution of difference between forecast and actual demand; during the lead time.

To illustrate this principle, the optimum batch size was calculated solely on the basis of Camp's formula, which only applies subject to certain conditions.

The practicability of combining inventory control with intermittent production per article and with production control, taking the limitation of productive capacity into account, is discussed in 'An Introduction to Production and Inventory Control' with the aid of an example.

The idea that every system should include standards of stock level, change-over costs, number of rush shipments and so on was also elaborated.

A complete chapter of that volume was devoted to stock chain problems, with special reference to the results of Forrester's investigations into the problems of stocks in series combined with continuous production (that is, including all the articles of the assortment).

In conclusion, the principal rules of planning were discussed:

— deliver promptly at the agreed time;
— deliver fast;
— react quickly but smoothly;
— plan with due regard to the possible effect upon costs.

A simple example illustrating these points is considered in 'An Introduction to Production and Inventory Control'.

2 General remarks on planning

2.1 The development of ideas in the planning sector

The pattern of co-operation in modern industry has become more complex as a result of an increase in the range of products and the increasing technical complexity of the production processes. The whole scale of events has widened, raising problems which were not even perceived, let alone solved, up till now.

Technical complexities foster specialization; the majority of the people involved are only concerned with an individual phase of the overall production process, so that it is necessary to organize a system of communication between people or between groups of people. To quote Verburg: 'Organization is the efficient arrangement of activities and resources'; or according to Limperg 'the creation of efficient relationships' [Ve 3].

As regards planning, promotion of efficiency will have to be focused primarily upon cost price, quantity and delivery date of the product, or in other words an answer will have to be found to the question: 'when and how should given quantities of a product be purchased, produced or distributed?'. At the same time, the difficulty of planning and controlling the development, production, sale and distribution of goods mainly arises from the complex structure of our industries.

Industrial growth has made development in the planning sector essential. This has been amply demonstrated in practice, as we may infer from the volume of literature on the subject which has appeared in recent years. However, a study of this literature soon reveals a considerable diversity of opinion as to the best way of solving planning problems, and at the same time creates a distinct suspicion that many of the theories expressed have not been subjected to adequate practical tests. It follows that the essence of the planning problem has not yet been clearly defined, which is not really surprising considering that this subject has only been under examination on a large scale for some ten to fifteen years.

The importance of studying this problem is made evident by the balance sheets of companies, large and small. It is by no means exceptional for an amount constituting more than 30% of the total capital to be invested in stocks of materials, components and end products.

More detailed studies reveal that these stocks are not always located in the right place, so that production is held up by a lack of components and the distribution channel is partly cluttered with unsaleable products. These problems have not been rendered any less obscure by the almost boundless enthusiasm for introducing electronic computers into industry which has manifested itself in the last five to ten years.

This innovation would have been more effective had a clearer distinction been made between the computer as a 'calculator' and as a means of process 'control'. 'Calculation' here means the successive execution of a series of mathematical operations which merely result in a transformation of figures. 'Control' means a very much more difficult process, namely the comparison of a norm with the (measured) reality and the preparation of a decision based on the result of this comparison. The control of *stochastic* processes is probably the most complex of all and it is precisely these processes which occur most often in production control.

Frequent attempts have been made to use the computer for both functions at once, which in many cases proved too drastic a measure. The computer specialists with their powerful aids and the planning experts with their (still) involved theories are slow in coming together, whilst both factions are convinced that their own approach is the right one, and the more important of the two. Between them is the executive, who asks for clear and if possible simple rules and directives which he can comprehend without an excessive amount of retraining. He does not get a great deal of help from difficult and still largely unproven theories, nor from pronouncements about all the wonderful things which computers can do now, or rather, will be able to do in the future.

Here we have two techniques of comparatively recent origin harnessed to a very much older skill which has fallen into disuse. The most serious outcome of this neglect, which strikes at the very essence of planning, is of course that insufficient attention has been given to the creation of training facilities. The present generation of planners are self-taught and it is therefore not surprising that no generally accepted planning doctrine has been developed so far. In order to stimulate creative thinking on a par with that which is now current in the purely technical sector, a great deal of attention will have to be given to:

a. acquiring a better understanding of the fundamentals of planning;
b. formulating rules based on this improved insight;
c. training planners at all levels;
d. defining the proper function of computers in the planning sector.

The authors' aim has been to help solve the first three problems and they trust that their two books on production and inventory control will also contribute in some measure to the fulfilment of the task mentioned in c. Only when industry is able to obtain the services of enough people with thorough training in this field will it be possible to raise the general standard of planning and control to a reasonable level.

We have not yet reached the stage at which it will be possible to provide a really comprehensive set of rules and define the exact scope of same. Nevertheless, we should be able to define the basic rules and principles more precisely than has been done so far. Further simplification will have to await the translation of these principles into accepted rules and procedures applicable to many different situations in industry. Therefore the present somewhat strained relations between the planner and the designer of planning rules are likely to persist for a considerable time.

2.2 Long-term and short-term planning

There is no point in trying to indicate, in general terms, how many years a long-term, short-term, or possibly a medium-term, plan should cover. The fact is that the forecast period depends mainly upon the production process and upon the resources, e.g. buildings, plant, scope, planned for. Because of the great diversity of processes, there will also be major differences in the *lengths* of the long-term and short-term planning periods.

A trading company engaged in buying, storing and selling has a relatively simple 'production process' with a through-put time of, perhaps, a few months. A long-term plan for such a company will cover a shorter period than one for a company which makes assemblies, manufactures components and buys materials. Although it is in many cases difficult to stipulate the required planning periods with any certainty, one or two characteristic phases can nevertheless be indicated.

The primary requirement is information as to the demand for the products which are to be sold. An inherent feature of this is that our control over the demand is only partial and that the best we can do is to try to learn as much as we can about it beforehand. An attempt can be made to influence the demand, say, by launching an advertising campaign, but here again the effect can only be estimated. The overall scope of the market will also have to be predicted.

Since various uncommitted institutions such as the national planning bureau produce forecasts of this kind, it is usually possible to arrive at a reasonably accurate estimate. In many cases this is a safe course, because the total market is often more stable than a company's individual share of it. The demand for hearing aids, say, is a good example; this demand is very stable and therefore readily predictable. However, our individual share of the market is very much more difficult to forecast; hence we often discover that our expectation has erred systematically on the high side. The total market and the individual share of same together constitute the selling plan. The selling plan is not a datum; it is a target in respect of which methods have to be worked out to enable the planned share of the market to be realized. The content of the selling plan will have to be known, or in other words it will have to be translated into terms of capital, space, man hours, machine hours and sales capacity required. For this we require characteristic values and standards reflecting the relationship between these quantities and the products. The expression will be very approximate initially, but will become more detailed as it approaches realization.

The growth of efficiency is certainly a factor of major importance in planning for several years ahead. It is known that this growth is also often subject to a certain natural law, namely that the production costs associated with mechanization and increased productivity are a negative exponential function of time. In a fast expanding market the adverse effects of errors in the forecast and in the calculation of capacity are less noticeable because any capacity acquired prematurely (i.e. temporary over-capacity) quickly becomes productive as a result of this rapid growth. Very much greater accuracy is necessary in a more gradually expanding market where, say, failure to take the predictable long-term increase in efficiency into account may result in over-capacity persisting for some time.

How accurate the forecast should be therefore depends very much upon the market. The forecast may be mainly quantitative or mainly qualitative, depending upon the nature of the product.

Quantity forecasting is particularly important in the case of stock and catalogue goods such as domestic appliances, entertainment products and consumer goods. On the other hand, quality is more important than quantity in the production of, say, professional products in small quantities. Here it is as important to plan the development as the production; generally speaking, such planning will cover a longer period than for products produced in large quantities.

In the latter case development is followed by mass production, the two being planned separately, whereas in the former case development, production and testing are all included in the overall project plan.

Another term used in the literature as well as 'production planning' is 'production *control*'. The two have different meanings. Production planning means, of course, the formulation of a plan, or in other words marking out a specific course of action to be followed exactly. 'Control' means directing, governing, guiding and supervising. Accordingly, production control may be defined as: directing or guiding the production process so that this keeps as closely as possible to the original plan.

There is also a difference in the relative intricacy of the two tasks. Planning may become intricate owing to the use of exacting mathematical methods. This is so with mathematical programming, for example linear programming as a means of establishing an optimum production plan or calculating growth curves involving many different influential factors which may themselves be complex functions. Translating the plan into terms of components required or into man and machine-hours may also be an intricate and therefore very exacting task.

Control involves altogether different problems. As applied to production, control usually means the continual (dynamic) regulation of processes affected by chance (stochastic processes). This implies that a knowledge of processes and the laws governing them is indispensable and that some practical experience of controlling stochastic processes is also necessary to the people concerned with these matters. Solving these problems of control and adapting the solution to practical situations is usually more difficult than the task of preparing the original plan.

Acquiring the ability to detect and recognize incidental or random variations in production processes and sales is an important step towards solving production control problems. This means accepting the fact that plans rarely work out exactly and that forecasts are never entirely accurate. The greatest need for effective control procedures exists where incidental variations occur most frequently. Systematic measurement of differences between plan and reality coupled with the use of decision rules to ensure that these differences react with the original plan so as to restore the process to an optimum level was unheard of until recently.

The definition of situations subject to random variations is the special function of statistics; statistics would be meaningless without the concept of the 'standard deviation', and the involvement of statistics in production control is merely a natural outcome of the recognition and acceptance of random deviations between plan and reality.

The longer the period covered by the survey, the less significant will any individual deviation become, because positive and negative deviations then tend to strike a balance. The principal task in long-term surveys will be to modify the plan in response to recognized *systematic* deviations, whereas in the short term it will be more important to adjust the process in response to random deviations.

The latter procedure, in particular, has received a great deal of attention in recent studies of planning problems; statistics are an essential feature of this approach. 'Production control' of this kind will be discussed at length later in this volume.

Stock builds up because, for technical reasons, two consecutive phases of production are not synchronized exactly or cannot be brought into exact balance, or because in the circumstances it costs less to tolerate this build-up than to insist on a balance. Another reason is that the impracticability of exact forecasting makes stock holding essential in order to allow for random deviations. Hence inventory 'control' is a rather more passive process than the production control mentioned earlier, although in essence the two are very much the same.

2.3 Planning and control of production and development

The object of planning, whether for production or for development, is to ensure that the necessary resources are made available at the right time. In both cases, norms have to be established for man-hours and for machine-hours; such norms are an essential feature of reliable planning. They are more difficult to determine in the development sector than for ordinary manual work, but special planning techniques, like PERT, nevertheless give a great deal of scope for devising reliable plans and for forecasting the probable consequences of errors in timing.

Apart from the calculation and co-ordination of resources, cost factors also play a major part in production planning, and should be given due consideration in the determination of production runs and production levels. As the range of planning and control methods involving the principal influential factors widens, it will become possible to evaluate these cost factors more systematically.

The above technical approach to control is becoming more and more prevalent in mass production and long-run production. The elements of uncertainty in forecasting, rejects and tempo (or rate of output) are being processed statistically in production and inventory control.

In contrast to mass production is the planning and control of a one-off project, such as the construction of a ship, a building, etc. Here, a more deterministic approach is employed, e.g. with the aid of *critical path* planning methods. Elements of uncertainty as regards time and resources required can be introduced through individual activities, but are very much less important than the random variables involved in the control of mass production processes. The approach is highly deterministic; focused upon detail. There is a wide range of variants between project planning and the planning of mass production processes.

Should the short-term planning (plant planning, scheduling) of a metalware factory or engineering works handling hundreds of batches or orders per week be approached statistically or as a project? There are tendencies in both directions. In an 'engineering works' type of factory, orders can be controlled through the use of 'priority rules' as they are called. These rules (in fact 'decision rules') govern the sequence in which the orders should be processed in each phase of production in order to achieve the end in view.

This end may be: a high level of plant utilization, a short order-throughput time or a minimum of variation in the difference between the forecast and attainable throughput times per order. These priority rules are based upon a statistical analysis of the future pattern of incoming orders, the number of operations involved, the distribution of the operation times, the operation-sequence pattern and so on. With the aid of such analysis, parameters are established in the decision rules. The order-flow control rules thus obtained are based upon a statistical approximation.

The deterministic approach (e.g. critical path methods) is at present developing from a single-project system to one involving the simultaneous planning and control of more than one project. Interest is now focused on an approach whereby several projects can be planned with due regard to the resources of the departments concerned. Where several projects, together comprising a large number of individual activities, are to run side by side, there is distinct evidence of a trend away from the traditional one-off project towards the sort of system which exists in large engineering works, which have to deal with a variety of jobs using various groups of resources.

The machine allocation and timing of the operations involved in each job have to be decided beforehand.

Of course, the statistical approach also requires a knowledge of the number and sequence of operations and of elementary plant planning.

The control function is exercised mainly in accordance with the above priority rules and therefore allows the official concerned a good deal of latitude. In the deterministic approach more emphasis is placed upon the anticipation of details and interactions in order to arrive at, say, a more detailed specification of plant utilization; on the one hand this allows the manager less latitude, but on the other hand it enables more factors to be processed systematically in order to achieve greater economy. The processing of large quantities of information (e.g. by means of a computer) is expensive. The costs involved will have to be weighed against the gains in terms of increased efficiency of operators and plant.

The amount of detail to be aimed at in planning will therefore be governed by the costs of information processing and the efficiency of the plant available.

2.4 Flexibility

What does flexibility mean and why is it necessary?

The answers lie in the fact that it is impossible to forecast the total demand from customers exactly, so that companies catering for this demand will have to be able to respond quickly to unforeseen changes. To be successful commercially, they must keep pace as far as possible with such changes in order to avoid having to disappoint customers through inability to meet their requirements promptly, since failure to do so would mean forfeiting both sales and good will. Accordingly, the production process will have to be adaptable, or, as we usually put it, flexible. We use this word 'flexible' in a more restricted sense than Malotaux [Ma 2] and Verburg [Ve 2], who give it the wider meaning of exploiting new opportunities in a particular market sector, new technical developments and so on. Nevertheless, many of the remarks made by these two writers are valid in our case also. For example, although optimum, rather than maximum, flexibility should be the aim, we entirely agree with Verburg [Ve 2] that: 'In very many cases, flexibility tends to be below, rather than above the optimum level'.

If flexibility in the present sense may be taken to mean the speed of reaction to a sudden change or trend, then the following is a suitable measure of it: the interval between the occurrence of a systematic effect and the resultant change of production level. To achieve a high degree of flexibility, then, we must:

— recognize systematic deviations promptly
— adjust the process as quickly as possible to the new level of demand.

Of course, increased flexibility is not achieved without effort. Short preparation times, reaction times, throughput times and lead times make for greater flexibility. Therefore, the obvious way to make the process more flexible is to find ways of *shortening* these times or if possible *eliminating* them altogether. This is usually done by first analyzing the procedures involved and then simplifying and accelerating them. Motion time standards for simple administrative work should be given due consideration in this process. Another way is to introduce planning procedures ensuring shorter throughput times.

Eliminating some of the times is often simply a matter of reorganizing, particularly as regards:

— the linking of activities in parallel
— the elimination of redundant activities
— the elimination of activities through changes in the system of organization.

This approach is particularly effective in dealing with production processes in which there are many consecutive links. Such long chains not only react relatively slowly, but are also prone to produce an ominous build-up at the end of the chain when the reaction to sales variations is too abrupt. Accordingly, chain problems are well worth studying; Forrester's work 'Industrial Dynamics' provides much useful information on this subject.

Consideration of the technical and commercial aspects of flexibility together leads us to a remarkable and very significant conclusion. Whereas some flexibility in the production process is essential owing to the inherent inaccuracy of forecasts, the need for flexibility is inversely proportional to the accuracy of the forecast. Technically, flexibility is governed by lead times and throughput times in the production process. The shorter these times, the greater the flexibility. Shorter reaction times resulting in increased flexibility enable the forecast period to be reduced, which in turn increases the accuracy of the forecast and makes the flexibility of the process less critical.

Shortening throughput and lead times thus greatly enhances the overall flexibility on the one hand by making flexibility *less critical* from the commercial point of view and on the other hand by increasing the *technical* flexibility. This goes a long way towards bridging the gap between what is technically possible and what is commercially desirable. An important factor in the elimination of throughput times and lead times is delivery from stock.

As explained in 'An Introduction to Production and Inventory Control', 'stock' is equivalent to 'production capacity shifted in time'. To put it in another way, delivery from stock means, in effect, that production reacts to forecasts of demand in advance of the actual demand. The result is that not only the production times, but also the waiting times (which together constitute the 'lead time') are eliminated altogether.

The reaction times of chains consisting of sales — assembly — sub-assemblies — components — materials can be shortened by holding stocks of components and materials. When the flexibility is improved in this way, the necessary materials, components and assemblies can be divided into different categories, expensive or inexpensive and specific or universal.

Whether a component is classified as specific or universal usually depends mainly on the predictability of the demand for it. The catch-phrase: 'universal components may properly be held in stock' simply means that: 'because universal components are widely used, the demand for them can be forecast with reasonable accuracy so that there can be no harm in building up a stock of them'. Predictability is therefore the criterion and the descriptions 'universal' and 'specific' are merely indications of this.

Inventory and production control as applied to inexpensive, universal articles present no problem; the rules governing them can safely be generalized and simplified considerably.

Expensive universal articles have to be studied more carefully and require more precise methods of calculation.

Still more careful forecasting of demand is necessary in the case of inexpensive, but specific components; the quantity required can probably be calculated on the basis of the demand as deduced from the assembly plan. If so, the forecast thus obtained will enable the components to this class to be controlled in the same way as inexpensive, universal components.

Usually, the group of expensive, specific components constitutes only a small fraction of the whole. No general pronouncements can be made concerning them.

With the aid of the ideas defined in this book, then, it will often be possible to make an approximate estimate covering much of the overall assortment of articles. To sum up, different combinations of the following aspects will have to be considered:

TABLE 2

	Use of the particular material, component or assembly is:	
	specific	universal
Inexpensive	in stock; careful forecasting	in stock; simple rules governing forecasting and inventory control
Expensive	special arrangements depending upon product and production process	in stock; inventory control governed by more complex rules involving many cost factors

2.5 Chains; information and stocks

Control of production levels in production processes involving numerous phases (chains) has been discussed in detail by Magee [Ma 1] in 1958, by Forrester [Fo 1] in 1961 and by Brown [Br 1] in 1963. Control is obtained mainly through good inventory control and through the correct interpretation of reliable information. Each link in the chain may be regarded as a process comprising: demand, stock, production.

When a link in the chain solely issues orders (derived from the stock and the demand) to its predecessor and if each link employs this procedure, then the links at the end of the chain will no longer be able to form a reliable estimate of the actual demand. Brown demonstrates this with the aid of an example. He regards the entire inventory system in the chain as a pipeline with the manufacturer pumping goods into it at one end and the customer extracting them from the other end. Any delay in response to the customer's demand, together with the individual delays occurring in each link (amongst other things owing to the existing stock), causes a disastrous pile-up. The effect is comparable to what happens to a car at the end of a file which suddenly accelerates or stops (chain collision). His comment:

'It may be cheaper in the long run to pay for a watermeter at the far end than to try elaborate techniques of forecasting from poor data'.

The propagation of, and reaction to, real demand is a matter of prime importance. New aids to information processing now give scope for rapid expression and dissemination of this information.

Reaction to possible fluctuations in demand will have to be smoothed, while the links nearest the customer will have to keep stocks at the lowest possible level.

2.6 The application of electronic data processing

Side by side with the development of insight into planning and control systems, the present generation has seen the creation of progressively more and better aids to data processing. Although so far it is not clear just how far the range of computer applications is likely to extend, there is every reason to suppose that there will be an even more marked increase in the use of computers in the years immediately ahead.

In order to find the most rational approach to a wider use of computers, it is useful to define one or two characteristic features of these devices.

— very fast calculation;
— great accuracy;
— ability to make 'logical decisions';
— ability to complete a long and complex programme of calculation without human intervention;
— capacity to store a considerable volume of data in the 'memory' (or store) in such a way that this is readily accessible.

It will be evident from this summary that the machine is capable of performing some tasks faster and more accurately than a human being. Our aim must be to make the most effective use of these facilities. There is nothing essentially new in this idea, since mechanization and automation were introduced in the technical sector some considerable time ago. Because theories as to the correct use of machines were also evolved in that sector, a great deal can be learned from a comparison of mechanization there and as applied to information processing.

Some of the facts which emerge from this comparison are: the degree of mechanization required; the risks involved in imitating the existing process with the aid of machines; the need to introduce mechanization by degrees, starting with the simplest operations. The main advantage of this comparison is that it enables us to learn from mistakes made in the past and thus save time and money. Perhaps the most important lesson of all is that human beings must be given time to accustom themselves to mechanization before they can be expected to recognize its value. The step-by-step approach offers most opportunity for this.

Note

The purpose of presenting a more or less general outline of the situation in this chapter is to enable the reader to place the material dealt with in this book in its correct context. The subjects discussed come mainly under the heading of 'control' and therefore refer in the main to short-term problems. The intention is to give a general insight into such matters rather than general rules applicable to them.

Section II: Statistical Inventory Control

3 The importance of mathematical statistics

We have shown in 'An Introduction to Production and Inventory Control' how important it is to acquire a proper understanding of probability theory and a knowledge of statistical laws as applied to production and inventory control. Natural laws were discussed in Chapter 3 of that book, the cumulation of deviations was covered whilst the terms 'standard deviation' and 'fluctuations' were defined in connection with the re-order level.

A separate chapter of the present volume is devoted to 'statistical inventory control'. This will not be presented as a concise course in statistics, since that subject has already been dealt with very thoroughly in the literature. Instead we have decided to base our remarks on the assumption that the reader is familiar with the basic principles of the theory of probability and mathematical statistics as discussed, say, by Moroney [Mo 1]. In the coming chapters, therefore, we shall merely:

— redefine one or two of the terms employed, at the same time discussing the notation;
— talk about one or two relatively novel frequency distributions particularly suitable for our purpose;
— lead up to the specific applications which we shall be discussing later.

At the same time, we feel obliged to take this opportunity to stress the importance of statistics, as follows.

Anyone who has been in any way involved in the planning of a project will have heard the exasperated exclamation of the practical man faced with yet another detailed piece of planning or sales forecasting: 'All this is just guesswork. We all know it never works out in practice'. True enough. Statistics confirm it. In a way, statistics could be defined as 'the theory of practical matters'.

Thus statistics prove that the practical man is right to rebel against the unwarranted suggestion of accuracy and reliability implicit in plans and forecasts. But they do not bear him out if he adds 'You can't plan an industry like ours. There are too many variables and figures tell us nothing'. It is the final statement that 'figures tell us nothing' which is disputed by statisticians.

As explained in Chapter 3 of 'An Introduction to Production and Inventory

Control', the object of statistics is to define natural laws which exist in, and despite, all forms of irregularity. The following example illustrates this point.

An assembly plant produces relatively few end products; each of them is manufactured continuously, or in other words a certain assembly capacity is devoted continuously day after day to the same product. Let us examine one of these products more closely. The planned assembly output for the weeks ahead is invariably 120.

Now, what happens in reality?

The real production is brought forward from week to week, producing the survey given in Table 3. It is therefore quite true to say that 'none of it tallies', since there is not one week in which exactly 120 products were assembled. But do the figures really 'tell us nothing'? Those who check the deviations line by line with the departmental supervisor do in fact incline towards that opinion.

A surplus left over from the previous week was finished in week 1. Most of the work had already been done, but one component was lacking.

In week 2 a slow-down occurred owing to defects discovered in a batch of components, which added to the time required for assembly.

In week 3 in order to make up some of the time lost the previous week special attention was given to the speed aspect of performance.

In week 4, one of the assemblers was absent through illness. She was back at work in week 5. Another girl became ill in week 6, followed almost immediately by still another. Since the other departments were also being plagued by illness, it was impossible to 'borrow' a replacement.

TABLE 3
OUTPUT, PLAN AND REALITY

Week no.	Plan	Reality	Deviation
1	120	122	+ 2
2	120	115	− 5
3	120	124	+ 4
4	120	115	− 5
5	120	122	+ 2
6	120	105	−15
7	120	91	−29
8	120	115	− 5
9	120	111	− 9
10	120	123	+ 3
11	120	128	+ 8
12	120	118	− 2
13	120	125	+ 5

The worst blow came in week 7, when the assembly line was held up for an entire day owing to a shortage of one of the principal components. In week 8 one of the girls was still away ill and the others showed very little zest for work. This situation persisted throughout week 9.

In week 10 the target was reached again for the first time since the troubles began and in week 11 a girl from another department gave a certain amount of help; output might have been higher in week 11, but for a persistent delay in the delivery of one of the components.

Similar explanations can be found for subsequent deviations. Every deviation has its story or stories and the reason why things went as they did is always perfectly clear after the event.

Another thing which is always obvious in retrospect is that the particular turn of events could never have been foreseen. And this is true enough. No one could have foreseen that a given girl would be ill on a given day; or that a given component would be conspicuous by its absence on a given day. In this sense the situation is indeed unpredictable.

But a different kind of forecast can certainly be made. After studying the given output figures and others of a similar nature for this and other products over a somewhat longer period, it is possible to make a pronouncement of the following kind:

Next week the real output will be not less than 100 or more than 140; there is only about one chance in twenty that this forcast will prove to be incorrect.

Pronouncements of this kind are precisely what is required, and vitally so, for stock calculations.

Similar natural laws enabled the French police to predict in 1965 that traffic accidents would claim about 4000 victims during the holiday period; of course, they were unable to produce a list of names beforehand.

An understanding of statistical phenomena and a knowledge of the principal laws of statistics and its methods are therefore essential for establishing realistic systems of production and inventory control.

4 Stochastic quantities, probability distributions and moments

We shall confine ourselves as far as possible to the notation advocated in the Netherlands by, amongst others the 'Mathematisch Centrum' (Mathematics Centre) (M.C.) in Amsterdam [Kr 1].

Stochastic (or random) variables will be denoted by italics (e.g. x or d) underlined. A stochastic variable is one whose value is entirely a matter of chance (like the number which turns up when a dice is thrown).

If a stochastic variable x can only assume discrete values (for example: the number of orders per week), then $P(x) = P[x = x]$ is the probability that the variable x will assume a specific value x.

Since the number of possible values of x_i is infinite in theory and the sum of all the probabilities must be unity, we have

$$\sum_{i=0}^{\infty} P(x_i) = 1 \tag{1}$$

The stochastic variable x then has a discrete or discontinuous probability distribution.

The 'distribution function' of x is given by

$$F(x) = P[x \leqslant x] \tag{2}$$

For a discontinuous probability distribution, the distribution function is of course a step function.

The continuous probability distributions mentioned in this book are probability distributions in which the variable can assume any of the values throughout a given range continuously, whilst $F(x)$ is continuous and differentiable for all these values.

The density function $f(x)$ of the distribution is defined by

$$f(x) = \frac{\mathrm{d}}{\mathrm{d}x} F(x) \tag{3}$$

now we have

$$\int_{-\infty}^{+\infty} f(x)\, dx = 1 \tag{4}$$

and

$$P[x_1 \leqslant \underline{x} \leqslant x_2] = \int_{x_1}^{x_2} f(x)\, dx = F(x_2) - F(x_1) \tag{5}$$

The mathematical probability $E(\phi\,(\underline{x}))$ of a function of a stochastic variable is defined by

$$E(\phi(x)) = \sum_{i=-\infty}^{+\infty} \phi(x_i)P(x_i) \tag{6}$$

for a discrete probability distribution and by

$$E(\phi\,(\underline{x})) = \int_{-\infty}^{+\infty} \phi(x)f(x)\, dx \tag{7}$$

for a continuous distribution.

The following are special cases:
1. The mean value of $\underline{x}$ itself (denoted by μ)

$$\mu = E(\underline{x}) = \sum_{i=-\infty}^{+\infty} x_i P(x_i) \tag{8}$$

and

$$\mu = E(x) = \int_{-\infty}^{+\infty} x f(x)\, dx \tag{9}$$

2. The variance σ^2 of $\underline{x}$. This, as we have seen, is deduced from

$$\sigma^2 = E\{(\underline{x} - E(\underline{x}))^2\} \tag{10}$$

For a discrete probability distribution, then, we have

$$\sigma^2 = \sum_{i=-\infty}^{+\infty} = (x_i - \mu)^2 P(x_i) \tag{11}$$

For a continuous probability distribution

$$\sigma^2 = \int_{-\infty}^{+\infty} (\underline{x} - \mu)^2 f(x)\, dx \tag{12}$$

An alternative expression for (10), which we shall require later, is obtained as follows

$$\sigma^2 = E(\underline{x}^2) - (E(\underline{x}))^2 \tag{13}$$

or
$$E(\underline{x}^2) = \sigma^2 + (E(\underline{x}))^2 \tag{14}$$

5 Some theoretical distributions

5.1 Exponential distribution

Let us now consider the distribution density of the interval t between two consecutive events in circumstances identical with those in which the number of
events per time unit follows a Poisson distribution:

$$P(0) = e^{-\mu} \qquad (15)$$

The probability that no event will take place in t consecutive periods is equivalent to $(e^{-\mu})^t = e^{-\mu t}$.

The probability that the interval $\underline{t}$ is between the values t and $t + dt$ is equal to
the probability that no event will take place during t time units, multiplied by
the probability that an event will occur in the subsequent short time span dt.

Formulated

$$f(t)\,dt = e^{-\mu t}\,\mu\,dt = \mu\,e^{-\mu t}\,dt \qquad (16)$$

This distribution, which is continuous, is called the (negative) exponential distribution. From definitions (9) and (12) and by means of partial integration, we can
readily ascertain that for this distribution

$$E(\underline{t}) = \frac{1}{\mu} \qquad (17)$$

and $\qquad \sqrt{(E\{\underline{t} - E(\underline{t})\}^2)} = 1/\mu \qquad (18)$

Accordingly, an exponential distribution with mean and standard deviation a
can be formulated as follows

$$f(t) = \left(\frac{1}{a}\right) e^{-t/a} \qquad (19)$$

The curve in Fig. 5 shows the shape of such a probability distribution. This
diagram illustrates, for classes of a width a, the probability that the variable t will
assume a value within the class.

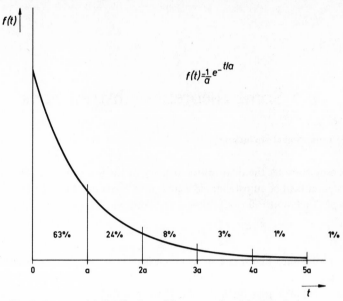

Fig. 5 Exponential distribution with mean and standard deviation α.

The distribution function $F(t)$ is readily established as follows

$$F(t) = \int_0^t \mu e^{-\mu\tau}\, d\tau = 1 - e^{-\mu t} \qquad (20)$$

Therefore $\qquad\qquad\qquad P[\underline{t} > t] = e^{-\mu t} \qquad\qquad\qquad (21)$

As an initial indication of whether a collection of observations encountered in practice bears any resemblance to an exponential distribution, $P[\underline{t} > t]$ can be plotted against t on single log paper. The line thus obtained should be virtually straight, since from (21) we have

$$\log P[\underline{t} > t] = -t\mu \log e \qquad (22)$$

Because the probability that an event will occur in the future does not depend upon what has happened in the past, the negative exponential distribution constitutes the probability distribution not only for the interval between two consecutive events, but also for the interval between any given moment and the next event to occur after this.

A table of powers of e is appended (appendix no. 3).

5.2 The gamma distribution

A theoretical distribution having many uses in studies of waiting times and stocks is what is known as the gamma distribution. This is a single-peaked, continuous frequency distribution, whose coefficient of variation can be varied between 1 and 0. Moreover, this distribution lends itself well to mathematical treatment [Kl 2].

We shall employ only those gamma distributions whose starting points are at 0. The general form of these distributions is as follows.

$$f(x) = Ax^{n-1} e^{-x/a}, \ x \geqslant 0 \tag{23}$$

where a is the scale parameter governing the mean value for a given form. The parameter n is called the form parameter and governs the shape of the curve. For integral values of n, A takes the form

$$A = \frac{1}{a^n (n-1)!} \tag{24}$$

The gamma distribution may be regarded as the distribution of the sum of n independent values drawn at random from an integral exponential distribution having a mean a.

From (23) and (24), a gamma distribution with $n = 2$ is

$$f(x) = \mu^2 x e^{-\mu x}, \ x \geqslant 0$$

It can also be shown that the sum of two quantities following gamma distributions, having the same scale parameter a but with form parameters n_1 and n_2, itself follows a gamma distribution with a scale parameter a and a form parameter $(n_1 + n_2)$. Other equations applicable to the gamma distribution are $E(x) = an$ and

$$\sigma^2 = E\{x - E(\underline{x})\}^2 = na^2$$

It is often convenient to determine the chances of excess for the gamma distribution by making use of the relationship between this and the χ^2 distribution (chi-square distribution) [Pr 2].

The reason is that $\chi^2 = \frac{2x}{a}$ is found to follow an χ^2 distribution having $2n$ degrees of freedom, if $\underline{x}$ follows a gamma distribution with parameters a and n. A table of chances of excess for the gamma distribution is given in Appendix 4. The usual problem encountered in practice is that of adapting a gamma distribution to a number of observations. If the mean $\bar{x}$ and standard deviation s of these observations have been calculated, then the simplest way to adapt a gamma distribution is as follows

calculate n from
$$n = \left(\frac{\bar{x}}{s}\right)^2$$

and then a from
$$a = \left(\frac{\bar{x}}{n}\right)$$

Although this is not the most efficient method statistically, it is nevertheless preferable to others in view of its simplicity [Ho 1].

Towards higher values of n, a normal distribution provides a better approximation of the gamma distribution; for the purposes of stock control, a sufficiently close approximation is usually obtained above $n = 20$; a different limit of $n = 50$ is required only for the tail of the distribution (probabilities of error 1% and lower) (see also Appendix 4).

6 Fluctuation of demand per product

In industrial practice, demand is invariably defined as a quantity per period. The succession of figures representing the demand for a given product constitutes a time series. Let d_t denote the demand in period t.

A time series usually has three components:

— a trend, defined by M. G. Kendal [Ke 1] as 'a smooth, broad motion of the system over a long term of years', whereby the definition of long depends, as Kendal rightly remarks, upon the time span covered by our study. We can never be sure that a trend is not itself part of a long-term fluctuation;
— cyclic motions, or oscillations, taking place more or less regularly about the trend;
— random fluctuations which may be regarded as values drawn, possibly independently, from a given frequency distribution.

Incidental effects also occur, albeit rarely; for instance an increased demand for TV receivers before the Olympic Games.

One or two simple and fairly common instances of demand behaviour will now be discussed, beginning with those which do not involve a trend or cycle.

6.1 Stable situation

A situation will be described as stable if the successive demand figures may all be regarded as drawn from the same frequency distribution, or in other words if neither trend nor cyclic effects are involved. Thus the expected demand is not a function of time.

Three special instances of this stable situation are particularly worth mentioning.

6.1.1 The Poisson process

In some cases, successive demand figures behave as though drawn *independently* from a Poisson distribution. The interval between two consecutive customers

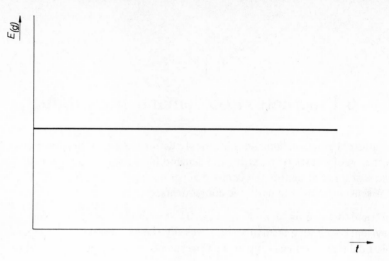

Fig. 6 Stable situation.

follows an exponential distribution and the 'demand' of each customer is for 1 product.

According to Goudriaan [Go 1], examples of such behaviour are to be found in the demand for medicines, coats, shoes, toasters, bicycles, machine tools and so on.

If the weekly demand follows a Poisson distribution, so also (in the stable situation) does the fortnightly and monthly demand.

In such a situation, then, we have

$$\sigma_t(d) = \sigma_1(d)\sqrt{t} = \mu\sqrt{t}$$

where $\sigma_1(d)$ is the standard deviation of the demand in a period;
$\sigma_t(d)$ is the standard deviation of the demand in a time span equivalent to t periods;
μ is the average demand in one period.

We must emphasize that this formula holds good only on the above assumption that successive demand figures are drawn independently.

Fig. 7 illustrates the relationship between t and $\sigma_t(d)$. If μ itself were to follow a trend or cycle, then $\sigma_t(d)$ would of course increase more steeply than Fig. 7 suggests.

A variant of the Poisson process is the situation in which the number of customers does in fact follow a Poisson distribution, but the order quantity is other than unity. At the same time the order quantity is constant.

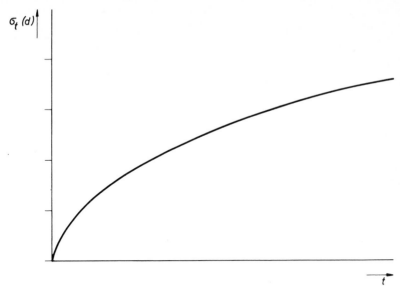

Fig. 7 Relationship between t and $\sigma_t(d)$ when the demand
follows a Poisson distribution.

This situation arises when products are sold in standard unit packages each
containing P products.

If the frequency distribution of the number of orders follows a Poisson distribution with mean μ, then the following applies to the frequency distribution of
the number of products sold

$$E(\underline{d}) = \mu P$$
$$\sigma(\underline{d}) = P\sqrt{\mu}$$

Here we have a Poisson distribution with a transformed x-axis; see Goudriaan [Go 1],
Marshall and Boggess [Ma 3], and Bosch [Bo 3].

Bosch has the following to say on the subject of inventory control as applied
to spare parts:

'The system outlined here and the associated tables are based on the assumption that the usage per time unit (e.g. one week), expressed in terms of a suitable
unit of quantity, follows a Poisson distribution, at any rate approximately.

When the average usage for each individual repair is chosen as the unit of quantity
it is found to meet this requirement very well.

From this point of view, then, one withdrawal of 100 parts is by no means the
same thing as ten withdrawals totalling 100 parts.

Accordingly, an estimated annual usage of 200 kg should be expressed as 20 × 10 kg, where 10 kg is the unit and 20 the annual usage'. Marshall and Boggess explain how we should go about determining the 'unit of demand' after the event, should this unit not be self-evident.

6.1.2 Pseudo-Poisson process

In practical situations we must be careful not to confuse a real Poisson process with what may be described as a pseudo-Poisson process. Smith and Cox [Co 1] have shown that the sum of a number of processes involving events taking place in a fixed cycle soon approaches a Poisson process, in the sense that the frequency distribution of the intervals between two consecutive events of the sum process fairly soon approaches an exponential distribution.

6.1.3 General formula

Let us now consider a formula which can be used to define the demand per period.

Assume that the number of orders per period A follows a known (discontinuous) probability distribution (μ_A, σ_A).

Also that the order (or re-order) quantity B follows a likewise known probability distribution (μ_B, σ_B).

Provided that A and B are entirely independent of each other and have no autocorrelation, the demand C in terms of quantity per period may be formulated as follows

$$\mu_C = \mu_A \mu_B \tag{25}$$

and

$$\sigma_C{}^2 = \mu_A \sigma_B{}^2 + \mu_B{}^2 \sigma_A{}^2 \tag{26}$$

The derivation of this is given in Appendix 5.

If you are surprised to find that this formula is not symmetrical, then you should remember that what we are considering here is *not* the situation $C = AB$.

The process taking place may be described as follows: make a withdrawal A from (μ_A, σ_A); make A withdrawals from (μ_B, σ_B). The sum of these A orders is C.

In one or two special cases it is at once apparent that (26) will produce correct results.

When the re-order quantity is constant, so that $\sigma_B = 0$, we have $\sigma_C = \sigma_A \mu_B$. The standard deviation of the demand therefore equals the standard deviation of the number of orders, barring the scale factor μ_B.

If the number of orders is constant, $\sigma_A = 0$, the demand C is the sum of a constant number μ_A of draws $\underline{B}$. Accordingly, we find that

$$\sigma_C = \sigma_B \sqrt{\mu_A}$$

This formula will be encountered later in another form, applicable where the number of orders follows a Poisson distribution, that is when $\sigma_A{}^2 = \mu_A$. In that case

$$\sigma_C{}^2 = \sigma_A{}^2 (\sigma_B{}^2 + \mu_B{}^2) \tag{27}$$

6.1.4 Form of the frequency distribution of the demand

Paragraph 6.1.3 contains formulae for determining the first and second moments about the mean in the general case. We now have to decide how far we can go towards defining the higher moments, or in other words the shape of the frequency distribution.

In the experience of the authors, and others,† the demand figures often behave to all intents and purposes like independent draws from a gamma distribution. In some cases a lognormal distribution is a better approximation. The Poisson distribution can also be used now and then if the demand is expressed, not in terms of the actual number of items, but as an adapted unit. If the frequency distribution of demand shows a marked asymmetry, this may be due to distinct differences between large and small customers or to major differences between large and small orders, whereby chain effects sometimes occur.

6.2 The non-stationary situation

We shall adopt Brown's [Br 1] theory that in most cases the short-term behaviour of the average demand as a function of time can be grouped under one of the following models.

a. *Linear model*

$$E(\underline{d_t}) = a + bt$$

b. *Quadratic model*

$$E(\underline{d_t}) = a + bt + ct^2$$

† See Holt, C. C. and Modigliani, F. [Ho 1], ibid. page 288.

c. *Exponential model*

$$\log E(\underline{d_t}) = a + bt$$

d. *Trigonometric model*

$$E(\underline{d_t}) = a + b \cos \frac{2\pi t}{T_0}$$

where T_0 is the length of a cycle.

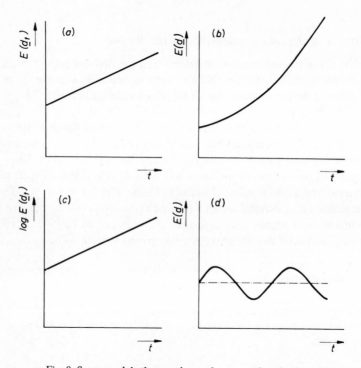

Fig. 8 Some models that can be used representing the demand.

Brown does not mean to imply that the long-term behaviour of the demand will follow a given model, but rather that it may often be assumed to do so in the short term.

When stocks and operations (or transports) are linked 'in series', the original pattern of demand may undergo considerable distortion, depending upon the re-order systems employed. This will be discussed more fully under the heading of 'chain problems'.

6.3 Autocorrelation

If d_t is the observed demand in the period t (and d_{t+1} is the observed demand in the period $t + 1$), then the possibility that a correlation exists between d_{t+1} and d_t, for a whole range of values of t, is also worth examining. This would constitute what is known as autocorrelation; the autocorrelation coefficient can be determined.

To the extent that the autocorrelation can be established for an inverval 1 (e.g. between d_t and d_{t+1}), it is also possible to determine, in general terms, the autocorrelation coefficient for the interval i (as between d_t and d_{t+i}). The correlation coefficients found can be plotted against i and then give some idea of the character of the time series investigated (Figs. 9a' and b').

R. G. Brown [Br 2], amongst others, has indicated how the autocorrelation can be analyzed and what its consequences are. At the same time he rightly points out that series of values long enough to give scope for thorough analysis are rarely available in practice.

Where stock problems are concerned, a great deal of attention should be given to autocorrelation, for two reasons.

First, a time series having a high degree of autocorrelation will require an entirely different method of forecasting than a series without autocorrelation; in the one case the last observed values provide a good indication for the immediate future, whereas in the other case a long-term average is more reliable.

Second, due consideration will have to be given to autocorrelation in the calculation of buffer stocks. This calculation is usually based upon the assumption that the deviations from the forecast demand occurring in two consecutive periods are entirely independent of one another; this is by no means always so, however, since positive or negative autocorrelation is often involved.

Positive autocorrelation in the demand figures themselves may occur, say, when a seasonal pattern is present. If this seasonal pattern is not taken into account, or at any rate not sufficiently so, in forecasting the demand, then there is a risk of systematic error in the forecast and of autocorrelation in the errors which occur in the forecast.

Autocorrelation of the forecast errors may also occur, if forecasts are invariably made for a number of future periods simultaneously; in this case it often happens that if an error is made in the forecast, the deviation of the real, from the forecast demand is in the same direction in all those periods for which a common forecast was made.

Negative autocorrelation of the demand figures may occur if the overall usage of a component is very regular, but an intermediate store transmits the demand intermittently.

It is perhaps also worth mentioning that when time series involving a seasonal pattern or trend are examined for possible autocorrelation without eliminating the seasonal element or trend beforehand, they show a typical pattern. This is illustrated by Fig. 9a to Fig. 9d inclusive, borrowed from Brown.

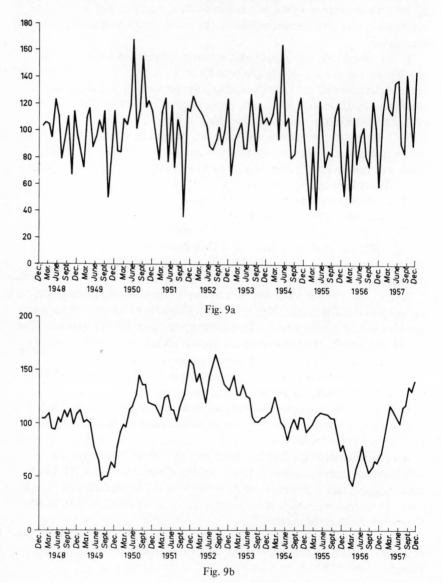

Fig. 9a

Fig. 9b

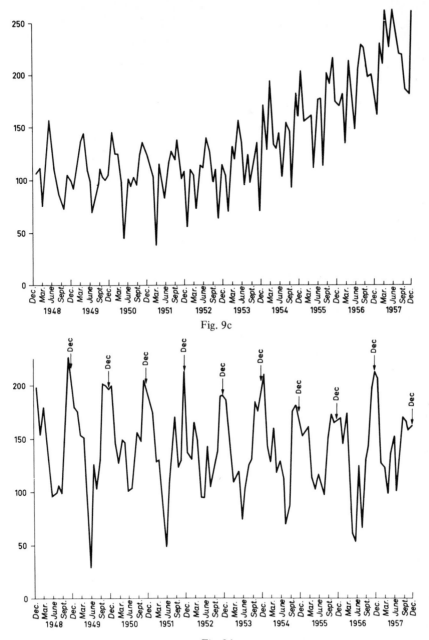

Fig. 9c

Fig. 9d

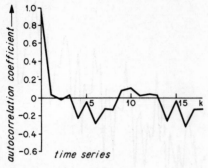

time series

Fig. 9a'

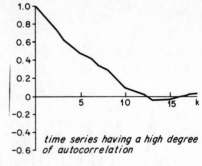

time series having a high degree of autocorrelation

Fig. 9b'

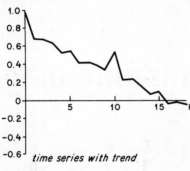

time series with trend

Fig. 9c'

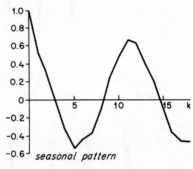

seasonal pattern

Fig. 9d'

7 Natural laws affecting a large group of articles

7.1 Uses of the lognormal distribution

Examination of the annual turnover figures of an assortment of products (individually in the case of comparable products, in terms of money in the case of others) often reveals that these figures follow a curve which is a reasonable approximation of a lognormal distribution. The cumulative distribution, plotted on a logarithmic scale, will then constitute a straight line. For example, Fig. 10 illustrates the conversion of the lognormal, skew, distribution of the annual turnover figures D, through the different transformations and transitional stages, into a straight line for the cumulative distribution.

Fig. 10 d is reproduced on a larger scale in Fig. 11, together with an additional feature which will be discussed later. The straight line in Fig. 10 d is the same as that marked 'articles' in Fig. 11. For example, the following information can be read from this diagram:

— 5% of the articles have an annual turnover of more than 30 000;
— 60% of the articles have an annual turnover of fewer than 1000.

This brings us to the following problem: if we take the overall turnover in terms of individual items of those articles whose annual turnover exceeds the value G, what proportion of the total turnover will this represent?

The total turnover amounts to

$$N \int_0^\infty D f(D) \, dD$$

The overall turnover of those articles whose annual turnover exceeds the value G amounts to

$$N \int_G^\infty D f(D) \, dD$$

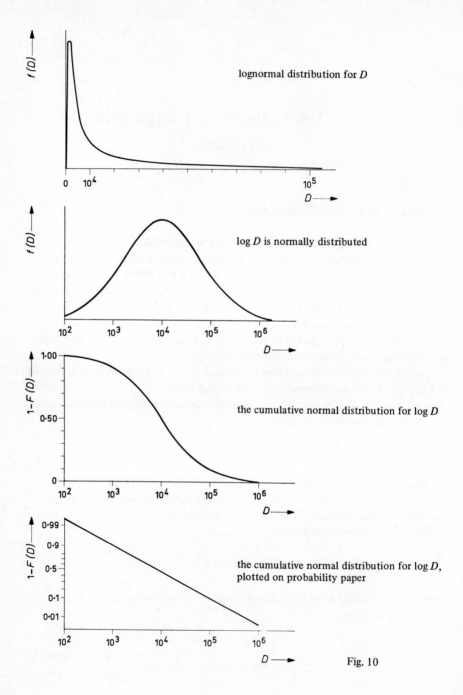

lognormal distribution for D

$\log D$ is normally distributed

the cumulative normal distribution for $\log D$

the cumulative normal distribution for $\log D$, plotted on probability paper

Fig. 10

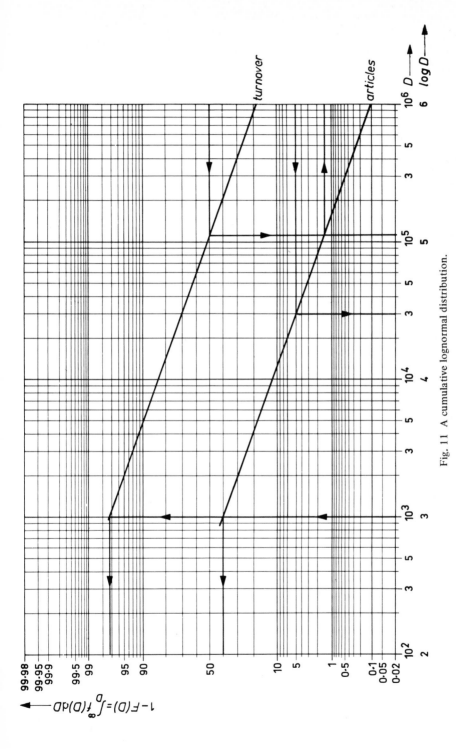

Fig. 11 A cumulative lognormal distribution.

$$\nu = \frac{\displaystyle\int_G^\infty D f(D)\, dD}{\displaystyle\int_0^\infty D f(D)\, dD}$$

Now, the ratio

can be plotted against G or against $\log G$; the latter has been done in Fig. 11, where it is represented by the line marked 'turnover'. As a result, the following information can also be read from Fig. 11:

— the articles having an annual turnover of 30 000 or more together comprise 72% of the total turnover;
— about 50% of the total turnover is accounted for by those articles whose annual turnover exceeds 100 000;
— those articles of which the annual turnover is less than 1000 account for only 3% of the total turnover.

A more conventional representation is the chart in which the ratio ν is plotted, not against G or $\log G$, but against $1 - F(G)$, or in other words against

$$\int_G^\infty f(D)\, dD$$

Here, ν and $1 - F(G)$ are both shown on the normal scale. Thus we obtain what is known as the Lorenz or Pareto curve. Fig. 9 in 'An Introduction to Production and Inventory Control', provides an example of this; $100(1 - F(G))$ can be defined in words as 'percentage of the types' and $100\,\nu$ as 'percentage of the turnover'.

A Lorenz curve is plotted in Fig. 12.

It can be shown that there is a direct relationship between the standard deviation σ of the normal distribution for $\log D$ and the shape of the Lorenz curve.

The following table [Mu 1] illustrates this.

TABLE 4

% of the articles $100(1 - F(G))$	% of the turnover $100\,\nu$		
	$\sigma = 1{\cdot}00$	$\sigma = 1{\cdot}684$	$\sigma = 2{\cdot}3$
1%	9·2%	26·0%	49·0%
5%	25·9%	51·6%	74·4%
10%	38·9%	65·6%	84·6%
20%	56·3%	80·0%	92·8%
50%	84·1%	95·4%	98·9%

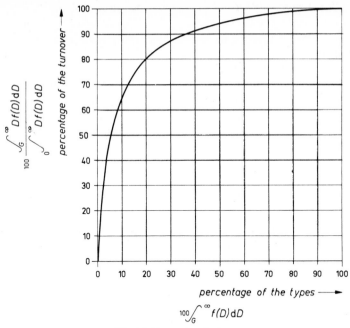

Fig. 12 Example of a Lorenz curve.

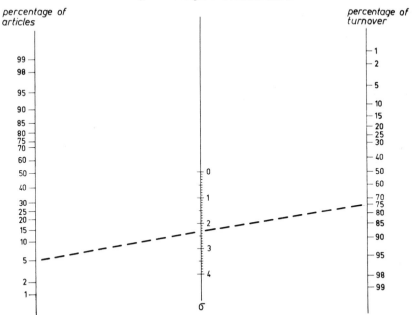

Fig. 13 Nomogram for Lorenz curves.

Fig. 13 is a nomogram evolved by Muyen, from which the relationships listed in Table 4 can be read.

According to Brown [Br 2], the value of σ for sales to industrial customers or wholesalers should be in the region of 2·3; for retail sales, σ should be about 1·0 (to the base e). This is based on his experience with many (mainly American) companies. He attempts to explain this on the grounds that the size of British and American companies likewise follows a lognormal distribution, with $\sigma = 2·3$, as do private incomes in the United States, albeit with $\sigma = 0·9$.

7.2 The relationship between average demand and standard deviation of demand

It is often found that within a given homogeneous assortment of articles, those articles for which the level of demand is relatively high also show a relatively greater variation in demand as between successive periods. In such cases the increase in the standard deviation is usually absolute, whereas the decrease in it is relative. The fact that the same relationship has been noted by different authors suggests that it is not uncommon.

The term 'homogeneous' is difficult to define exactly. A grocer's shop, for example, stocks and sells articles of many different types. In this case the curves obtained by plotting the annual turnover of each article against the standard deviation of the weekly sales cannot be expected to reveal a high degree of correlation. The immediate difficulty lies in choosing the correct units. A turn-over of 100 pots of jam per year should not be plotted at the same point on a scale as an annual turnover of 100 packets of coffee, 100 pounds of sugar or 100 packages of salt.

To avoid undue digression at this stage, we shall postpone further discussion of the possible correlation between demand and standard deviation to those sections of this book which deal with the determination of the re-order level (see Chapter 17 up to 22 inclusive).

8 The idea of dynamic programming as applied to multi-stage decisions

The idea of dynamic programming was conceived by Bellman and developed by Howard [Ho 2], amongst others, into a method of analysis for discrete problems which is particularly useful in dealing with numerical data. Its scope is not confined to the applications discussed in this book. A brief, general introduction to the subject is provided by Van der Veen [Ve 1] and by Kaufmann/Faure [Ka 2]. Bellman's principle of optimality plays a fundamental part in this: a problem which is insoluble in itself and involves an object function of n variables, can be overcome by solving n problems, each with one variable, one after another.

Dynamic programming is highly effective as applied to multi-stage decisions, whereby, as the name implies, opportunities to revise previous decisions occur time and again, eliminating the need for a single once-and-for-all decision. For this reason, dynamic programming also has one or two possible applications in the theory of inventory control. For instance, in the determination of the levels s and S in an (s, S) system and in the calculation of optimum production levels. In this introductory paragraph we shall merely provide a general outline of the subject.

In order to lead up to this, however, it is necessary to consider first of all the following problem†, which on the face of it has nothing whatever to do with stock control. A gambler plays dice according to the following rules. He makes a number of throws. After each throw there are two alternatives:

— the number which comes up is the same as after the previous throw. If this happens the game ends and the gambler is paid a sum in florins equal to half the number of points concerned;
— the number which comes up is different from that produced by the previous thow.
  If this happens the player can choose between two alternatives:
— stop playing. In which case he is paid a sum in florins equal to the last number cast;
— continue playing.

† Example given by Muyen.

What decision rules should be employed by the gambler? The reader should be able to work this out for himself from the knowledge of the theory of probabilities which we have assumed him to possess. However, the calculation involved is rather laborious.

Within the scope of dynamic programming, the problem can be approached in two ways; we shall discuss them both, beginning with the method of 'value-determination' and proceeding to that of 'policy-iteration' (to use the terms employed by Howard).

8.1 The value-determination method

After each throw, the game presents one of the following 12 situations:

— the last throw is the same as the previous one and is 1, 2, ... 6. This situation is represented by the notation 11, 22, ... 66.
— the last throw is different from the previous one and is 1, 2, ... 6. This situation is represented by the notation 1, 2, ... 6.

Example

1st throw is 1; situation 1 then obtains
2nd throw is 5; bringing us to situation 5
3rd throw is again 5, which brings us to situation 55.

According to the rules of the game, this ends when the situations 11, 22 up to and including 66 are reached; in the other six situations, it depends upon the decision rule (strategy) followed by the player. A strategy is a set of decision rules according to which the player stipulates exactly how he will act in any given situation. Thus his strategy may be: 'keep the game going as long as possible', but may equally well be: 'only go on if the number thrown is less than 3'.

For a given strategy, certain values V_i and V_{ii} may be assigned to the different situations i and ii; these values represent the winnings to be expected from the game in the particular situation provided that the strategy adopted is in fact followed.

It will be evident that according to the rules of the game, the following applies whatever the strategy adopted by the player

$$V_{ii} = \tfrac{1}{2} i$$

If the player follows the (rather stupid) strategy of 'keeping the game going as long as possible', the game will end after an average of seven throws (the reader can verify this fairly simply for himself). With any other strategy the game will, on average, be shorter.

We may assume, without affecting the outcome appreciably, that the player will not continue the game beyond 100 throws, but gives up at this point whatever happens (if this is considered to show undue impatience on the part of the player, we can easily set a limit of 1000 throws; or make a rule: the game shall end after 100 throws).

Let us assume that the game has reached the 100th throw and that this has just been made. Since the game ends at this juncture, the value of the situations V_i will now be known, as

$$V_i = i$$

Besides the rule $V_{ii} = \dfrac{i}{2}$ applies here also.

Let us now turn our attention to the previous throw, namely the 99th. Assume that the player has just made the 99th throw; what, then, is his best strategy? If the number thrown is i (the 98th throw was $j \neq i$) and the player decides to go on with the game, then the expected winnings from the remainder of the game, that is from the 100th and last throw, will be

$$W_i = \tfrac{1}{6}(V_{ii} + V_1 + V_2 + V_3 + V_4 + V_5 + V_6 - V_i)$$

If the 99th throw produced, say, 3, then the situation reached after 99 throws is 3 and the value is

$$W_3 = \tfrac{1}{6}(V_1 + V_2 + V_{33} + V_4 + V_5 + V_6) = \tfrac{1}{6}(1 + 2 + \tfrac{3}{2} + 4 + 5 + 6) = 3 \cdot 25$$

If the player decides to stop playing in the same situation, then the expected value (or in other words the least that the player can be certain of receiving after the 99th throw) is

$$W_i = i$$

The optimum decision as between stopping or continuing can thus be established for every i. The results of the calculation are given in Table 5.

The last column indicates the value associated with the correct strategy; we shall use V_i to denote this value. This set of values can then be used to calculate the optimum strategy for the situations 1 to 6 inclusive and to evaluate the different situations, after the 98th throw. To illustrate this, the calculation will now be carried out in full for one specific case.

Assume that the 98th throw was 3 (and the 97th throw was other than 3). If

TABLE 5

i	W_i (stop)	W_i (continue)	best decision	V_i = value for best decision
1	1	3·42	combine	3·42
2	2	3·33	combine	3·33
3	3	3·25	combine	3·25
4	4	3·17	stop	4
5	5	3·08	stop	5
6	6	3·00	stop	6

the player decides to stop the game, the winnings will be 3. If he decides to continue, the expected winnings will be

$$W_3 = \tfrac{1}{6}(V_1 + V_2 + V_3 + V_4 + V_5 + V_6) = \tfrac{1}{6}(3\cdot42 + 3\cdot33 + 1\cdot5 + 4 + 5 + 6) = 3\cdot88$$

The advantage of this method of calculation is that all we need to know are the possible states of the game after the 98th throw; we already know what the value in the particular situation will be, assuming that the player has followed the best strategy.

In the same way, we calculate further and further back, in the manner indicated in the following table:

TABLE 6

number of throws remaining to the end of the game	V_1	V_2	V_3	V_4	V_5	V_6
0	1·00000	2·00000	3·00000	4·00000	5·00000	6·00000
1	3·41667	3·33333	3·25000	4·00000	5·00000	6·00000
2	3·68056	3·77778	3·87500	4·00000	5·00000	6·00000
3	3·85880	3·92593	3·99306	4·05556	5·00000	6·00000
4	3·91242	3·98457	4·05671	4·12963	5·00000	6·00000
5	3·94515	4·01646	4·08777	4·15895	5·00000	6·00000
10	3·97521	4·04664	4·11807	4·18950	5·00000	6·00000
15	3·97616	4·04759	4·11902	4·19045	5·00000	6·00000
20	3·97619	4·04762	4·11905	4·19048	5·00000	6·00000
50	3·97619	4·04762	4·11905	4·19048	5·00000	6·00000

It can be deduced from the table that as from the third iteration (3 or more throws before the game definitely ends), the best strategy will be:

— go on playing if a 1, 2, 3 or 4 is thrown (and, therefore, if the situation 1, 2, 3 or 4 is reached);
— stop if a 5 or 6 is thrown.

It will also be evident that the *values* quickly approach a limit; in other words, the arbitrary ending of the game after the 100th throw affects the calculation less and less, the further we get away from it. When it not longer affects the outcome at all, what is known as the 'steady state' is reached; unfortunately this does not happen as quickly in every case as it has in the example discussed here.

Another question of importance to the gambler has yet to be answered, namely: what are the expected winnings from the game? It is useful to know this before beginning the game!

The expected yield can be determined at the start of the game by middling the limit values of V_1 to V_6 inclusive, since, the first throw cannot, of course, produce a 'double'.

Accordingly, the expected winnings are $V_0 = 4 \cdot 55556$.

8.2 The policy-iteration method

Let us now apply the policy-iteration method to the same problem. This method operates directly from the steady state. In this situation the values of the different states associated with a given strategy can be determined. Conversely, given a set of values, it is possible to ascertain whether the associated strategy can be improved: if so, a better strategy can be established and if not, then the existing strategy and its associated values are known to be the optimum. How does this process work?

Firstly, we can begin either from an arbitrary strategy or from an arbitrary set of values; let us choose the first alternative. Accordingly, our strategy will be only to stop voluntarily after throwing a 6, or in other words in situation (or state) 6. Then

$$V_6 = 6$$

and at the same time $V_{ii} = \frac{1}{2}i$ continues to apply.

Now V_1 up to and including V_5 still have to be determined. In the steady state the values are the same after each throw, so that the following equations can be constructed

$$V_1 = \frac{1}{6}(V_{11} + V_2 + V_3 + V_4 + V_5 + V_6)$$
$$V_2 = \frac{1}{6}(V_1 + V_{22} + V_3 + V_4 + V_5 + V_6)$$
$$V_3 = \frac{1}{6}(V_1 + V_2 + V_{33} + V_4 + V_5 + V_6)$$
$$V_4 = \frac{1}{6}(V_1 + V_2 + V_3 + V_{44} + V_5 + V_6)$$
$$V_5 = \frac{1}{6}(V_1 + V_2 + V_3 + V_4 + V_{55} + V_6)$$

The structure of this set of equations is such as to enable us to arrive at a solution very quickly. By adding all the equations and multiplying the result by three, we obtain

$$(V_1 + V_2 + V_3 + V_4 + V_5) = \tfrac{1}{2}(V_{11} + V_{22} + V_{33} + V_{44} + V_{55} + 5 V_6)$$

Since the right-hand side of this equation is known, the left-hand side is readily determined. The remainder of the calculation is self-evident. The result is

$$V_1 = 3 \cdot 607$$
$$V_2 = 3 \cdot 679$$
$$V_3 = 3 \cdot 750$$
$$V_4 = 3 \cdot 821$$
$$V_5 = 3 \cdot 893$$

and we already know that $V_6 = 6$.

So much for the values, or winnings to be expected if the above strategy is followed. Let us now try to improve the strategy.

With this in view we shall consider the following alternatives for the states 1 to 6 inclusive:

— stop the game; the value is then $W_i = i$;
— continue the game; the value is then

$$W_i = \tfrac{1}{6}(V_{ii} + V_1 + V_2 + V_3 + V_4 + V_5 + V_6 - V_i)$$

We choose for each i the decision concomitant with the highest value of W_i; thus we obtain the best set of decisions or in other words the best strategy.

The results are given in Table 7.

TABLE 7

i	W_i (stop)	W_i (continue)	best decision	V_i (= W_i value for best decision)
1	1	3·607	continue	3·607
2	2	3·679	continue	3·679
3	3	3·750	continue	3·750
4	4	3·821	stop	4
5	5	3·893	stop	5
6	6	3·625	stop	6

This completes the first iteration.

We now proceed to determine the steady state values again, this time with V_1, V_2 and V_3 as unknown quantities, giving

$$V_1 = 3\cdot929; \quad V_2 = 4\cdot000; \quad V_3 = 4\cdot071$$
$$V_4 = 4 \quad ; \quad V_5 = 5 \quad ; \quad V_6 = 6$$

Next we try to improve the strategy a second time, in the manner already described. The results are given in Table 8.

TABLE 8

i	W_i (stop)	W_i (continue)	best decision	V_i
1	1	3·929	continue	3·929
2	2	4·000	continue	4·000
3	3	4·071	continue	4·071
4	4	4·167	continue	4·167
5	5	4·083	stop	5
6	6	4·000	stop	6

For the third time we begin an iteration by solving a set of equations (four of them in this case), and thus arrive at the following result

$$V_1 = 3\cdot976; \quad V_2 = 4\cdot048; \quad V_3 = 4\cdot119$$
$$V_4 = 4\cdot190; \quad V_5 = 5 \quad ; \quad V_6 = 6$$

The third strategy improvement obtained is shown in Table 9.

TABLE 9

i	W_i (stop)	W_i (continue)	best decision	V_i
1	1	3·976	continue	3·976
2	2	4·048	continue	4·048
3	3	4·119	continue	4·119
4	4	4·190	continue	4·190
5	5	4·083	stop	5
6	6	4·056	stop	6

Comparison of the alternatives then reveals that the strategy cannot be improved any further. The set of values and the strategy thus established therefore represent the optimum.

8.3 General remarks

To conclude this chapter there now follow one or two remarks concerning dynamic programming in general and the procedures employed in this.

A major advantage of dynamic programming is that it is not necessary to establish the form of the decision rules in defining the particular problem, so that both the form and any parameters involved can be optimized.

In the problem of the dice player, we distinguish between 6 different states of the system. Practical problems are likely to involve many times this number of states, depending upon the complexity of the model.

In fact the number of states may well attain such proportions that even the most modern of calculating machines would be unable to handle the calculations involved. Therefore the uses of D.P. will have to be confined to relatively simple models.

On the other hand, development of D.P. is still proceeding and problems previously considered insoluble have been solved by this method. In general the two techniques mentioned in the example are not easy to compare.

A drawback of the first of them (value determination) is that it is sometimes difficult to ascertain whether the limit of strategy and values has been approximated to the desired degree of accuracy. In policy iteration, the task of resolving the values from a set of equations may take rather a long time.

In the end, choice of method will depend upon the particular problem and upon the assistance available in the form of computer programmes.

Section III: Forecasting (Plans and Predictions)

9 Introduction

9.1 Why forecasting is necessary

Humanity has been making predictions for hundreds of years, and employing some very strange devices for the purpose. It is common knowledge that the solar system, for example, has always appealed tremendously to the imagination of human beings, some of whom have ventured to make pronouncements concerning future events, based upon certain astronomical phenomena. At the same time, we would be very surprised to read an advertisement in which astrologers were asked to apply for the position of 'forecaster' in an industrial company.

A closer examination of this subject soon reveals that the method of prediction depends very much upon its object. For example, anyone wishing to get an idea of the number of traffic accidents likely to result from a steady increase in traffic density would be ill-advised to try to get this information by circulating enquiry forms in which people are asked to state whether they plan to be involved in a traffic accident during the coming months. On the other hand, an opinion poll is almost the only way of forecasting the result of an election.

Thus the method of forecasting will depend upon its object. The period covered by the forecast will also depend upon the purpose for which it is to be used. A large industrial concern will have to look ahead at least four years in planning its expansion policy, since this is the period they will require to build up the necessary production capacity (in the form of buildings, plant, finance, scope and so on). If the same company wants to purchase a supply of standard nuts and bolts, however, it will only have to forecast its needs over a very much shorter period, since the delivery time for these items is short. The need for forecasting is implicit in all this; decision taking usually involves making such pronouncements as: build a new factory; buy nuts and bolts; raise the production level; launch a publicity campaign, etc.

Because all these activities take *time to prepare*, it is necessary to look ahead over a period at least equal to this set-up time. To put it in another way, because all decisions take a certain time (= the set-up time) to execute, it will be necessary to make a forecast covering a period at least as long as this set-up time.

It follows that the formulation of expectations concerning future developments is a matter of the greatest importance to every industrial activity.

This explains the major efforts in the field of 'forecasting techniques' which are part and parcel of the present marked industrial growth. At this juncture we should perhaps draw a distinction between two forms of prognostication, namely the more or less visionary foresight into social, political and economic development, based on insight and intuition into matters not readily expressed in quantitative terms (called 'prediction' in the literature†) and prognostication based on natural laws which can be deduced from the behaviour of the object itself or from past records (called 'forecasting' in the literature).

An example of 'prediction' thus defined is a pronouncement concerning the difference in wage level in the countries of Western Europe in seven years time; 'forecasting' is what is done by someone who *calculates* a seasonal pattern on the basis of past records and makes use of this to determine the probable sales in the coming season. Forecasting in this sense is very much more exact than in the ordinary sense of the word, therefore, it is not surprising that physicists and mathematicians have become concerned with prognostication of this kind. Nevertheless, the idea of mathematics as an aid to industrial forecasting strikes some people as being just as ridiculous as that of astrology as a means of predicting the future. Nothing is further from the truth. Experience has shown that the behaviour of large groups of consumers follows certain laws, from which the pattern of demand for a new product can be deduced mathematically. An example of this is a growth curve in the form of a 'logistic curve'. A growth curve depicts the total quantity of products sold as a function of time. The growth (or in other words the *increase* in the quantity sold) is slight at first, but subsequently builds up steadily to a saturation level of, say, 50% (at which the product concerned is in the possession of half the potential customers), whence it falls off again and then approaches, asymptotically, a saturation level of 100%. Hypotheses can be evolved which explain this behaviour and enable this logistic curve to be formulated mathematically.

Thorough mathematical-statistical analyses have also demonstrated that much can be learned from past records which is useful in defining future expectations. For instance, it is found that random variations occur about a given sales pattern, which are comparable to 'noise' in electrical engineering theory. These variations also conform to certain laws and knowledge of them is a major factor in efficient inventory control (see Chapter 6). Thus mathematics enters into the world of forecasting.

† According to the terminology of R. G. Brown.

9.2 The reliability of forecasting

Good forecasting is therefore of major importance in industry. However, this statement at once invites the question:

'What is a *good* forecast?'

The quality of a forecast is governed primarily by the *forecasting error*; that is the difference between the forecast and the actual value. All this may appear self-evident; however, *systematic* measurement of this forecasting error is surprisingly rare in practice. This may be partly because such error detection is of no real value unless it is linked with systematic forecasting, thus enabling the information concerning the forecasting error to be used as a means of revising the forecasting system. The object of this revision should be to eliminate, or at any rate reduce, the forecasting error and thus improve the quality of the forecast. An indifferent forecast will make it difficult to 'hazard' subsequent forecasts on the basis of the error detected, because owing to the lack of system it is not possible to define the relationship between the method of forecasting and the error involved.

Regardless of the method, however, it is always desirable to know how reliable the forecast is.

A very simple visual check can be carried out by plotting the forecast and actual values in a graph (see Fig. 14). The more closely the accumulation of dots is concentrated about the straight line (having an angle of inclination whose tangent is unity), the smaller the error in the forecast.

This relationship between forecast and reality is expressed in quantitative terms by calculating the correlation coefficient.

It would be dangerous to commit oneself to any rash statement in connection with this correlation coefficient (p) [Mo 1]. For instance, Fig. 15 assigns a high

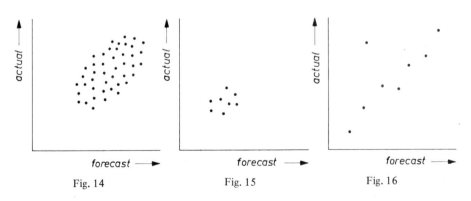

Fig. 14   Fig. 15   Fig. 16

Relationship between correlation coefficient and forecast

value to p, whilst the method of forecasting employed was unreliable; on the other hand, Fig. 16 gives p a low value, although the forecasts were accurate barring one overestimate. Not only the measurement, but also the interpretation of the errors is important.

9.3 The length of the forecast period

That 'the forecast period should not be longer than strictly necessary' may seem, on the face of it, obvious enough, but experience shows that it is not. The truth of this statement can be verified by studying plans produced in practice. It often happens that the amount of detail in them is the same, whether they be short-term, medium-term or long-term plans. In many cases, two-year or longer fore-casts concerning a given *article* are of no particular interest and information con-cerning a whole group of articles is all that is required. Undue insistance upon detail in such cases merely produces a volume of information which is not only useless, but also, most probably, unreliable.

How long a period should the forecast cover and what are the factors govern-ing its length? As we have seen, the forecast should contain enough informa-tion to provide a basis for making, and acting upon, a decision. If one year is to be allowed for the development of a new product, the associated sales forecast will have to cover more than one year. Not that it is necessary to know all the details concerning, say, the finish of the article at this stage. If the preparations for applying the colour will take one month, then the colour aspects of the sales programme will have to be established at least a month beforehand. The set-up (or make-ready) times of the various phases of the production process govern the 'horizon' of the forecast (that is the period which the forecast must cover).

The following example illustrates this (see Fig. 17).

A company decides to market a certain kind of plastic article. The production process involves extrusion of the plastic. Metal parts are placed in the mould prior to extrusion. To be able to make the product the company requires workers and factory space, plant, tools (moulds), parts and moulding compound (plastic). The delivery times for all these items are indicated in Fig. 17.

If it is known (forecast) what the sales of the total range of articles of the product groups $A + B$ will be in about $1\frac{1}{2}$ years time, then this information can be used as a means of estimating the number of sq. metres of floor space and the number of man-hours required. Since the make-ready time required for this is 16 months, the forecast will have a horizon of 16 months.

The overall assortment is divided into large products A and smaller ones b. These groups of products require different machines (delivery time 12 months).

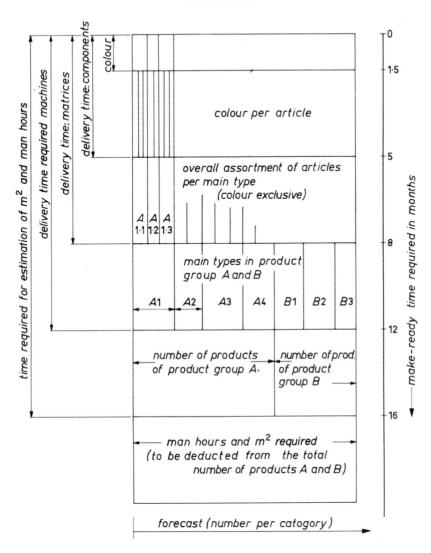

Fig. 17 Decreasing abstraction of information.

Therefore the forecast horizon referred to the individual product groups *A* and *B* is 12 months.

All the articles of a given (main) type (Ai, Bi) are similarly shaped. The moulds for each main type have delivery times of 8 months, so that the forecast per main type has a horizon of 8 months. Because the parts have a delivery time of 5 months, the overall technical specification will have to be established 5 months prior to production. Accordingly, the forecasts per article will have to cover at least 5 months. One and a half months is allowed for imparting the correct colour to the moulding compound, so that the quantities per article, including particulars of colour, will have to be fully established not more than one and a half months prior to production.

In this case, a planner who analyses, say, the colour distribution within the assortment of articles to be marketed more than a year ahead is doing unnecessary work and thus wasting time and money.

It will be evident from this example that the forecast horizon required depends upon the nature of the article and the production process.

9.4   Method of forecasting

There are two groups of methods of short-term forecasting:
  – Extrapolation methods. For particulars see the relevant references, namely
    Fraser and Van Winkel [Fr1] and ICI monographs [I 1] no. 2 and no. 3.
    These books also deal with methods of checking the quality of the forecast.
  – The explosion method. This will now be discussed in rather more detail.
In industries involving the assembly of products from numerous components, it is customary in many cases to calculate the quantity of components and sub-assemblies required on the basis of the assembly plan and the list of parts per product. This calculation of requirements is simple in principle and in fact amounts to nothing more than multiplying the assembly plan by the parts list.

A careful search for the most suitable inventory structure is particularly important where electronic computers are employed, since it can then save a very large amount of computer time. The calculation of requirements thus described is sometimes called 'explosion' because it involves 'exploding' each product into all its component parts. After this explosion per product the quantities of similar components and assemblies required are added together to provide an estimate of the total requirement per product.

This method of calculation in fact constitutes a translation of the original 'forecast' in terms of end products into another 'forecast' for the demand for components.

Because, for technical reasons, the key to the *translation* (= the parts list) is very exact, there is a risk that this may create the impression that the result of the calculation is likewise exact, whereas in reality it is only as accurate as the assembly plan of the end products. Moreover, the accuracy of the forecast is also affected adversely by fluctuations which occur in the percentages of defectives. It is therefore also advisable to establish confidence limits for the results of these calculations, in order to allow for variations in the assembly plan, the percentage defective and the working tempo.

9.5 Choice between extrapolation and explosion

The demand for components can be established by extrapolation of the usage figures of the components or by exploding an assembly of end products. This assembly plan is derived from a forecast of the demand for end products and the explosion method is therefore likewise based upon figures obtained by extrapolation. At the same time the latter extrapolation has then taken place at one or two higher levels.

The factors governing the choice between extrapolation and explosion are as follows:

— the forecast of the end products is more accurate than an extrapolation of the usage figures of the components;
— the explosion method may or may not cost less than the extrapolation of the usage figures of the components.

The whole object of the choice, then, is to obtain a forecast which is accurate within specific limits, without overspending. This therefore boils down to a question of costs; the greater the error in the forecast, the larger the inventory and the greater the risk of obsolescence, whereas increasing the accuracy of the forecast increases its cost, owing to the more or less complex data processing involved.

Another point to be considered in making this choice is the universality of the components, or in other words the frequency with which a particular component occurs in different end products. The usage of a component occurring in equal quantities in all the end products will depend very little upon the types of end product produced; instead it will be for all practical purposes constant. Explosion is superfluous for this particular component; a simple form of extrapolation will produce equally accurate results and will usually cost far less. This argument applies to many inexpensive standard articles.

If a component is specific, or in other words if it occurs in only one or in only a few end products, then there will be very distinct discontinuities in the pattern of demand; these discontinuities are caused by the starting or stopping of the end-product in which the specific component occurs. Mere extrapolation in this case gives rise to shortages during the initial manufacture of the end product and results in obsolescent stocks (unsaleable) because the demand abruptly ceases or falls to a low level when the production of the end product is halted.

In the case of expensive specific components having a long lead time, explosion is the only effective solution, even if it involves a relatively large volume of data processing.

Explosion also has advantages in the event of technical changes being made in the end product or components, because the calculation of requirements then preserves the original relationship between end product and component. There is a wide range of gradation between the inexpensive universal component and the expensive, specific one. The logical solution would therefore be to base a carefully considered system of requirements calculation partly upon extrapolation and partly upon explosion. The choice between the two is based upon the above cost considerations.

10 Distinction between categories of customers or orders

So far we have discussed one or two methods of forecasting the expected demand. We wish to emphasize that in a given concrete case, all the customers, orders or articles need not necessarily be treated in exactly the same way.

If a number of articles in a range have different sales channels, this may be reason enough to employ a different method of forecasting. A range of components required for the assembly of a number of end products may include some which are so universal in scope that the demand can be forecast as effectively, and very much more cheaply, say, by the single smoothing method as by the explosion method. If a large, but irregular, part of the demand for a given article is furnished by a small group of customers, it may well be worth while to try to obtain further information from these customers concerning their share of the demand, whilst forecasting the remainder of the demand according to an extrapolation method.

In a discussion which took place some years ago, Goudriaan [Go 2] had the following to say on this point: 'The extreme skew distributions† should be avoided by making a fundamental distinction between stocks to serve a large group of small customers and stocks for a small group of major customers – which is in fact merely the naturally evolved division of labour between wholesale and retail trade'.

Although it may not always appear advisable to keep separate stocks for different purposes, it is sometimes possible to combine different methods of forecasting. For example, there is the situation in which stock components are supplied not only to the assembly belt, but also to the development and service departments. The assembly demand can then be determined by explosion (at any rate in the case of large assemblies planned sufficiently far in advance) and the remainder of the demand (probably: the relatively smaller quantities required) can be estimated by extrapolation methods. In these circumstances it may be advisable from the organizational point of view, to keep a separate 'petty stock' for the minor sources of demand, which is then replenished periodically from the central stock.

---

† Of size order or of monthly demand figures.

Section IV: Calculations Associated with Re-order Systems and Production Batches; Intermittent Supply

11 Introduction

11.1 General survey of this sector

In every system of stock replenishment it is necessary to calculate the re-order quantity and the re-order date. There are numerous factors which may add to the difficulty of this calculation. Some of them will now be defined. In the short term there may be limitations in the form of money shortage or lack of space, or other resources. The re-order quantity (chosen by the customer) affects the buffer stock which the supplier must maintain. Nor would it be in the interests of the customer himself to calculate the re-order date and the re-order quantity independently, since both affect the costs of placing an order, stock keeping and stockout, or the avoidance of same. Again, much depends upon the re-order system employed, whilst the stock variation and associated costs also depend upon a variety of factors, so that it is necessary to formulate rules covering various circumstances. Last but by no means least, there is the question of the values to be substituted for the different factors in the formula.

Our approach to this complex problem will be as follows.

First we shall discuss the situation in which a stock point may be considered in isolation from all the other stock points linked to it in series or in parallel. Within the limits imposed by this situation we shall first demonstrate the relationship between the re-order quantity or production quantity on the one hand and the buffer stock on the other hand by means of a greatly simplified example, and then calculate the two separately as entirely independent quantities. Different formulae for calculating the batch quantity are discussed, and methods of evaluating the factors in these formulae are given, in Chapter 14. Instructions as to the use of the derived formulae for periodic re-order systems are also provided (Chapter 15). The buffer stock is dealt with in the same way in Chapters 17 to 22 inclusive.

A cost function for a (B, Q) system, in which B and Q occur together, is deduced and discussed, again under otherwise simplified conditions in Chapter 23. A (s, S) system will then be treated in the same way in Chapter 24. In Chapters 25 to 27 inclusive we shall then deal with certain problems which arise when the other stock points, linked in series or in parallel, are taken into account.

In conclusion we shall explain how stock norms should be calculated for an assortment of products.

11.2 One stock point: demand known and constant

In practice this is a rare situation. However, our intention in presenting it is to show that the formulae constructed to cover this situation may often be used as approximations in other situations.

Now we shall assume that:

— the entire quantity Q enters the stores;
— the storage space is unlimited;
— there is no discount;
— there is no need for rounding on account of packing units, life of tools, etc.

In the first calculation we shall also assume that there are only three kinds of variable costs:

— the costs of ordering, or re-ordering, involving an amount F on each occasion;
— the costs of maintaining stock in stores, an amount c_i per item;
— the costs of stockout, representing an amount N per year and per product.
    To put this in another way, a negative stock (or lag in delivery) of 1 product persisting throughout a whole year costs an amount N.

Another assumption which we shall make is that any cumulative lag in the deliveries is brought up to date as soon as the new replenishment quantity Q arrives. Thus the stock becomes a quantity which may be either positive or negative. Positive and negative stocks alike involve certain costs per time unit. This hypothesis will be discussed more fully in Section 18.1

Fig. 18 illustrates the situation described. As hitherto in this discussion, the letter Q is used to denote the batch quantity and the letter b to denote the (in this case negative) buffer stock.

The stock is positive for part of the time. This period is represented by ED/EC or, as will be evident from the similarity between triangles FED and FBA

$$\frac{ED}{EC} = \frac{ED}{AB} = \frac{EF}{BF} = \frac{Q-b}{Q}$$

The average stock during the time that this is positive is $\frac{1}{2}EF$, or $\frac{1}{2}(Q-b)$.

Accordingly, the annual costs of maintaining stock are

$$\left(\frac{Q-b}{Q}\right)\tfrac{1}{2}(Q-b)c_i = \frac{(Q-b)^2}{2Q}c_i$$

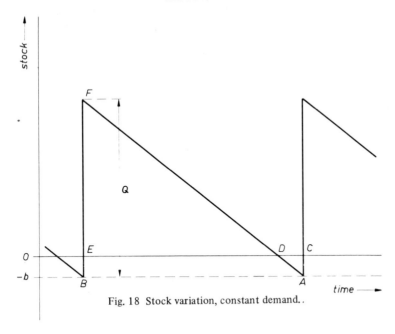

Fig. 18 Stock variation, constant demand..

The stock is negative during a part of the year equivalent to DC/EC, so that the costs, determined as above, become

$$\left(\frac{b}{Q}\right)\tfrac{1}{2}bN = \left(\frac{b^2}{2Q}\right)N$$

The total variable costs per year are then found to be

$$C = \left(\frac{D}{Q}\right)F + \frac{(Q-b)^2 c_i}{2Q} + \left(\frac{b^2}{2Q}\right)N \tag{1}$$

By differentiating with respect to Q or b and taking the differential quotients to be zero, we obtain, after a certain amount of simplification

$$\frac{C}{Q} = -2DF + Q^2 c_i - b^2(c_i + N) = 0 \tag{2}$$

$$\frac{C}{b} = b(c_i + N) - Qc_i = 0 \tag{3}$$

Equation (3) can also be written as $\dfrac{b}{Q} = \dfrac{c_i}{c_i + N}$ (4)

Finally, substitution of the value $b(c_i + N) = c_i Q$ (according to (3)) in (2) produces

$$bQ = \frac{Q^2 c_i - 2DF}{c_i}$$

By multiplying this result for bQ by $\frac{Q}{b} = \frac{c_i + N}{c_i}$ (see (4)), we obtain

$$Q^* = \sqrt{\left(\frac{2DF}{c_i} \cdot \frac{c_i + N}{N}\right)} \qquad (5)$$

$$\frac{b^*}{Q^*} = \frac{c_i}{c_i + N} \qquad (4)$$

Since in most cases $\frac{c_i + N}{N}$ will be relatively close to unity, there is little difference between the value of Q^* thus established and that resulting from Camp's formula. At the same time we must point out that the one is invariably higher than the other.

If we stipulate that under otherwise constant conditions no negative stock may occur, then this means in fact that $N = \infty$.

The result is that

$$Q^* = \sqrt{\left(\frac{2DF}{c_i}\right)} \quad \text{(Camp)}$$

$$b^* = 0$$

The following is also worth mentioning concerning the results obtained. It may well seem surprising that in the (otherwise purely theoretical) case $N = 0$ the results are that both Q^* and b^* have to be infinitely high, whilst according to this assumption the solution would be: allow the stock to decline, regardless of its initial level, so that it ultimately becomes more and more negative, but never re-order. However, it should be remembered that this solution is ruled out by the manner in which Fig. 18 has been drawn and equation (1) formulated.

The following is a more important consideration. It sometimes happens in practice that precise information available as to the future demand for components covers a period longer than the lead time. The question is, would it be advisable in such cases to allow the stock to fall to just below zero before the replenishment batch arrives? If not, there must be a fallacy somewhere in our argument, and what is it? In our view, the answer is that in such cases the ratio N/c_i will be so high that we may assume, for all practical purposes at any rate, that $N = +\infty$.

12 Calculation of the optimum batch size Q^*

12.1 Camp's formula

Camp's formula, discussed in 'An Introduction to Production and Inventory Control', will now be briefly re-iterated. We shall do so on the same assumptions as in Section 1.1 and add that $N = +\infty$, thereby eliminating the risk of stockout ($b^* = 0$).

Now
$$C = \frac{D}{Q}F + \frac{Q}{2}c_i$$

and
$$Q^* = \sqrt{\left(\frac{2DF}{c_i}\right)}$$

The dependence of Q^* upon D and of $\dfrac{Q^*}{D}$ upon D is demonstrated by means of an example in 'An Introduction to Production and Inventory Control', where it is also stated that the costs are not affected to any appreciable extent by deviations from the optimum batch size.

We shall now go a little further into these matters.

The minimum value of the variable costs can be found by substituting the calculated value of Q^* in Q above.

$$C^* = \frac{D}{Q^*}\ F + \frac{Q^*}{2}\ c_i = \sqrt{2DFc_i}$$

From this we can see at once the true proportion of the variable, to the total costs. We may take as a criterion the ratio

$$\frac{C^*}{DK} = \sqrt{\left(\frac{2Fc_i}{DK^2}\right)} \qquad\qquad (K = \text{cost price})$$

If δK is introduced instead of c_i, this ratio can be defined as follows

$$\frac{C^*}{DK} = \sqrt{\left(\frac{2F\delta}{DK}\right)}$$

In Fig. 19, $\dfrac{C^*}{DK}$ is plotted against DK for one or two values of F on the assumption that $\delta = 20\%$.

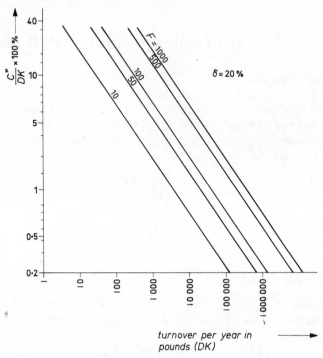

Fig. 19 The optimal inventory costs and re-order costs as percentage of the cost price dependent on annual turnover and re-order costs.

The following arithmetical example is employed in 'An Introduction to Production and Inventory Control'

$$c_i = £4; \quad K = £20; \; F = £40; \; D = 50\,000; \quad \delta = 0\cdot2$$

We find that
$$\frac{C^*}{DK} = \sqrt{\left(\frac{2 \times 40 \times 0\cdot2}{50\,000 \times 20}\right)} = 0\cdot004$$

Accordingly, the lowest value attainable for the sum of inventory costs and re-order costs is $0\cdot4\%$ of the purchase value. This result reflects the importance of the costs discussed here. Moreover this can be used as a measure of the real costs.

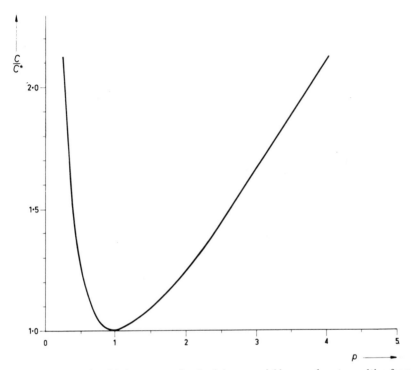

Fig. 20 The relationship between real and minimum variable annual costs resulting from deviation from the optimum batch size.

12.2 Costs increase resulting from deviations from $Q*$

In practice it is sometimes desirable or even essential for various reasons to deviate from the calculated $Q*$. It is therefore necessary to understand the consequences of such divergence.

Let us assume that the actual batch size employed is $pQ*$. The value then attained by the total variable costs C may be defined as follows

$$C = \frac{D}{pQ*} F + \tfrac{1}{2}pQ*c_i = \frac{1}{2}\left(\frac{1}{p} + p\right) \sqrt{(2DFc_i)}$$

or: $C = C*\frac{1}{2}\left(p + \frac{1}{p}\right)$, where $p = \dfrac{Q}{Q*}$

The effect of a batch Q of twice the optimum batch size is to increase the variable costs by a factor of $\tfrac{1}{2}(2 + \tfrac{1}{2}) = 1 \cdot 25$ relative to the minimum. The reader can readily ascertain that the equation now formulated constitutes the basis of Table 9 in 'An Introduction to Production and Inventory Control'; instead of repeating this, we give its graphical equivalent (Fig. 20).

13 Definition of the factors occurring in Camp's formula

13.1 General introduction

The factors occurring in Camp's formula, discussed in 'An Introduction to Production and Inventory Control', will now be explained more fully.

The formula $Q = \sqrt{\left(\dfrac{2DF}{c_i}\right)}$ contains the following factors:

D = number of items per year (annual programme)
F = re-order costs per batch
c_i = inventory costs per item per time unit,

    where $c_i = \delta K + sp$

δ = profitability factor (as a fraction of unity)
K = fraction of the cost price per product affected by the inventory
sp = costs of space per product per year

As regards the accuracy with which each of these factors should be determined, the following applies.

The effect upon the costs of the error involved in assuming, say, a value F_1 in place of the real value of the factor F, is readily deduced from the previous information. The argument is as follows:

F represents the re-order costs. The optimum batch size is therefore

$Q^* = \sqrt{\left(\dfrac{2DF}{c_i}\right)}$, and the minimum value of the variable costs is $C^* = \sqrt{(2DFc_i)}$. The

re-order costs are assumed, in error, to be F_1. Accordingly, the batch Q found on

this basis will differ from Q^*, i.e. $Q = \sqrt{\left(\dfrac{2DF_1}{c_i}\right)}$, which is equivalent in effect to

$Q = pQ^*$, where $p = \sqrt{\left(\dfrac{F_1}{F}\right)}$.

This leads to $\quad C = C^* \dfrac{1}{2}\left[\sqrt{\left(\dfrac{F_1}{F}\right)} + \sqrt{\left(\dfrac{F}{F_1}\right)}\right] = C^* \dfrac{1}{2}\left[\dfrac{F + F_1}{\sqrt{(FF_1)}}\right]$

A wrong assumption that $F = £20$ instead of the real value of £40 boosts costs

by a factor of $\dfrac{1}{2} \dfrac{20 + 40}{\sqrt{(20 \times 40)}} = 1\cdot06$, and therefore an error of 50% in F produces

an error of only 6% in the variable costs (we can, of course, reach the same conclusion via the calculation $p = \sqrt{0\cdot5} = 0\cdot705$).

The degree of accuracy desirable in determining the factors in the formula can thus be established on the basis of the error acceptable in the calculation of the minimum costs.

13.2 Calculation of the annual programme (*D*)

In the explanation of Camp's formula the annual programme was assumed to be constant and devoid of any seasonal pattern or trend. When the pattern of demand shows a seasonal variation, there are two alternative possibilities to consider:

a. The variation is in goods purchased.
In this case the turnover in a given period must be converted to an annual basis.

Example

annual usage 18 000
(1) turnover in period October to December inclusive 9000
(2) turnover in period January to September inclusive 9000

Annual usage deduced from (1) $\frac{12}{3}$ x 9000 = 36 000

With: $F = £4\cdot72$

$\delta K + sp = 8\cdot5$p

$$Q_1 = \sqrt{\left(\frac{2 \times 36\ 000 \times 4\cdot72}{0\cdot085}\right)} = 2000$$

(= one batch every 20 days)

Annual usage deduced from (2) $\frac{12}{9}$ x 9000 = 12 000

$$Q_2 = \sqrt{\left(\frac{2 \times 12\ 000 \times 4\cdot72}{0\cdot085}\right)} = 1130$$

(= one batch every 35 days)

b. The variation is in goods produced.

b.i. It may then be that only a few products show a seasonal pattern or that all the products have different seasonal patterns, with the nett result that the total demand for the products of a certain factory has no seasonal pattern. In this case we can proceed in exactly the same way as for the first alternative.
b.ii. It may also happen that all the articles made in a given factory show the same seasonal pattern. In this case the overall demand is also seasonal.

The company may respond to this with a uniform output, with the result that stock builds up during the slack period (low demand). This provides the opportunity to make large batches precisely during the period of low demand.

Alternatively, the company might keep its capacity in step with the demand by producing more in the period when this is high. However, the stock build-up involved in producing relatively larger batches in the period of maximum demand would lead to additional fluctuations in the overall productive capacity.

We shall not go any further into this matter at the moment, since it is primarily a problem of batch size. The annual programme employed at a given time of year is here of secondary importance and the principal problem concerns the total demand, the total capacity and the total inventory. In order to calculate the batch size stock required on average, it is permissible to take the annual programme for D.

If the demand is concentrated into one batch (military requisitions, etc.), Camp's formula must not be employed, since it assumes a uniform demand. It is necessary to make a clear distinction between this case and that of a producer within a concern who delivers all his products in one batch to a user within the same concern, who in turn spreads the use of them uniformly over a period. Even if the producer and the user here are financed separately, the producer must arrange his batch size as though he were himself the stokkeeper, and in consultation with the user.

However, if the particular product runs for a period of a few months only, so that there is no specific annual programme, then this should be determined as though production were to continue throughout the year at the same rate of demand. The simulated annual programme is then several times the total run. Of course, in such a case the result for Q should be equated to the total demand still to be expected, so as to avoid being left with any obsolescent stock. We shall come back to this when discussing the risk of obsolescence.

13.3 General remarks concerning the cost factors

Although when we come to demonstrate the costs factors in the formula we shall do so by means of an example based upon only one of them, it is perhaps advisable to discuss beforehand certain general considerations applicable to all these factors.

In the first place it is worth mentioning that the analysis of costs factors is strictly a matter of industrial economy, so that it is most advisable to approach this task in co-operation with a specialist on the subject or even to leave it entirely to such a specialist. At the same time it is most important to keep the purpose for which this costs information is required continually in mind, or in other words to remember the specific questions which require an answer. We must therefore emphasize that the object here is *not* to calculate a cost price, but to influence costs and appraise them from the point of view of management.

Our responsibility is to decide upon a batch size and our choice of same must be governed by an understanding of its effect upon the different kinds of costs involved. Costs which are not affected and therefore constitute fixed costs† in relation to the batch size, can safely be ignored. For example, the direct labour, direct machine hours and direct material costs are immaterial throughout a wide range of alternative batch sizes, because they are not affected by the batch size within this range. A given workpiece may take, say, two minutes to turn on a lathe and this time does not vary, whatever the size of the production run.

What happens if we choose a different machine for the relatively longer production runs is an entirely different problem which will be discussed separately later.

Those costs which vary in direct proportion to the derived variables in our present problem are the easiest to deal with. The batch size may itself be regarded as an independent variable and the derived variables are:

— the number of orders D/Q
— the average stock level $Q/2$.

If we look for them it is always possible to find costs which, considered per time unit, are proportional to the number of orders. If each order requires one sheet of paper, then the amount of paper used per period constitutes such an item. However, there are also other kinds of costs which, although variable in principle, are neither continuously nor discontinuously so; if a number of buyers are busy placing orders, then the size of the group of buyers may remain constant throughout a wide range of batch sizes, or number of orders, for some time, after which it abruptly 'steps up' through the appointment of one additional buyer. Again, there are other costs whose variation is continuous, but not proportional. The point is that we are not concerned with the average costs of a conversion or the average costs of the inventory. Instead, the calculation which we have to carry out may be considered as a survey of all the alternative batch sizes from the

† Fixed costs per time unit is here synonymous with fixed costs per product, since considerations of batch size are invariably based upon the same demand per period.

smallest to the largest. Thus each step brings us to a slightly larger batch; this means there are slightly fewer orders from one year to the next, but the stock builds up slightly. Invariably, the question is whether the next step will lead to a cost reduction or not. As we have seen, we are not concerned with the average costs of a conversion; what we have to determine is the saving which can be achieved through dispensing with one conversion. In other words a marginal cost analysis is necessary. For further development and elaboration of these ideas, see the literature on industrial economics [Sc 1].

Two examples will now be given to illustrate what has been said so far.

A stock controller has a number of articles in stock. Replenishment is by purchase from outside sources. Most of the stock is in an old warehouse owned by the company. The accounts show that this warehouse costs £1·50 per square metre per year. Owing to lack of space in this old warehouse, however, extra space is rented every year in a large warehouse owned by another company. The rent is £3 per square metre per year. On average, 75% of the stock is in the old, and 25% in the new, warehouse. What price per square metre should be taken into account in calculating the batch size. The answer is, of course, that the rent of £3 should be employed in this calculation, since every additional square metre costs the company £3 per year and every square metre less saves a like amount. A different method is used for the cost price calculation. Here it is established that storage space costs the company on average $0·75 \times 1·5 + 0·25 \times 3 =$ £1·875 per square metre per year.

In the same stores, orders are placed by a staff of thirty order clerks. The placing of one order is found to take ten minutes. The inclusive hourly rate of an order clerk is 42p and this rate therefore contributes, on the face of it, about 7p to the cost of placing an order. However, the question is: will an increase in the number of orders necessitate taking on more order clerks? We may assume that the answer is in the affirmative. Although the increase in the number of order clerks is discontinuous, the step size 1 is small in relation to the existing 'capacity' of 30.

Another point to consider is: the sum of 42p includes a general allowance designed to take the management costs into account in the cost price calculation. This allowance must be eliminated, since the size of the management does not depend upon the number of orders.

Our second and final example again refers to the costs per square metre in the above situation. The following may happen.

The batch size is calculated on the basis of a sum of £1·50 as the costs per square metre. On calculating the total area required we come to the conclusion that the batches calculated are so much smaller than those at present employed that they would not even fill all the space available in the old warehouse. In this situation it is no longer permissible to calculate the cost of storage space at £3 per square metre, since the saving per square metre in the old store is less than this amount. If the extra space available in the old warehouse cannot be rented to others and if the company itself has no real use for it, then this means that this space is for all practical purposes wasted. Accordingly, one square metre of space released constitutes no real saving whatsoever. The batch calculation then has to be repeated, with the price per square metre reduced to zero. If the space requirement according to the result of this calculation is still less than the capacity of the old warehouse, the problem is solved. If the space required is

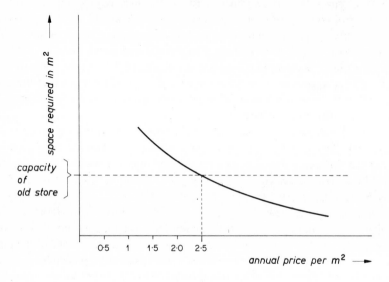

Fig. 21 Costs resulting from limited storage accommodation.

more than the old warehouse can provide, then the problem will have to be considered as one in which the space available is limited.

The method of solving this problem by means of the 'Lagrange multiplier' is discussed in Section 27.2. The underlying principle of this method may also be explained as follows: assume, that the relationship between the price per square metre taken into account in the batch calculations, and the total space requirement indicated by the result of these calculations has been determined for the entire assortment of products; also that this relationship is represented by the curve in Fig. 21.

In the circumstances postulated, the marginal value of 1 square metre is £2·50. Calculated on the basis of £2·50 per square metre per year, the available space is barely utilized. If the company is offered alternative warehouse space at less than this figure, the offer should be accepted (subject to other considerations such as geographical location, floor load, etc.).

So much for the main problems likely to be encountered. The order costs and inventory costs will now be discussed separately.

13.4 Calculation of the re-order costs

A distinction may be made between the following two cases:

a. optimum lot size for the acquisition of goods (from other companies or from sources within our own company),
b. optimum batch size for the manufacture of goods.

13.4.1 Acquisition of goods

When acquiring goods to be used, say, in an assembly, the manufacturer should weigh the costs of carrying inventory against the costs of placing an order. The costs of placing an order comprise:

— the costs of issuing the order;
— the costs of receiving the goods ordered.

a. The costs of issuing the order

In most cases, the order will originate with an official in a 'production office' or 'purchasing department'. The costs usually relate to:

— writing an order;
— determining the size of the order;
— where an internal supplier is concerned (within the company), receipt and processing of the order voucher in the stores whence the goods are to be dispatched, and writing the invoice.

It is advisable to find out what other departments (accounts) are involved in the order-placing procedure. Often, the times required to perform the above tasks will have to be analysed separately. The time thus established will have to be charged at an hourly rate which includes indirect costs (vouchers, papers, etc.), but does not include allowances for overheads not affected by the lot size. In some cases the above costs may be lower if the order quantity is scheduled for delivery when called for. In these circumstances, the completion of the order should not be confused with the delivery of lots on call within a given schedule; in fixing the lot size to be delivered when called for, we are concerned with the costs of such a call.

b. Costs of receiving the goods ordered

The receipt of the goods ordered will involve costs relating to:

— the arrival of the goods in the stores;
— the receipt of the invoice;
— the further processing of the invoice.

The costs of individual inspection, where this takes place, should not be included in the order costs, since they are not fixed costs per lot. Instead they are analogous to the costs of processing a product, and should therefore be incorporated in the factor K (see Section 13.5).

When the user is part of a company and obtains his goods from a supplier within the same company, which cannot supply them from stock, then he must take into account the order costs incurred by the supplier. If the supplier does carry stock within the company, then the user need only take the administrative order costs of the supplier into account, since the other order costs do not depend upon the demand from any single user (or customer). It will be sound policy on the part of the supplier to apportion his costs in the same way and make this known in his delivery conditions. Of course, the same applies when there is a separate financial responsibility as between supplier and user within the company.

This brings us to a question which invariably arises in calculations of savings: if the working time required to place an order costs 50 p and it is decided that two hundred fewer orders should be placed per year, then do we in fact save 50 p on each order? In most cases it will be necessary to proceed on the assumption that this is so, although it does not necessarily result in an immediate saving of staff or the release of staff for other duties. The reason is that a subsequent calculation of savings carried out in the same way may well show a profit higher than expected, because by this time the work saved is just equivalent to that of one staff member. As we have already seen the relative size of the step is an important factor in the expansion of capacity.

13.4.2 Optimum batch size in the manufacture of goods

The order costs of a production run may comprise:

— set-up costs, machine;
— change-over costs, man;

— restarting costs;
— administrative order costs.

Such costs can be determined by various methods, which often have to be combined, amongst other things:

(i) Comparison of budgets.
    The principle of this is:
— take the current factory budget;
— with the assistance of the experts on the spot, prepare a new budget for a hypothetical factory involving far fewer changeovers, for example a factory which makes each product only once a year;
— determine the difference between the two budgets and divide this by the difference in the number of changeovers. This produces an upper limit for the costs per changeover. In calculations of this kind, particular attention must be given to all indirect costs, to rejects and to stoppages, and also to the production method. We shall return to the latter point later.

(ii) Comparison of different machines, different departments, or even factories making similar products, but in different batches. The effect of the number of changeovers upon the total cost can be ascertained by means of the correlation calculation. Often, however, the variation through other causes is such as to rule out any reliable result.

(iii) The 'summation method'. The different factors are established one after another by method study and then added together. The result is usually on the low side, because 'concealed effects' are ignored.

a. Set-up costs, machine

These include the costs of the machine and the machine setter during the set-up time (tools, belts). It may happen that the waiting time of the machine for the setter (or vice versa),has to be taken into account. For the procedure to be employed in charging the machine hours: see next page.

b. Changeover costs, man

Changeover costs are incurred because the direct worker needs time to get fresh instructions from his foreman.

As a rule, the set-up time will not be the same as the changeover time. If the 'direct' worker does not set up the machine himself and is to be put to work on the same machine after this has been set up, but remains virtually idle until this has been done, then the set-up time equals the changeover time. Here again, the rule applies: first subtract from the wage or machine costs the allowances given for those overheads which are not affected by the choice of the batch size.

c. Restarting costs

The costs of restarting (slower pace, more rejects) will account for a substantial part of the order costs, particularly where assembly work is concerned. (These costs should not be confused with the initial costs, which occur only once at the start of the production of a newly developed product.) Sometimes, costs of this kind can be determined only by statistical methods. Also, an increase in the frequency of repairs to the product and/or machine is to be expected soon after the changeover.

The man-hours or machine-hours lost through changeover can be charged:

– at the particular man-hour or machine-hour rate;
– at (number of products lost) x (added value per product);
– at man-hour or machine-hour rate + (number of products lost) x (extra price of products purchased to fill the deficiency).

The method of calculation chosen depends upon whether the particular department studied does or does not constitute a bottleneck. See also Section 13.5.

d. Administrative order costs

Some of the tasks of ancillary departments such as the production office, time-study department, administration and indirect production personnel, depend upon the re-order frequency. Any increase in the number of production batches adds to the number of tasks they have to perform. It may happen that there are costs which depend only partly upon the batch size. For instance:

– costs of sample testing. Although an increase in the batch size will necessitate taking a larger sample, doubling the batch size does not mean that the size of the sample has to be doubled;
– starting costs of a production quantity. As the batch size for a given cycle time increases, so the interval between the end of one production batch and the start of the next will widen and as it does so, more and more will be forgotten, which adds to the restarting costs. At the same time, doubling the batch size does not mean that the restarting costs are twice as much as they were before.

The above factors can be defined, approximately at any rate, by means of the formula $F = f + (a/b) Q$ (Fig. 22).

The order costs per year are then

$$F\left(\frac{D}{Q}\right) = \left(\frac{D}{Q}\right)\left(f + \frac{a}{b}\, Q\right) = \left(\frac{Df}{Q}\right) + \left(\frac{aD}{b}\right)$$

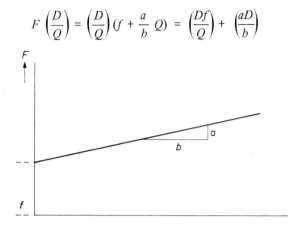

Fig. 22 Order costs as a function of the batch size.

Increase or decrease in Q does not affect $(a/b)D$. Conversely, Q^* is not influenced by a/b, so that only the term f has to be included in the variable order costs.

13.4.3 The coincidence of order costs of production batch and order costs of placing an order.

It may happen that the material required for a production batch has to be ordered separately. To the order costs of the batch there should then be added the order costs of *ordering* the *material*.

13.5 Inventory costs

13.5.1 Profitability

The required yield from capital invested in inventory has been the subject of much controversy in the literature and in practice also, opinions concerning it tend to differ widely. In principle, however, this problem can be defined in exactly the same way as the problem of the available space.

If a maximum of £G is available for investment in (batch size) stocks, exactly the same method of calculation can be employed as for the space costs: in principle, the relationship between the required profitability δ on the one hand

and the total capital to be invested in batches of different sizes on the other hand is

$$\sum_i \frac{Q_i}{2} K_i = I = f(\delta)$$

That value of δ whereby I assumes the value represented by G, is the marginal profitability. Substitution of this value of δ in Camp's formula reveals that, on average, G represents the exact capital required. If a value of δ below the normal rate of interest on bank loans is found, then it will probably be more sensible to take δ equal to the bank loan interest and invest the remainder of the money elsewhere.

The calculation of δ^* is a problem of industrial economy and we shall not have a great deal to say about it here; at the same time, the significance of δ will be explained in some detail.

(i) For example, by taking $\delta = 18\%$, we stipulate an extra profit margin of $18\% - 5\% = 13\%$ over and above the normal bank rate, assuming this to be 5%.
(ii) We consider δ to be very much more important as a means of bringing the inventory system under better control, than as a means of establishing the precise optimum. By means of the prescribed δ it is possible to obtain direct control over the amount of capital invested in replenishment batches.

There are two important points to consider in this connection:

— the decision and feedback mechanism must function smoothly;
— it is necessary to know something about the dynamics of an abrupt change in δ, in order to avoid setting up internal 'shock waves' of the kind mentioned on page 142 of 'An Introduction to Production and Inventory Control'.

(iii) Taking $\delta = 18\%$ and substituting this value in Camp's formula (or variants of this) does not mean that the capital investment yields an average of 18%, but instead that the marginal yield of the last pound invested is 18%. On average, the profitability is very much greater.

This may be illustrated by means of the following calculation, referring to one article.

The variable annual costs involved in a given annual programme are

$$C_{\text{tot}} = \frac{D}{Q} F + \frac{Q}{2} \{c_w + K(\alpha + \rho)\}$$

where c_w = costs of space per item per year
    α = normal bank rate
    ρ = risk per product per year, expressed as a fraction of the cost price.

Accordingly, only the normal *interest* is taken into account in the calculation of these costs, not the stipulated extra profit margin. Averaged over a period, the investment in stock amounts to $(F/2) + (Q/2)K$ (since the costs per item are $K + (F/Q)$).

The question is, what is the cost reduction obtained through an increase in the investment?

Let x equal the variable† investment, which amounts to $(Q/2)K$, so that $Q = (2x/K)$.

We may then write

$$C_{tot} = \left(\frac{DFK}{2x}\right) + \frac{x}{K} \left\{ c_w + K(\alpha + \rho) \right\}$$

The increase in costs per unit invested amounts to $\dfrac{dC_{tot}}{dx}$.

The decrease in costs‡ is then

$$-\frac{dC_{tot}}{dx} = \frac{DFK}{2x^2} - \left(\frac{c_w}{K} + \alpha + \rho\right)$$

By plotting the cost reduction against the number of units invested we obtain a hyperbola, as shown in Fig. 23.

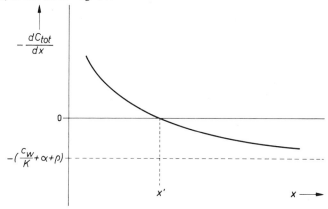

Fig. 23 Cost reduction against the number of units invested.

The asymptotes of this hyperbola are the y-axis (upon which $\dfrac{-dC_{tot}}{dx}$ is plotted) and the line $y = -\left(\dfrac{c_w}{K} + \alpha + \rho\right)$.

† Variable through the choice of Q.
‡ Here identical with profit increase, since neither the turnover nor the selling price is affected.

For the point x' in the diagram, we have

$$\frac{-dC_{tot}}{dx} = 0$$

therefore the associated value of Q is

$$Q' = \sqrt{\left(\frac{2DF}{c_w + K(\alpha + \rho)}\right)}$$

Accordingly, investment should certainly not be continued beyond the value Q', since any further investment will merely produce a rise in costs. But is Q' the 'optimum batch size'?

If the particular company can borrow unlimited funds at an interest rate of α, then Q' is in fact also the optimum batch size $Q*$.

However, it is a fair assumption that only a limited amount of money will be available, slightly in excess of x'. We may also assume that there is alternative scope for investment within the same company (e.g. gradual modernization of the plant). Let us further assume that over a wide range of values, every pound invested in the plant produces not only the normal interest α, but also an extra margin of profit $(\delta - \alpha)$, making the total yield per pound thus invested δ. Therefore every pound invested in the stock is diverted from the alternative investment and constitutes a loss of potential income δ, which is more than the normal interest α.

This situation can be demonstrated in two ways:

– by plotting the level $(\delta - \alpha)$ as in Fig. 23; as soon as the costs fall below $(\delta - \alpha)$, investment should be discontinued, since beyond this point the fall in costs does not compensate the loss incurred through the withholding of capital from the alternative investment;
– or, to put it in another way

$$C_i = c_w + K(\alpha + \rho)$$

no longer applies, therefore we should take

$$C_i = c_w + K(\delta + \rho)$$

in order to determine the optimum batch size for these circumstances.

Of course, both methods produce the same result, namely

$$Q* = \sqrt{\left(\frac{2DF}{c_w + K(\delta + \rho)}\right)}$$

Accordingly, the optimum batch size is established by substituting in the formula for δ, the required profit margin of the capital investment.

Example

annual programme	100 000
order costs per batch	£10
interest percentage	5
profitability percentage	20
part of cost price influenced by	£0·10
stock policy	
space costs: negligible	

D.C. = 100 000 x 0·10p =	£10 000
Specific tools and initial costs	£ 2 900
Total production costs (stock + order costs)	£12 900

Total yield

at $\delta = 0.05$ we have $Q = \sqrt{\left(\dfrac{2 \times 10^5 \times 10}{0.20 \times 0.1}\right)} = 20\,000$, therefore $\dfrac{100\,000}{20\,000} = 5$ batches per year.

The order costs are: $5 \times 10 = £50$
The inventory costs are: $\frac{1}{2} \times 20\,000 \times 0.10$ at $5\% = £50$.
Hence the overall costs are

order costs	inventory costs	other production costs	total costs
£50	£50	£12 900	£13 000

With $\delta = 0.20$ we have $Q = \sqrt{\left(\dfrac{2 \times 10^5 \times 10}{0.20 \times 0.1}\right)} = 10\,000$, therefore 10 batches per year.

The order costs are: $10 \times 10 \times 10 = £100$.
The inventory costs are: $\frac{1}{2} \times 10\,000 \times 0.10$ at $5\% = £25$.
Therefore the overall costs are

order costs	inventory costs	other production costs	total costs
£100	£25	£12 900	£13 025

With $\delta = 0.05$ the profit is $14\,300 - 13\,000 = £1300$.
With $\delta = 0.20$ the profit is $14\,300 - 13\,025 = £1275$.

The profit related to the product costs (maximum return) is

with $\delta = 0.05$: $\dfrac{1300}{13\,000} \times 100\% = 10\%$

with $\delta = 0.20$: $\dfrac{1275}{13\,025} \times 100\% = 9.8\%$.

Accordingly, both the profit and the maximum return are higher with $\delta = 0.05$ than with $\delta = 0.20$.

Where the object is to attain the highest possible profitability level, however, the capital assets have to be taken into account.

Assuming that the investments in plant and buildings are worth £5750, then with $\delta = 0.05$ we have

Assets	Yield	Costs	Profit	Profitability
Buildings, plant £5750 Inventory £1000 _____ total £6750	14 300	13 000	1300	$\dfrac{1300}{6750} = 19.3\%$

and with $\delta = 0.20$

Assets	Yield	Costs	Profit	Profitability
Buildings, plant £5750 Inventory £ 550	14 300	13 025	1275	
Alternative assets £ 500	100	25	75	
total £6750	14 400	13 050	1350	$\dfrac{1350}{6750} = 20\%$

Philips employ the profitability factor.

It will be evident from the figures given so far that any deviation from the optimum batch size reduces the profitability; the following table (Table 10) also illustrates this fact.

TABLE 10

Batch size	Order costs	Inventory costs at 5% interest	Yield (order and inventory costs)	Profit	Total capital	Profitability, %
20 000	50	50	1400	1300	6750	19·3
10 000	25	25	1475	1350	6750	20·0
5 000	12·5	12·5	1512·5	1300	6750	19·3

Reducing the batch size increases the total costs and raises the gross yield as a result of the liquidation of capital.

(iv) There remains the question: what is the (optimum) value of δ in a concrete situation?

As we have seen, this is a problem of industrial economy. The value of δ to be employed should be reviewed periodically, say, once a year, by management after it has been advised by a financial-planning department. The changes from year to year will probably be small enough to preclude the possibility of a shock-wave effect of the kind mentioned on page 142 of 'An Introduction to Production and Inventory Control'. As regards this point, however, the difference between two criteria need not give any cause for concern, provided that it remains within reasonable limits. Eilon [Ei 1] is quite right in saying that: 'The insensitivity of the model suggests that much of the controversy and arguments on the batch size theory are of an academic nature'. In practice, many companies adopt a value of δ in the region of 15 to 20%.

13.5.2 Costs of space

Space costs have already been mentioned under the heading of general remarks. The following is worth adding. We take as a starting point the variable costs per square metre, specifically:

— interest on and depreciation of buildings, fixtures and any storage devices such as pallets, racks, drums, tanks and so on;
— costs of security services, lighting, heating.

The other costs customarily included under the heading of storage costs need not be taken into account in the space costs as defined here.

The tasks of the stores personnel (fetching and carrying) and the quality and quantity control functions have to be carried out regardless and do not depend upon the time that the product remains in the stores.

The costs of inventory administration are included in the order costs. Insurance costs are taken into account in the 'risk' factor, as are the costs associated with products becoming obsolescent.

If several different articles are stored in the same warehouse and the space is found to be unduly limited, the par method of calculation may be employed. It may happen that the area required to store a batch remains constant throughout the usage of the batch. For instance, in the case of a stack of cardboard, the full batch occupies a height of 3 metres whilst its average height will be $1\frac{1}{2}$ metres.

Camp's formula is based upon an average stock of $\frac{1}{2}Q$, so that the average costs are $\frac{1}{2}Qsp$. In the above case this calculation is incorrect and the space occupied would have to be calculated on the basis of an average stock Q instead of $\frac{1}{2}Q$. In such a case the formula for the optimum batch size can remain unchanged if the calculation is based upon '2 sp', that is upon twice the space costs, instead of upon sp.

13.5.3 Determination of that component of the product costs which is sensitive to inventory costs (K)

Factor K is often defined in the literature in terms of the production costs not including ordering and inventory costs. Since this is not strictly correct, the costs components which constitute the cost price will now be discussed one after another:

(a) costs of material (including scrap, rejects, storage costs);
(b) processing costs (man–machine costs, including allowances and rejects);
(c) costs per order quantity;
(d) tool costs; initial costs (IK);
(e) overall allowances.

This explanation will be easier to follow if we consider the production factors involved in the manufacture of a product as quantities of work units, consumed as these units are absorbed in the product. The question is, whether work units are consumed in greater quantity or faster according as the value of Q is increased.

a. Material

Material may be divided into two categories, specific and universal. Specific material occurs in one type of product only, whereas universal material has general uses.

As a rule, specific material will be taken into stock shortly before the manufacture of a production batch is to begin. However, it also happens occasionally that the material has been stocked for some other reason (strategic and speculative considerations).

The number of work units of specific material absorbed in the product will increase with the batch size, due to the attendant increase in the stock of end products (see Fig. 24). When the specific material is already in stock, any increase in the batch size will be accompanied by a proportionate decrease in the stock of such material (see Fig. 25).

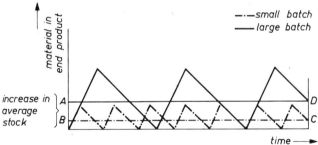

Fig. 24 Average stock level as a function of the batch size.

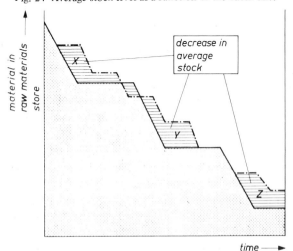

Fig. 25 Variation of stock with specific material.

The increase in the number of work units absorbed in the end product (equal to area ABCD in Fig. 24) is countered by an equivalent decrease in the amount of material (equal to area $X + Y + Z$) in Fig. 25.

Accordingly, the specific material item should not be included in K if this material is already in stock

Whether or not it should be included therefore depends upon the method of ordering specific material. The basic question invariably is: does the investment concerned increase with the batch size Q?

The situation with regard to universal material is entirely different; such material is (often) ordered regardless of the quantity available elsewhere in the same company.

The increase in the number of work units of material in the product which attends an increase in batch size is not countered by any additional fall-off in the stock. Hence the costs of universal material should be included in K. This will apply in most cases. This division of financial responsibility into separate sectors is also encountered in the inventory costs of the material (see ordering costs).

b. *Processes*

(i) *Labour costs*

Since labour as a production factor is not held in stock and is not specific in the sense that one worker can produce only one type of product, it has to be included in the factor K.

It is commonly asserted in the literature [Ma 1] that accommodation costs (of the building in which the products are made) and indirect labour costs (foreman, factory manager) are not part and parcel of the inventory costs, since they have to be paid throughout the year regardless of the batch size. In other words the amount of money that has to be found to pay for accommodation and so on does not become any less on account of an increase in the batch size. According to this argument such costs should be extracted from the hourly rate, since they do not contribute to the factor δK. This reasoning is erroneous, however, in that a certain amount of supervision on the part of indirect personnel, together with the use of buildings, etc. has gone into the making of the stock of products.

As will be demonstrated in the following example, increasing the batch size also adds to the out-of-pocket expenses.

Assume that three products A, B and C are manufactured and sold. Each of them contributes equally to the above overheads. Accordingly, one product involves indirect costs amounting to

$$\frac{£1080}{3 \times 3600} = 10p$$

Let the batch size be 300, making one batch of each product per month; A on the first of each month, B on the eleventh and C on the twenty-first of each month. Hence each batch of 300 takes ten days to produce.

The inventory costs of A in terms of overhead work units are

$$\tfrac{1}{2}Q(1 - D/P)\delta K = \tfrac{1}{2} \times 300(1 - \tfrac{1}{3}) \times 0{\cdot}2 \times 1 = £10$$

(for the factor $(1 - D/P)$ see Section 14.1).

The inventory costs of A, B and C are therefore

$$£2 + £2 + £2 = £6$$

Doubling the batch size from 300 to 600 also doubles the inventory costs from £6 to £12. Our object is to show that the difference of £6 also represents an out-of-pocket expense.

When the manufacture of product A in batches of 600 begins on the first of the month, the batch takes 20 days to complete. Production of batch B or batch C can be begun on the 20th of the month. If batch C is chosen, a month will elapse during which no products B are available for sale, since according to the old schedule, production of B should begin on the eleventh day of the second month, whereas according to the new schedule it will not begin until the eleventh day of the third month (Fig. 26).

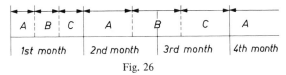

Fig. 26

A similar argument holds good if batch B is chosen for the second month instead of batch C.

The sales period of one month corresponds to ten days' production. The overheads for these ten days will vary depending upon the circumstances of production. For example, overtime will boost some indirect costs (overtime paid to foremen, etc.) and reduce others (no overtime paid to management). Assuming that the cost of overheads remains the same, then ten days will cost

$$\frac{10}{360} \times £1080 = £30$$

Interest on this at the profitability percentage of 20% amounts to £6.

Accordingly, the difference of £6 calculated above is revealed as an out-of-pocket expense.

(ii) *Machine costs*

As before it is necessary to differentiate between specific and universal machines. Specific machines are those machine and machine tools which can be used only for one specific type of product. Universal machines can be used for several different types of product.

An increase in the batch size will produce an increase in the number of specific machine work units absorbed in the product, since the inventory production increases. At the same time, the stock of work units embodied in the specific machine production factor will fall off more steeply (see argument under a and Fig. 25). An increase in the stock of work units in the product is thus balanced by an equivalent decrease in the stock of work units in the means of production (when the batch size increases). If the technical life of the specific machine is the limiting factor, the costs of this machine should not be included in K. Machines used for only one specific product are rare in practice.

On the other hand the costs of universal machines should be included in K.

c. Costs per order quantity

This item was discussed under the heading of ordering costs (F). What we now have to decide is whether the ordering costs assigned to each product (F/Q) should also be included in K.

Let us assume that the ordering costs (F/Q) are *not* included in K. These costs may then be formulated as follows

$$\tfrac{1}{2}Q\delta(K + F/Q), \quad \text{or} \quad \tfrac{1}{2}Q\delta K + \tfrac{1}{2}\delta F$$

The term $\tfrac{1}{2}\delta F$ does not depend upon Q, which indicates that the inventory costs are not affected by F.

> *Accordingly, the factor F should not be included in the factor K*

The following example illustrates this:
ordering costs £100 per batch,
batch of 1000 produces an average stock of 500 products.

ordering costs per individual product $\dfrac{£100}{1000} = 10p$

stock of 500 at 10p each = £50
batch of 200 produces an average stock of 100 individual products,

ordering costs per product $\dfrac{£100}{200} = 50p$

stock of 100 at 50p each = £50.

d. Initial costs and tool costs

What has been said concerning specific machines also applies to initial and specific tool costs. As production batches become larger, fewer work units are accounted for by the initial costs and specific tools, whereas more work units are absorbed by the product (see remarks concerning universal material). Therefore these costs should not be included.

e. Overall allowances

As a rule these allowances cover those costs whose relation to the complete article produced is more or less causal. Accordingly, these costs have a bearing upon K and F alike. When this is the case there is no point in including these costs in K, since to do so would necessitate increasing the factor F in the numerator by the same percentage. Therefore these allowances should not be included in the factor as a rule.

f. Determination of the factor K in practice

As we have seen, not all the items constituting the cost price of the product have to be taken into account in the calculation of the factor K. In practice, K can be deduced from the calculation method as follows.

Material data: sum for material + rejects + machine costs. If specific material is in stock, this should not be included. Do not forget packing material.
Processing data: sum for processing costs (including rejects). If the administrative ordering costs are incorporated in the hourly rate, then these costs, including allowance percentages, should be subtracted.
Tools and initial costs: sum for universal tools. Special tools and initial costs should not be included. Finishing and packing costs are made up of material and processing costs, and therefore covered by the remarks concerning the latter.

14 Variants of the simple batch size formula

14.1 Effect of the rate of production (P)

Effect of the rate of production (P) upon the stock level

The stock variation associated with production for stock and with abrupt replenishment of the stock with a batch size Q^* has been described earlier. It was then assumed that the stock replenishment takes place in a very short time, or in other words that the ratio of the rate of usage (D) to the rate of production (P) is zero ($D/P = 0$), D representing the usage per time unit and P the production per time unit (e.g. per year). In reality the production of a replenishment order may take some time, so that this assumption is no longer valid.

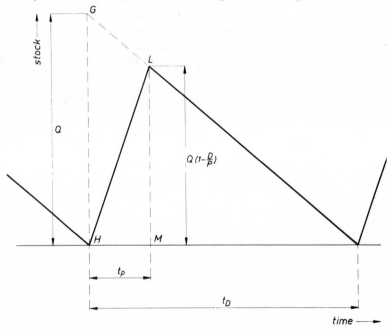

Fig. 27 Stock level as a function of the rate of production P.

Fig. 27, which illustrates this, is itself based on the assumption that the first product completed does not have to await the last before being delivered, or in other words that from time H to time M, delivery to the stores takes place at a constant rate P.

Fig. 27 shows that the maximum stock level drops when the ratio of the rate of demand (D) to the rate of production (P) increases. In the diagram, t_D represents the time required to consume the quantity Q.

It is reasonable to suppose that the time required for production (t_p) decreases towards higher rates of production (P); t_p equals Q/P. If the rate of demand (D) is high, then the usage time (t_D) will be short, so that t_D is equivalent to Q/D. During t_p, a quantity Q will be produced and a quantity $Q/P.D$ will be consumed.

In the diagram, the following applies

$$Q:LM = t_D:(t_D - t_p)$$

$$LM = Q\,\frac{Q/D - Q/P}{Q/D} = Q(1 - D/P)$$

Accordingly, the maximum stock is $Q(1 - D/P)$.

In the derivation of Camp's formula, the inventory costs per year are equivalent to $\frac{1}{2}Qc_i$; logically, this now changes to $\frac{1}{2}Q(1 - D/P)c_i$. Thus the formula becomes

$$Q^* = \sqrt{\left(\frac{2DF}{c_i(1 - D/P)}\right)}$$

In the case that $D/P = 0$, Camp's formula is restored to its original form. This happens when the rate of production is infinitely high (e.g. on ordering). If $P = D$, on the other hand, then $(1 - D/P)$ is zero and Q becomes infinitely large. This is likewise a rational solution in that it constitutes continuous production whereby the rate of production equals the rate of demand. Thus production continues without interruption and the batch is then 'infinitely large'.

14.2 Effect of in process stocks

Another assumption made in the derivation of Camp's formula is that the variation of the stock of end products follows a saw-toothed line (see Fig. 28a). Only the stock of end products, amounting on average to $Q/2$ and therefore costing $(Q/2)\delta K$, is considered. The assumption therefore is that a consignment Q is delivered to the stores and at once becomes available in its entirety, whereupon the amount $Q \times K$ is invested immediately.

Of course this does not hold good in reality. In the case of production batches, and with order batches for that matter, there may be an interval between the moment at which the money is invested and the moment at which the stock replenishment becomes available. Because this interval affects mainly production batches, however, it will be discussed here in terms of the effect on stocks.

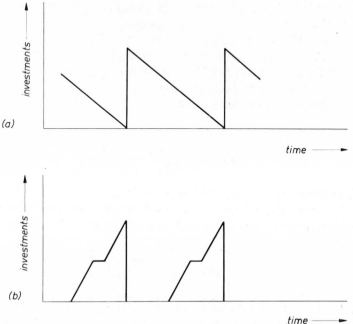

Fig. 28 Variation of investments in stock of end products (*a*) and in buffer stock (*b*).

First of all it can be shown that the batch size calculation does not require correction if the throughput time of a batch in the factory does not depend upon the batch size.

Assume that an ordered quantity Q is paid for in cash on delivery to the factory, but that (for some reason, e.g. delays in the paperwork) M weeks elapse before the goods are actually 'on the shelf' in the stores. The result is that an in process stock is created in addition to the stock of end products in the stores.

What will be the annual cost of this in process stock?

The costs per batch amount to $Q \times \dfrac{M}{52} \times \delta K$ (for a given article). The costs per year per article are

$$\frac{D}{Q} \times Q \times \frac{M}{52} \times \delta K = D \times \frac{M}{52} \times \delta K$$

Of course, Q is eliminated from this, since each product has to remain in stock for an extra M weeks regardless of Q.

The following argument also applies: at any given moment the in process stock contains that quantity of goods which will enter the stores in the coming period of M weeks and this quantity (regardless of the batch sizes chosen) will constitute, on average, a fraction $\frac{M}{52}$ of the annual turnover in terms of money.

A different situation occurs, however, if the throughput time M becomes dependent upon Q, so that $M = M(Q)$. In many cases it is reasonable to suppose that a batch passes through the factory as a unit and that the total throughput time is proportional to the processing time; the processing time, in turn, will be for all practical purposes proportional to the batch size [Ra 1].

Imagine, for instance, the situation in a press shop, where waiting times may be ignored. A whole batch Q of a given article is first blanked from strip material. When the batch has been completed in this way, it is transferred (e.g. in a standard container) to the next operation, the actual pressing. On completion of this, the container carrying the whole batch is taken to the last operation. After this operation, which happens to be tapping in the present case, the whole batch is taken to the stores in one journey. Thus the stock of end products varies in the exact manner illustrated in Fig. 28a.

At the same time there is another stock which is governed by the choice of Q, namely the in process stock (Fig. 28b). What correction of the batch size formula is made necessary as a result of this?

Assume that the throughput time of a batch is fQ years and that the average value of a product in transit through the workshop is hK. For convenience, the inventory costs per product per year are again represented by δ (invested value).

The costs per batch of the in process stock are $QfQ\delta hK$. Per year, this becomes

$$\frac{D}{Q} \times fQ^2 \delta hK = DfQ\delta hK$$

The total variable annual costs are

$$C = \frac{D}{Q} \times F + \frac{Q}{2} \times \delta K + Df\delta hKQ$$

Applying the method previously described, we deduce from this that

$$Q^* = \sqrt{\left(\frac{2DF}{\delta K(1 + 2hDf)}\right)}$$

The factor f will have to be examined more closely. According to definition, fQ is the throughput time of a batch in years. Hence the dimension of f is years

per individual product. The value of f can be deduced from the available information concerning process times and throughput factors or from a routine study of
throughput times.

14.3 Substantial risk of obsolescence

14.3.1 Theoretical derivation

If the batches calculated by means of Camp's formula cover demand over a long
period, or if numerous modifications are to be expected (as in the case of a new
article), there will be some doubt as to whether the risk of obsolescence can be
fully covered merely by taking the current percentage allowed for this from the
administrative records and substituting this in the denominator of Camp's formula.
If the existing batch size does not differ very much from the calculated size, then
this method of calculation should produce a more or less accurate result; where
major differences occur, however, or where no reliable precedent exists, it will be
necessary to employ a different method of calculation. Strictly as a case in point

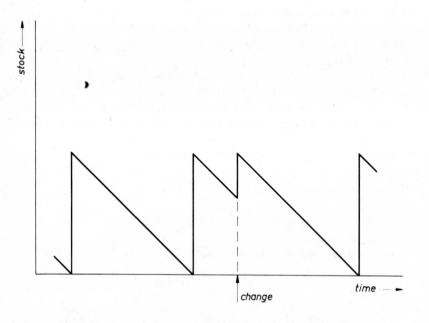

Fig. 29 Variation of stock of products that are object to changes.

and by no means as a general example, we shall now indicate a method of calculation based on certain extreme assumptions.

Assume that the number of design changes to be expected per year is known, that the changes may occur at any given moment (that is, regardless of the stock level) and that a change at once renders the existing stock valueless. The stock variation then follows the pattern illustrated in Fig. 29.

It is demonstrated in Appendix 8 that Camp's original formula has to be changed as follows in order to take account of the risk of obsolescence

$$Q^* = \lambda_1 \sqrt{\left(\frac{2DF}{(\delta + \beta)K + sp}\right)} \quad (\lambda_1 \leqslant 1)$$

where
  β is the number of changes to be expected in the next twelve months;
  λ_1 is a correcting factor.
In many cases λ_1 is found to be very close to unity (see Table 11), so that the following may be accepted as a very close approximation

$$Q^* = \sqrt{\left(\frac{2DF}{(\delta + \beta)K + sp}\right)}$$

The validity of this result can also be demonstrated directly. We began our calculation on the assumption that a change may take place at any given moment and that it automatically deprives the existing stock of all value. Unless β is unduly large, then, $\frac{1}{2}Q$ may be accepted as an approximation of the average stock at any given moment. The expected loss per change is then $\frac{1}{2}QK$ and the loss which may be expected to result from β changes per year is $\frac{1}{2}QK\beta$. This may be considered as an additional cost factor which, added to the inventory costs, produces $\frac{1}{2}Q(\alpha + \beta)K$. Since the changes add to the number of orders which have to be placed, the yearly total of the ordering costs is also increased, which raises the average stock level, and therefore increases the inventory costs to some extent. It is to take due account of these additional costs as well, that the factor λ_1 is introduced. The method of determining this factor is described in Table 11.

14.3.2. Application

The formula is applied as follows:

— estimate from past records the number of changes to be expected in the coming year. This establishes β;

— calculate Q_1 by means of the formula

$$Q_1 = \sqrt{\left(\frac{2DF}{(\delta + \beta)K + sp}\right)}$$

(in many cases this is a reasonable approximation of Q^*);

— then determine $m' = \frac{\beta Q_1}{D}$, where m' represents the average number of changes in the period of usage of Q_1;

— read the value of λ_1 associated with the particular value of m' from Table 11.

TABLE 11

m'	λ_1
0·19	0·97
0·20– 0·49	0·95
0·50– 0·79	0·90
0·80– 1·19	0·85
1·20– 1·69	0·80
1·70– 2·19	0·75
2·20– 2·89	0·70
2·90– 3·59	0·65
3·60– 4·69	0·60
4·70– 5·79	0·55
5·80– 7·29	0·50
7·30– 9·19	0·45
9·20–12·00	0·40

Note: λ_1 affects matters considerably if there is a large number of changes during the usage period of Q;

— calculate the optimum batch size from $Q^* = \lambda_1 Q_1$.

Example

This will now be illustrated by means of the following arithmetical example.
    Given:
changeover costs $F = £6$
annual usage $D = 10\,000$
cost price $K = 1·5p$
profitability factor $\delta = 0·20$
space costs $sp = 0$
factor $\beta = 1·00$ (one change is expected in the coming year).

Calculation

$$Q_1 = \sqrt{\left(\frac{2 \times 6 \times 10\,000}{0\cdot20 + 100)\,0\cdot015}\right)} = 2600$$

$$m = \frac{1\cdot00 \times 2600}{10\,000} = 0\cdot26$$

from Table 11, value of λ associated with $m' = 0\cdot26$ is $0\cdot95$, so that

$$Q^* = 0\cdot95 \times 2600 = 2460$$

Leaving the risk of obsolescence out of account, we have

$$Q = \sqrt{\left(\frac{2 \times 6 \times 10\,000}{0\cdot20 \times 0\cdot015}\right)} = 6300$$

In this situation, since $m < 0\cdot8$, it is reasonable to suppose that the average investment in inventory is $\frac{1}{2} \times 2460 \times 1\cdot5p = £18\cdot5$. Thus the loss to be expected due to obsolescence is $1 \times £18\cdot5 = £18\cdot5$.

Remarks

a. Practical experience in the use of the formula reveals that particularly with low values of β, λ invariably approaches unity. As a result, the correcting factor does not affect the batch size Q_1 appreciably and with values of β smaller than, or equal to unity the formula

$$Q^* = \sqrt{\left(\frac{2DF}{(\delta + \beta)K + sp}\right)}$$

can be used as it stands. The error involved is then negligible.
b. If the risk of obsolescence is taken into account in the formula, its effect upon the result is found to increase with the usage time of a batch.
c. The value of β may be greater or smaller than unity; with $\beta = \frac{1}{3}$, one-third of a change may be expected in the next twelve months, or in other words one change in the next three years.
d. Although by no means exact, the following approximation is nevertheless near enough for most practical purposes:

— estimate the value of β;
— calculate the optimum batch size without taking β into account ($\beta = 0$), thereby obtaining Q_0;
— the optimum batch size Q^*, taking β into account, then becomes $Q^* = \gamma Q_0$.

Here, γ depends upon β (see Table 12).

TABLE 12

β	γ
$\frac{1}{10}$	0·80
$\frac{1}{5}$	0·70
$\frac{1}{3}$	0·60
$\frac{1}{2}$	0·50
1	0·40
2	0·30
3	0·25
4	0·20
5	0·15

This method applied to the example given in 3.3 gives

$$Q_0 = 6300$$
$$Q^* = 0{\cdot}40 \times 6300 = 2520\,(\beta = 1)$$

Variation of obsolescence risk factor with time

It often happens that the risk of obsolescence changes with the passage of time. There is more likelihood of a change being made at the start, rather than at the end, of a production process. This is another point which will have to be taken into account in determining the batch size.

Example

Let us assume that the risk that a component will become obsolescent in the first two months is 25%. The corresponding risk in the period from the third to the twelfth month inclusive is likewise 25%.

Then
$$\beta_1 = \frac{12}{2} \times 25\% = 1{\cdot}5$$

$$\beta_2 = \frac{12}{10} \times 25\% = 0{\cdot}3$$

Now $D = 10^5$; $K = 10\text{p}$; $F = £3{\cdot}4$; $\delta = 0{\cdot}2$.
   Therefore during the first two months

$$Q_1^* = \sqrt{\left(\frac{2 \times 10^5 \times 3.4}{(0{\cdot}2 + 1{\cdot}5) \times 0{\cdot}1}\right)} = 2000 \text{ pieces}$$

and during the remaining ten months

$$Q_2^* = \sqrt{\left(\frac{2 \times 10^5 \times 3{\cdot}4}{(0{\cdot}2 + 0{\cdot}3) \times 0{\cdot}1}\right)} = 3650 \text{ pieces}$$

It will be evident that a high value of β should not be accepted without query. Also that even if β must of necessity assume a high value, a considerable saving in expenses can be achieved through the provision of adequate advance information and through correct timing of the particular change. Where such precautions are possible, it is no longer necessary to base the calculation of Q on the assumption that the change may take place at any given moment and that it will deprive the existing stock of all value.

What is the relationship between the value of β and the level of the risk of obsolescence which must be established for the cost price calculation?

For the cost price calculation, the risk of obsolescence is usually incorporated in the stores costs and expressed as a percentage of the amount invested per year.

Given a low value of m' (for instance $< 0{\cdot}8$) the following argument is more or less valid.

The average investment value is $(Q/2)K$.

The annual loss incurred through obsolescence of articles of a given type is found to be $x\%$ of the average investment value, or in the present case $(x/100) \times (Q/2)K$. If we simply add this risk percentage to the required profitability percentage, we obtain the following as the optimum batch size

$$Q^* = \sqrt{\left(\frac{2DF}{\left(\delta + \frac{x}{100}\right)K}\right)}$$

However, the annual loss expected can also be expressed as $\beta(Q/2)K$.
Thus we arrive at the equation

$$Q^* = \sqrt{\left(\frac{2DF}{(\delta + \beta)K}\right)}$$

To put it in another way, provided that there is no appreciable difference in risk of obsolescence as between the different products individually, Q^* may first be calculated by means of the percentage x as employed for the cost price calculation. After this the value m' will have to be checked; if $m' < 0{\cdot}8$, the result obtained for Q is accepted, but if not then the method of calculation previously described is used in order to obtain a better value of Q.

14.4 Problem of limited space

This problem only arises when several articles are stored in the same space. We shall therefore postpone discussion of it until we come to the relevant section (Chapter 27).

14.5 Discount on purchased quantities

It often happens that the price of the products depends upon the quantity purchased in a single order. This means, for example, that the price drops by a certain percentage if more than a given quantity of products is delivered. Such discount sometimes presents a problem when it comes to determining the correct batch size.

Various kinds of discount are known, but only one of them will be discussed here by way of an example.

Let us assume that the discount clause reads as follows: 'if the quantity ordered is greater than Q_k (discount point), then the purchase price K per individual product is reduced to

$$(1 - d/100)K, \text{ or in other words } d\% \text{ discount is allowed'}.$$

Three cases may arise.

Case A

Calculate the batch size Q_1^* on the basis of the purchasing costs K and compare it with the quantity which is subject to discount (the discount point Q_k). If Q_1^* is greater than Q_k, accept the discount and correct the calculated batch size. In this calculation, $(1 - d/100)K$ should be taken for K, whereby Q_2^* is established (see Fig. 30).

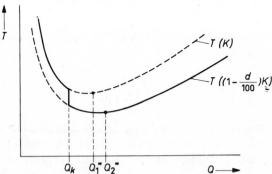

Fig. 30 The inventory costs and ordering costs for two cases, namely with purchase price K and purchase price $(1-d/100)K$ ($d\%$ discount).

Case B

Again calculate Q_1^* and compare this value with the discount point Q_k. If $Q_1^* < Q_k$ the matter of whether the discount should be accepted and whether Q_1^* should be increased to Q_k remains undecided. If the batch Q_1^* and therefore the purchase price K is employed, then the total variable costs are T^* (ordering, inventory and purchasing costs) (Fig. 31). On the other hand, if the batch size Q_k is employed, then the total variable costs are T_2 and the purchasing costs have dropped to $DK(1 - d/100)$.

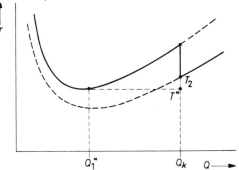

Fig. 31 As Fig. 30. The discount point lies in the neighbourhood of the optimum batch size.

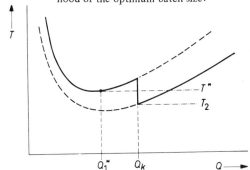

Fig. 32 As Fig. 31. The discount point, however, now lies higher.

In the situation that $T_2 > T^*$, Q_1^* should be chosen. A simple method of ascertaining whether this is so will be explained later.

Case C

It may happen that the discount point Q_k is greater than Q_1^* and that it is then more economical to increase the batch size (case $T^* > T_2$). This is illustrated in Fig. 32.

Derivation of formula for minimum discount limit

The total annual costs (ordering and inventory costs) T^* associated with the optimum batch size are

$$T^* = \frac{DF}{Q^*} + \tfrac{1}{2}Q^*\delta K$$

Because with Q^* the inventory costs are the same as the ordering costs, we may also write

$$T^* = 2(\tfrac{1}{2}Q^*\delta K) = Q^*\delta K$$

With $Q = (1 + u)Q^*$ instead of Q^*, the annual costs become

$$T = \frac{DF}{(1 + u)Q^*} + \tfrac{1}{2}Q^*(1 + u)\delta K$$

After conversion, this gives

$$T = Q^*\delta K \left\{1 + \frac{u^2}{2(1 + u)}\right\}$$

The costs increase resulting from the increase in Q is therefore

$$\frac{u^2}{1 + u} \times \frac{Q^*\delta K}{2}$$

The advantages to be gained from increasing Q^* to Q_k are a saving to the value of $(d/100)KD$ per year on the purchase price and a drop in the inventory costs due to the relatively lower purchase price amounting to

$$\left(\frac{d}{100}\right) \times \tfrac{1}{2}Q^*(1 + u)\delta K$$

If

$$\left(\frac{d}{100}\right)KD + \left(\frac{d}{100}\right) \times \frac{Q^*}{2}(1 + u)\delta K > \left(\frac{u^2}{1 + u}\right)\frac{Q^*}{2} \times \delta K$$

then it is more economical to increase the batch size to Q_k.

It follows from the above inequality that when

$$d > \frac{u^2}{1 + u} \times \frac{Q^*\delta 100}{2D + Q^*(1 + u)\delta}$$

Q^* should be changed to Q_k.

This expression can be further simplified by dividing both the numerator and the denominator by δQ^*, giving

$$d > \frac{u^2}{1+u} \times \frac{100}{\sqrt{\left(\frac{2DK}{\delta F}\right)} + 1 + u}$$

then $Q^* \to Q_k$.

Here u is the deviation of Q from Q^*. With $Q = 1400$ and $Q^* = 1000$, for example, we have

$$\frac{Q}{Q^*} = 1 + u = 1 \cdot 4$$

Therefore $u = 0 \cdot 4$.

Practical application

The following simple model (Fig. 33) can be followed in practice.

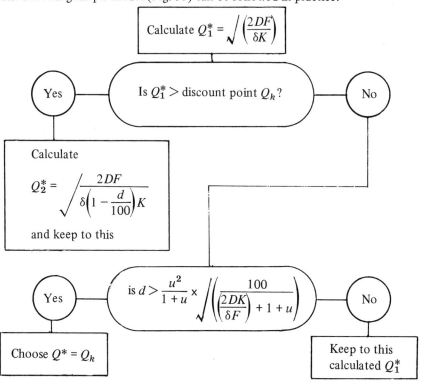

Example

The following complete example may serve to explain certain points more clearly.
Let $D = 50\,000$, $F = £40$, $K = £2$, $\delta = 0.20$.

What should the batch size be when 2% discount is given on

a. an order quantity of 750 items;
b. an order quantity of 3000 items;
c. an order quantity of 15 000 items?

Solution

a. Calculate $Q_1^* = \sqrt{\left(\dfrac{2DF}{\delta K}\right)}$

$$Q_1^* = \sqrt{\left(\frac{2 \times 50\,000 \times 40}{0.20 \times 20}\right)} = 1000 \text{ items}$$

Q_1^* is greater than Q_k ($Q_k = 750$).

Now calculate

$$Q_2^* = \sqrt{\left(\frac{2 \times 50\,000 \times 40}{0.20(1 - 0.20)20}\right)} = 1050$$

In this case, then, the optimum batch size is $Q^* = 1050$.

b. If Q_k equals 3000, then Q_1^* is not greater than Q_k (since $1000 < 3000$).
   The question now is whether

$$d > \frac{u^2}{1 + u} \times \frac{100}{\sqrt{\left(\dfrac{2DK}{\delta F}\right)} + 1 + u}$$

It is known that $Q_k = (1 + u)Q_1^*$, whence it follows that

$$u = \frac{Q_k}{Q_1^*} - 1 = \frac{3000}{1000} - 1 = 2$$

Now calculate

$$\frac{2^2}{1 + 2} \times \frac{100}{\sqrt{\left(\dfrac{2 \times 50\,000 \times 20}{0.20 \times 40}\right)} + 1 + 2} = \frac{4}{3} \times \frac{100}{500 + 3} = 0.26$$

Since $d = 2\%$, then, $d > 0.26\%$.
Accordingly, $Q^* = Q_k = 3000$ is chosen as the optimum batch size.

c. In this case, discount is given at $Q_k = 15\,000$.

As before, we find that $Q_1^* < Q_k$ (since $1000 < 15\,000$); the value of d is then compared with

$$\frac{14^2}{1+14} \times \frac{100}{\sqrt{\left(\frac{2 \times 50\,000 \times 40}{0\cdot20 \times 20}\right)} + 1 + 14} = \frac{196}{15} \times \frac{100}{500 + 15} = 2\cdot54$$

Since $d < 2\cdot54$, Q_1^* must be taken as the optimum batch size, therefore $Q^* = 1000$. In this case no use is made of the discount.

14.6 Tools with limited standing time†

Problem

Certain production processes involve the use of tools having only a limited standing time. Standing time may be defined as the time which elapses between set-up and failure of the tool. It may happen that the tool breaks before the calculated batch size (Camp's formula) has been reached. The defective tool can of course be removed and the batch continued with another tool of the same type, but alternatively the batch may be discontinued and a new product may be begun instead.

It will be evident that in the event of frequent stoppages it may be more economical to deviate from the batch calculated according to Camp's formula (which we shall call Q_0) and instead follow another rule. The theory of this is explained elsewhere [Mu 2].

Principle of the solution

The solution to the problem is based upon the following assumptions:

— the demand is stable;
— the lead time for an order is stable;
— spare tools are invariably on hand;
— the time of tool failure does not depend upon the time that the tool has been in use so far;
— if another product is begun after a stoppage, the sum of stoppage costs and ordering costs is less than it would be if the production of the original product was resumed and a different product was begun later.

† This section is written by A. R. W. Muyen.

An essential assumption is that the combination of a stoppage with a changeover is advantageous, as illustrated by the following simple example:

	Stoppage alone	Changeover alone	Combination of the two
Repair costs	50	–	50
Changeover costs	5	20	20
Administrative ordering costs	4	10	10
Total costs	$F_2 = 59$	$F_1 = 30$	$F_2' + F_1' = 80$

The saving thus obtainable by combination as compared with the changeover costs is

$$r' = \frac{59 + 30 - 80}{30} \approx 0{\cdot}3$$

where r' = saving factor.

There is another factor besides this saving r', namely the ratio of the batch size according to Camp (Q_0) to the average standing time in terms of quantity produced.

Assume that on average the quantity produced between two stoppages is 2800 and the calculated Q_0 is 6000; according to definition, then

$$\tau = \frac{Q_0}{\text{standing time (quantity produced)}} = \frac{6000}{2800} = 2{\cdot}14.$$

The deciding factors in this problem are r' and τ.

In essence, the rule to be followed states that two limits (Q_1 and Q_2), between which the stipulated batch size should lie, are defined instead of a fixed batch size Q_0; the position within these limits depends upon the time at which a stoppage occurs. The production is stopped and changed over to a different product when a quantity Q_2 has been made or if a stoppage occurs beyond Q_1, but before Q_2.

Application

The practical application of this rule will now be illustrated by means of an example.
    Let

the production rate $P = 300\,000$ per year;
the demand $D = 50\,000$ per year;
the inventory costs $c_i = 1\text{p}$ per item per year (δK);
the changeover costs $F_1 = £3$ per changeover.

The saving obtained through combining stoppage with changeover is estimated at £1, so that $r' = \frac{10}{30} = 0\cdot33$.

The average standing time is 2800 items.

The calculation is then as follows.

a. The optimum batch size according to Camp would be

$$Q_0 = \sqrt{\left(\frac{2 \times 50\,000 \times 30}{0\cdot10(1 - \frac{1}{6})}\right)} = 6000$$

It follows that

$$\tau = \frac{6000}{2800} = 2\cdot14$$

b. The saving obtainable by employing the 'variable batch size system' can be read from Fig. 34. The entries to the diagram are τ and r'. With $\tau = 2\cdot14$ and $r' = 0\cdot3$, the value read will be about 10%. This means that a saving of 10% in terms of inventory and changeover costs (T^*) is obtained through the use of the variable limits.

c. The value of Q_1 associated with known values of τ and r' can be read from Fig. 35. The value of Q_1 is expressed as a fraction of Q_0. With $\tau = 2\cdot14$ and $r' = 0\cdot3$, we have $Q_1/Q_0 = 0\cdot5$, so that $Q_1 = 0\cdot5 \times 6000 = 3000$.

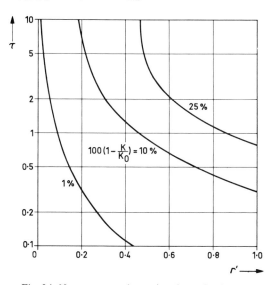

Fig. 34 Nomogram to determine the saving in costs.

d. Q_2 can be determined by means of Fig. 36. With the known values of τ and r' we find that $Q_2/Q_0 = 1\cdot25$; therefore $Q_2 = 1\cdot25 \times 6000 = 7500$.

The result of this calculation can be stated as follows.

'Stop the production and change to another product at the first tool failure after the output reaches 3000, or when the output reaches 7500.'

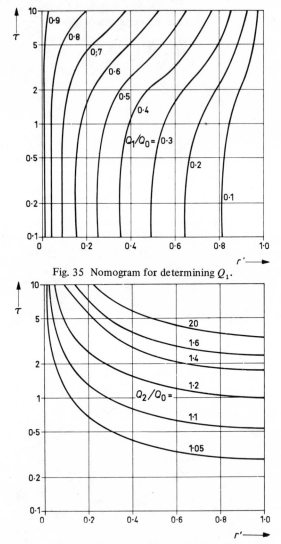

Fig. 35 Nomogram for determining Q_1.

Fig. 36 Nomogram for determining Q_2.

Effect of tool grinding upon the standing time

So far we have considered those stoppages which are due to tool failure in the form of breakage. For them, the number of products made in the interval between two stoppages does not depend on the number of products already made with the particular tool. The calculation relating to stoppages which occur owing to the fact that the tool requires regrinding after a certain period of wear is altogether different. In this case, the number of products made between two consecutive stoppages is more or less constant. That being so, the effect of the standing time may safely be ignored if the optimum batch size is very much smaller than the standing time. Otherwise, we must try to establish a production batch which is an exact multiple of the standing time; to put this in another way, the optimum batch size should be calculated by means of Camp's formula or a variant of this and then rounded to an exact multiple of the standing time.

In the event of additional stoppages owing to tool breakage, it will also be necessary to take into account the limits defined in the previous paragraph.

15 Batch size in the case of periodic re-ordering

So far, Q^* has been calculated on the assumption that the inventory is controlled according to a (B, Q) method and that B^* and Q^* are established independently of each other and separately for each article. We shall now define a suitable approach to the calculation of batch sizes in a periodic re-ordering system, for example a (s, S) method.

If the method of periodic replenishment is followed, when $s = S$, then the batch size Q is superseded as an independent variable by the interval m between two consecutive times.

For individual articles, the calculation of m^* proceeds on exactly the same lines as the calculation of Q^* in a (B, Q) system. The result is

$$m^* = \sqrt{\left(\frac{2F}{Dc_i}\right)}, \text{ with } m \text{ in years.}$$

However, the problem is that m is usually required to be *the same* for all the articles. It is then necessary to determine that value of m at which the sum of C_{tot} reaches a minimum for all the articles. A method of calculating this value is described amongst other things by Kleinmann and his associates [Kl 1].

If a (s, S) method is employed, whereby the interval m is the same for all the articles, and assuming that this interval is known, the following approach is possible.

Let the re-ordering frequency be low, namely one order, or less than one order, per four intervals, and assume that at time T the economic stock has fallen below s. The following then applies as an approximation: on average the stock will have passed the level s about midway through the preceding interval m between orders; from that moment until time T, the average usage will be $0{\cdot}5\,mD$. On the average, the re-order quantity in a (s, S) system will therefore be

$$Q = S - s + 0{\cdot}5mD \text{ (see Fig. 37).}$$

Next, Camp's formula or a variant of this can be employed.
Thus we obtain, say

$$S = s - 0{\cdot}5mD + \sqrt{\left(\frac{2DF}{c_i}\right)}$$

An approximate calculation of s^*, independent of S, is discussed in Chapter 22. For a calculation of s^* and S^*, interrelated, by means of dynamic programming methods, see Chapter 24.

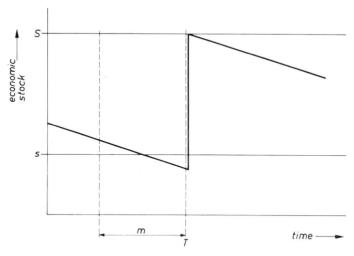

Fig. 37 The re-order quantity in an (s, S) system.

16 Simple aids to the calculation of batch size†

The batch size can be determined by means of certain techniques which, although they do not produce very exact results, are nevertheless very useful for practical purposes.

That the results are not exact usually does not matter very much, since in any case batch sizes are very rarely used exactly as indicated in the calculation 'by hand' or by the computer, but instead involve a certain amount of rounding. This rounding is more or less inherent in the methods which will now be described. To begin with, there is the table method.

16.1 Table

A table can be constructed for each group of articles subject to approximately the same costs per batch and the same percentage of interest for storage, etc. The two factors mentioned can then be regarded as a constant for the entire group of articles.

The formula for determining the batch size then becomes

$$Q^* = c\sqrt{\left(\frac{\text{demand}}{\text{price}}\right)}$$

where c is equal to $\sqrt{(2F/\delta)}$.

The demand and the price may then be employed as the two entries of a table. Something of the kind is done in 'An Introduction to Production and Inventory Control' (section 19.3), where the ordering costs between £2·50 and £4 are contained in the first part of the table and those between £4 and £6·30 in the second part of the table. The interest percentage for the table as a whole is 20%. Such tables are readily constructed and expanded in both directions by employing standard values from the R-series.

Examples of various R-series are given in Table 13.

† By J. W. M. van Houten.

TABLE 13

The *R*-series

The *R*-series are based upon the powers of 10.†
They can often be used in the construction of tables. The most widely used *R*-series are given below.

R5	R10	R20	R40
1	1	1	1
			1·06
		1·12	1·12
			1·18
	1·25	1·25	1·25
			1·32
		1·4	1·4
			1·5
1·6	1·6	1·6	1·6
			1·7
		1·8	1·8
			1·9
	2·0	2·0	2·0
			2·12
		2·24	2·24
			2·36
2·5	2·5	2·5	2·5
			2·65
		2·8	2·8
			3
	3·15	3·15	3·15
			3·35
		3·55	3·55
			3·75
4	4	4	4
			4·25
		4·5	4·5
			4·75
	5	5	5
			5·3
		5·6	5·6
			6
6·3	6·3	6·3	6·3
			6·7
		7·1	7·1
			7·5
	8	8	8
			8·5
		9	9
			9·5

† The *R*5-series comprises the results of $10^{1/5}$, $10^{2/5}$, $10^{3/5}$, $10^{4/5}$ and $10^{5/5}$, and the *R*10-series comprises the results of $10^{1/10}$, $10^{2/10}$, $10^{3/10}$, etc.

16.2 Nomograms

Nomograms, unlike graphs or charts, can accommodate several variables. They enable batch sizes to be worked out without prior calculation.

The use of the nomogram is explained by reference to Fig. 38.

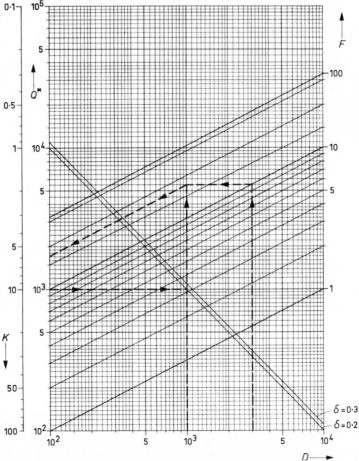

Fig. 38 Nomogram to determine the batch size.

1. Find the value of the annual turnover (*D*) on the bottom, horizontal axis.
2. Erect a vertical at the point where it intersects with the line representing the ordering costs to be employed (*F*).
3. Imagine a *horizontal* line through the point of intersection.

4. Find the value equivalent to the price per hundred products (*K*) on the left-hand *vertical line* (values increase downwards).
5. From this value, take an imaginary line horizontally to the right as far as the point of intersection with the line representing the desired δ.
6. Take an imaginary *vertical* line through this point.
7. The desired batch size can be found, parallel to the *F*-lines on the left-hand vertical axis, at the point of intersection of the imagined horizontal and vertical lines.

Example

Annual run	3000
Ordering costs	£10
δ	20 per cent
Price per hundred	£10

This example can be verified by means of the dotted lines in the nomogram. The result is a batch size of 1700.

However, the correct result should really be 1730, since

$$Q^* = \sqrt{\left(\frac{2 \times 3000 \times 10}{0 \cdot 2 \times 0 \cdot 1}\right)} = 1730$$

The reading error has the effect of producing a direct result in 'round figures', which is an advantage for the present purpose.

The procedure for determining the batch size with the aid of the nomogram in Fig. 39 is as follows. Draw a line from the point representing the changeover costs (*F*) on line *F* to the point representing the annual usage (*D*) on line *D*. Then draw another line from the appropriate point on the price line (*K*) to the point of intersection with the central line and extend it as far as line *Q**. The point of intersection on this line indicates the order quantity.

Example

Fixed costs per batch (*F*)	£6	
Annual usage	(*D*)	4500
Price per 100	(*K*)	£3
	(δ)	0·20

Draw a line from the *F*-value (6) to the *D*-value (4500).
Draw another line from *K* to the point of intersection on the central line and extend it as far as the *Q* line. The reading here is *Q** = 2500.

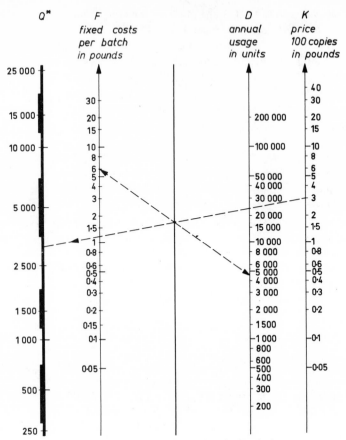

Fig. 39 Nomogram to determine the batch size.

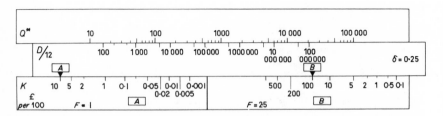

Fig. 40 An example of a slide rule designed by R. de Winter to calculate batch sizes.

16.3 Slide rules

Special slide rules have been designed for the calculation of batch sizes. Like the slide rules used in engineering, they are based on the principle that logarithmic multiplication and division are equivalent to addition and subtraction, respectively. Fig. 40 gives an example of such a slide rule.†

Using the slide rule

Firstly identify the group to which the article, whose batch size is to be determined, belongs. This may be, say, group A. Adjust the slide so that the arrow of group A is exactly opposite the price per 100 of the particular article. Read the batch size associated with the monthly usage.

As in Section 16.1 the design of this slide rule involves a constant equal to $\sqrt{(2F/\delta)}$. Accordingly, this leaves $\sqrt{(D/K)}$ to be calculated, which is readily accomplished by means of a slide rule.

The example on the previous page in fact involves four different constants, producing the groups A and B. The divisions and scales on the left-hand side are so chosen that the right-hand scales (monthly usage and optimum batch size) can be used for all the groups.

16.4 The chart

Charts are very useful as a means of determining batch sizes. Their advantage is that they are fairly simple to construct and produce results fast, particularly when they refer to groups of articles having the same profitability factor and the same set-up costs.

The first step is to establish a constant c_1, as in Section 16.1, which is equal to $\sqrt{(2F/\delta)}$. The formula $Q^* = c_1\sqrt{(D/K)}$ then applies, with K = price per item.

Formulated logarithmically, this will be found to correspond to the formula for the straight line $y = ax + b$

$$\log Q^* = \tfrac{1}{2} \log D/K + \log c_1$$

If a logarithmic scale is set out along the x-axis ($\log D/K$) and along the y-axis ($\log Q^*$), then the equation plotted with these co-ordinates will also produce a straight line, with $\tfrac{1}{2}$ as the tangent.

† Designed by R. de Winter.

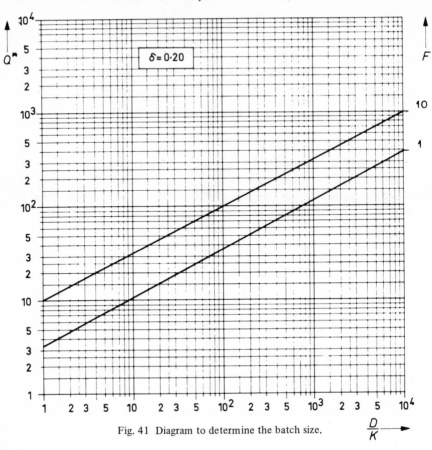

Fig. 41 Diagram to determine the batch size. $\dfrac{D}{K}$ ⟶

Another constant (c_2) can be calculated for groups of articles having different values of F. This produces a new line in the chart, parallel to the line of constant c_1. An example of such a chart is given in Fig. 41.

Construction of the chart

The chart can be constructed by calculating certain points on the straight line, for example for $D/K = 1$ and for $D/K = 100$.

In the one case we obtain the point on the Q^* axis having the value of the constant (c) and in the other case a point on the horizontal axis at the value 100 whereby the point on the vertical axis is a decuple of the previous point.

All the other lines relating to different values of $\sqrt{(2F/\delta)}$ run parallel to this line and can be constructed in the same way.

Another chart

Formula $Q^* = \sqrt{(2DF/c_i)}$ can be reduced to a formula expressing Q^* in terms of demand in weeks

$$Q_1^* = \frac{Q^*}{D} \; 52 \text{ weeks} = \sqrt{\left(\frac{2F}{c_i D}\right)} \times 52$$

Of course, the following also applies

$$\log Q_1^* = \log 52 + 0{\cdot}5 \log 2 + 0{\cdot}5 \log (F/c_i) - 0{\cdot}5 \log D$$

Q_1^* can be plotted on double log paper as a function of D for a number of values of F/c_i.

16.5 Muyen method

This method involves the use of what may be called an arithmetic code. We select the appropriate arithmetic code for each variable factor in the formula governing the batch size. An approximate value of the batch size is then found opposite the sum of these arithmetic codes.

Use of Table 14

The use of the table can best be explained by means of an example.

Data		Associated arithmetic code
Demand per year	4200 items	8
Ordering costs	£2·7	3
Inventory costs	20%	6
Price per 100	£0·8	11
	sum of arithmetic codes	28

The desired batch size of 3500 will be found in the appropriate column beside the value 28 in the column headed 'sum of arithmetic codes'. According to the formula this should be about 3700, but the answer given by the table is accurate enough for all practical purposes.

TABLE 14

Arith-metic code	Ordering costs in pounds (F)	Usage (or demand) per year (D)	Inventory costs in % δ	Price in pounds per 100 (K)	Sum of arith-metic codes	Batch size (Q)
	1	100		100	13	110
1					14	140
	1·6	160		63	15	180
2					16	220
	2·5	250	100	40	17	280
3					18	350
	4	400	63	25	19	450
4					20	560
	6·3	630	40	16	21	700
5					22	900
	10	1 000	25	10	23	1 100
6					24	1 400
	16	1 600	16	6·3	25	1 800
7					26	2 200
	25	2 500	10	4	27	2 800
8					28	3 500
	40	4 000		2·5	29	4 500
9					30	5 600
	63	6 300		1·6	31	7 000
10					32	9 000
	100	10 000		1	33	11 000
11					34	14 000
	160	16 000		0·63	35	18 000
12					36	22 000
	250	25 000		0·4	37	28 000
13					38	35 000
	400	40 000		0·25	39	45 000
14					40	56 000
	630	63 000		0·16	41	70 000
15					42	90 000
	1 000	100 000		0·1	43	110 000
16					44	140 000
		160 000		0·063	45	180 000
17					46	220 000
		250 000		0·04	47	280 000
18					48	350 000
		400 000		0·025	49	450 000
19					50	560 000
		630 000		0·016	51	700 000
20					52	900 000
		1 000 000		0·01	53	1 100 000

Standard series are employed in this table also, so that the reader can easily add to it if it proves inadequate for one of the factors.

17 Determination of the re-order level

17.1 Definitions. A simple example

The function of buffer stock and re-order level is explained fully in 'An Introduction to Production and Inventory Control'. To sum up.

If the economic stock falls below the re-order level B, a replenishment batch is ordered.

The technical stock which, on average, is present when a replenishment batch enters the stores, is the buffer stock b. The purpose of the buffer stock is to cover the maximum difference which may reasonably be expected to occur between the real demand and the forecast demand during the lead time t. If the frequency distribution of the difference between real and forecast demand during the lead time is known, then the buffer stock b is the value associated with that risk of excess which is equal to the acceptable risk of stockout per replenishment order.

The re-order level is calculated as $B = t\hat{d} + b$, where

t is the lead time in days (weeks, or months)
$\hat{d}$ is the expected demand per day (week, or month).

The calculation of the optimum re-order level B in a simple case will be explained firstly with the aid of an example, after which we shall discuss means of determining all the factors required in more complex situations.

Take, for instance, the situation described by Starr and Miller [St 1] as a 'static inventory problem under risk'; only one period is considered, and the entire frequency distribution of the demand is assumed to be known beforehand. The same problem is sometimes referred to in the literature as the problem of the newspaper vendor.

The newspaper vendor sells the current day's paper at his stall between seven o'clock in the morning and twelve noon. At 7 a.m. he must have enough papers in stock to satisfy the demand, since the stock cannot be replenished. His stock at 7 a.m. is comparable to the re-order level and will likewise be represented by B, whilst the period between 7 a.m. and 12 p.m. is comparable to the lead time. The question is: how many newspapers should the vendor have in stock at 7 a.m.?

Assume that the following are known.

$f(x)$ = the probability density of the demand x, which we shall consider to be continuously variable, in order to simplify matters;

TK = costs of every newspaper asked for after the vendor has sold out;

TV = costs of every newspaper remaining unsold.

ı TV and TK must be regarded as one symbol.

The variable costs per period from 7 a.m. to 12 p.m. are

$$C = TK \int_B^\infty (x - B)f(x)\,dx + TV \int_0^B (B - x)f(x)\,dx$$

We must now take $\dfrac{dC}{dB} = 0$. This is done as follows

$$C = TK \int_B^\infty xf(x)\,dx - TK \times B \int_B^\infty f(x)\,dx + TV \int_0^B Bf(x)\,dx - TV \int_0^B xf(x)\,dx$$

$$\frac{dC}{dB} = -TK \times Bf(b) - TK \int_B^\infty f(x)\,dx + TK \times Bf(B) + TV \int_0^B f(x)\,dx +$$

$$+ TV \times Bf(B) - TV \times Bf(B)$$

When worked out, this gives

$$\frac{dC}{dB} = -TK \int_B^\infty f(x)\,dx + TV \int_0^B f(x)\,dx$$

Of course $\displaystyle\int_0^B f(x)\,dx = 1 - \int_B^\infty f(x)\,dx$; substitution then gives

$$\boxed{\int_B^\infty f(x)\,dx = \frac{TV}{TK + TV}}$$

This means that B should be chosen so that the risk that the demand for newspapers between 7 a.m. and 12 a.m. will exceed B, is equal to

$$\frac{TV}{TK + TV}$$

This is illustrated graphically in Fig. 42.

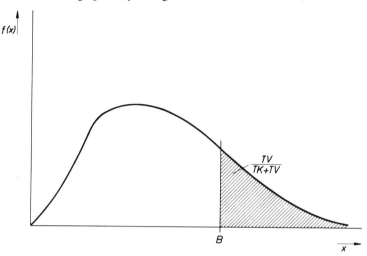

Fig. 42 Probability of running out-of-stock as a function of
inventory costs and cost of non-sellings.

Thus the newsvendor would be able to calculate the necessary initial stock B.
A similar procedure can be used to calculate B in a (B, Q) system, *if B and Q*
can be estasblished independently. 'All' that we now have to do is to ascertain
how the necessary costs data and the frequency distribution can be established
in practice and whether it is in fact desirable to do so.

18 Factors involved in the determination of the re-order level

18.1 Costs

The preceding example of the newspaper vendor involves two cost item, namely TK and TV. These amounts should be regarded as 'opportunity costs'; considerable discretion is called for in fixing these amounts, as explained in some detail by Starr and Miller [St 1]. The 'opportunity costs' TK and TV are established by solving an arithmetical problem, as follows (applicable to the situation of the newsvendor).

Our primary data are

K = purchase price per copy;
c_i = costs of holding 1 copy in stock from purchase to time of sale, or until 12 p.m.; a constant allowance c_i is made for this;
V = retail price per copy.

To determine TK and TV, first calculate the profit in the four possible situations. Assume that 1 copy or 2 copies of the newspaper are available at 7 a.m.; also that the number of copies asked for is 1 or 2. Accordingly, there are four possible combinations, and the profit for each of them is calculated in the following table.

TABLE 15

PROFIT VALUES

		Real demand	
		1	2
Number purchased	1	$V - c_i - K$	$V - c_i - K$
	2	$V - 2c_i - 2K$	$2V - 2c_i - 2K$

The 'opportunity costs' ('costs' of one too many or one too few) are then found by determining, per column, the difference in profit owing to failure to take what (afterwards) proved to be the correct decision. The values established in the table thus represent the profit forfeited, or in other words the 'costs' of an incorrect decision.

TABLE 16

PROFIT FORFEITED

		Real demand	
		1	2
Number purchased	1	0	$V - c_i - K$
	2	$c_i + K$	0

Thus TV and TK are determined.

Each product deficiency means a profit of $V - c_i - K$ forfeited and therefore costs $TK = V - c_i - K$.

Each surplus product means a profit of $c_i + K$ forfeited and therefore costs $TV = c_i + K$.

A very similar line of reasoning can be followed in the case of spare parts, the lack of which adds considerably to costs, instead of newspapers, which show a profit when sold. Let us assume that K and c_i mean the same as before but that c_u represents the loss incurred through the lack of a necessary spare part. Again, we construct two tables, in this case for costs and for additional costs relative to the correct decision.

TABLE 17

TOTAL COSTS

		Number required	
		1	2
Number purchased	1	$K + c_i$	$K + c_i + c_u$
	2	$2K + 2c_i$	$2K + 2c_i$

TABLE 18

ADDITIONAL COSTS

		Number required	
		1	2
Number purchased	1	0	$c_u - K - c_i$
	2	$K + c_i$	0

In these circumstances, then

$$TK = c_u - K - c_i$$

$$TV = K + c_i$$

The result obtained in the previous paragraph can also be formulated differently. From the problem of the newsvendor we have

$$\int_B^\infty f(x)\,dx = \frac{TV}{TK + TV} = \frac{K + c_i}{V}$$

and for the case of the spare parts

$$\int_B^\infty f(x)\,dx = \frac{TV}{TK + TV} = \frac{K + c_i}{c_u}$$

All the cost factors mentioned here have been discussed before in connection with the batch size calculation, with one exception, that is the loss due to stockout.

Loss due to stockout

Different hypotheses are to be found in the literature concerning the loss incurred through the late arrival of a replenishment order.

a. The loss is proportional to the number of stock items which should be, but are not in fact available for delivery from stores. In our opinion this is a valid starting point for a stock of end products. The basis of this theory is that the sales during a given time are 'negative'. This means either a number of sales (and probably customers) forfeited, or a number of 'back orders', or in other words orders booked for delivery only on arrival of the stock replenishment.
b. The loss is incurred whenever stockout occurs and does not depend upon the number of products in arrears. In our opinion this hypothesis reflects approximately the situation which arises in the inventory control of components. In the event of an *impending* stockout of a given component, certain precautions are taken, for example:

– factory is given first call on a production batch already ordered;
– batch already ordered may be sent by air instead of by sea (or by air over part of the route);
– telephone calls are made, telegrams are sent, talks are held.

c. The loss can be calculated as costs of holding a negative stock, or in other words the loss is calculated per product per time unit.

The costs are needed in order to arrive at the acceptable risk,

$$\int_B^\infty f(x)\,dx = z$$

Not infrequently, the determination of the cost factors is thought to be not worth the effort involved. A risk, considered acceptable, is then simply fixed arbitrarily, often described as the acceptable value of z. There are different ways of doing this. The same z can be chosen for all the products, or (from the theoretical knowledge acquired so far) a higher value of z can be assigned to articles having a high c_i or a relatively low c_u. The batch size employed, or in other words the number of orders per year, can also be taken into account.

Lastly, it is possible to establish values for the cost factors by reversing the calculation. Assume, for example, that the assumption made above under b appears to be the correct one, whilst the management are prepared to invest not more than A hundred pounds in buffer stocks. The amount to be accepted as the loss per individual stockout so as to arrive at a total investment of A hundred thousand pounds in buffer stock can then be determined by reversing the calculation. The amount thus established can be submitted to the person responsible for fixing the total investment in buffer stock (A hundred thousand) as evidence of the relationship between the buffer stock level and the costs of stockout. An insight into these matters should lead to better decisions despite the fact that the exact cost factors are not known.

18.2 Frequency distribution of usage during the lead time

18.2.1 Determination of the lead time

To be able to establish the frequency distribution of the usage during the lead time, it is necessary to know the lead time per product. In the absence of any specific and reliable agreement with the supplier as to the lead time, the first step is to find out whether there is any possibility of improving the situation. For example, a company controlling a stock of spare parts came to an arrangement with the factory supplying replenishments for this stock, whereby the latter agreed to guarantee their lead time (for example, the lead time attainable in 95% of the cases), in accordance with the following table:

TABLE 19

Category	Number of opera-tions or operation-equivalents	Lead time in months	
		Normal material	Specific material
1	1–3	3	5
2	4–6	4	6
3	7–9	5	7
4	10–12	6	8
5	13–15	7	9

A considerable variation in the lead time for a particular product is sometimes unavoidable; such variation should then be taken into account in the calculation of the variation in demand during the lead time (see Chapter 28). In most cases, however, we must agree with Goudriaan [Go 2] that:

In my opinion it is either unnecessary or unprofitable to take a variable lead time into account. Unnecessary when the variability is relatively small; in view of the general custom of totalling the squares of the coefficients of variation, minor coefficients of variation of the lead time can safely be ignored. On the other hand, instead of merely including *major coefficients of variation* in the calculations, we should do our utmost *to combat and eliminate them by all the legitimate means at our disposal.* At all events, I feel that the consequent stock expansion should not be undertaken without prior consent of the management.

Where statistical analysis of lead times, as carried out in the past, reveals considerable variation, it should be borne in mind that the user himself may well be responsible for this. It may well be that the short lead times are a result of shortening the normal lead-time (at the request of the customer), say, by expediting the particular work and thereby automatically extending the lead time for other products.

In this connection, it may be useful to say something about the different types of contract which may exist between a customer and his suppliers; Seebach even wrote a 145-page thesis on this subject. He divided long-term delivery contracts into different categories, namely 'Sukzessivlieferungsverträge' (contracts for delivery by instalments), 'Rahmenverträge' (skeleton contracts), 'Abrufaufträge' (contracts for delivery on call); he observed however: 'The specific types of contract described here are far less common in practice than a very wide variety of combinations of them' [Se 1].

What particularly interests us with regard to the lead time as we understand the term at present is: for how far ahead has the customer contracted to place an order which will be binding on him? Take for example the type of contract regarded by *Seebach* as a form of contract to deliver on call.

Company A (customer) agrees with company L (supplier) that for the duration of the contract, A shall order from L all the components of code number XYZ which A requires. On the other hand, L undertakes to deliver the quantities asked for at the specified time, subject to the following conditions: firm orders shall invariably be placed two months in advance, together with an estimate of requirements for the following three months.

This contract means that in fixing his buffer stock level, A must proceed on the understanding that the lead time will, as a rule, be two months. Depending upon the wording employed to describe the ordering procedure in the contract, the calculations will have to be carried out in exactly same way as for a (B, Q), or a (s, S), system with a lead time of two months.

We deliberately stipulated that this two-month lead time should be considered to hold good *as a rule*; although the customer can take measures if stockout appears really imminent, this is precisely the situation referred to under *b* on page 138.

18.2.2 Determining the frequency distribution of usage per time unit or per lead time

Last but not least, we require an insight into the frequency distribution of the difference between the estimated and the real usage per lead time. Some methods employ the frequency distribution of the usage per time unit as a link for two reasons:

— this datum is readily established in most cases;
— it can be used as a basis for calculations relating to different values of the lead time, so that it is not necessary to collect data all over again in the event of a change in the lead time.

The frequency distribution is needed as a means of determining the values of buffer stock and re-order level associated with a given value of z. This can be accomplished in two ways.

a. The graphical-empirical method.
The value of the re-order level appropriate to a given risk of excess, is determined empirically.
b. Analytical methods. They usually involve estimating the second moment of the distribution and then attempting to match some theoretical frequency distribution to this.

The two methods will now be discussed in more detail.

18.2.3 Practical measurement of lead time

Measurement of lead time may be carried out as part of a single investigation, or may be one feature of a system designed to bring lead times under control. The following plan proved successful in one specific case.

To get a better idea of the extent to which its suppliers could be relied upon for prompt delivery, a company sought the co-operation of these suppliers in evolving a test method. It goes without saying that this measurement is simple, is within the powers of each supplier and gives scope for comparing individual results.

In principle, the supplier undertakes to deliver the agreed quantities in the period (week, fortnight, month) promised by him. The difference between the agreed and real times of delivery is then measured. Because this measurement is carried out by the customer and the supplier, an insight is obtained into the behaviour of the transport time between supplier and customer.

This method involves measurement per delivery. A delivery is defined as the quantity constituting more than 90% and less than 110% of the weekly, fortnightly or monthly instalment called for on an order or code number per customer.

This measurement of undertaking, less realization, can be carried out in two ways, namely:

a. On the basis of the *undertakings* within a given period, by ascertaining at the end of this period how many of the promised deliveries have been realized. The unfulfilled promises are 'premature' or 'late' deliveries, in respect of which the difference between undertaking and realization is established.
b. On the basis of the *deliveries* within a given period. The difference between undertaking and realization is determined for each delivery.

The first method at once focuses attention upon the undertakings not yet realized, but is less simple to carry out than the other. On the other hand, the second method involves a certain amount of delay, but is simpler as regards the provision of warning signals.

Which of the two methods is chosen will depend upon the particular system of administration. The schedule in Table 20 simplifies the measurement. If necessary for the purpose of further analysis, some particulars of the 'premature' and/or 'late' deliveries can be recorded in a separate survey, e.g. number, code number, destination and promised delivery period.

The visual display of the differences in Table 20 provides an incentive to improvement of the delivery discipline. Practical experience has shown that there is usually no relationship whatever between the length of the prescribed lead time and the reliability of deliveries.

'Bad' suppliers simply cannot be relied upon to deliver on time, regardless of the lead time allowed, whereas 'good' suppliers can be relied upon for prompt delivery even when the lead time is relatively short. The reason is that the latter do not quote a delivery time unless they are certain that they can keep to it. Their behaviour with regard to deliveries is based upon carefully considered undertakings.

TABLE 20

RELIABILITY WITH REGARD TO DELIVERIES				
of: the article group, the supplier, the associated factory: . . . . in the period: . . . -71 to . . . -71, compiled by:				
Time:		number of deliveries	total	in %
premature	weeks			
	8			
	4 − 8			
	2 − 4			
	1 − 2			
	0 − 1			
on time (= within the agreed week, fortnight or month)				
late	0 − 1			
	1 − 2			
	2 − 4			
	4 − 8			
	8			
	weeks	total		100

19 The graphical-empirical method

19.1 Principle

A number of variants of the graphical-empirical method are described in the literature. It is the simplest and most understandable, but in most cases also the most laborious method. Despite this drawback, however, the graphical-empirical method constitutes an excellent introductory study not only for those engaged in mastering the principles of inventory control, but also for companies planning to introduce these principles for the first time, since it provides a step-by-step analysis of events. At the same time, every effort should be made to ensure an eventual change to one of the other methods, described later, since they are less time-consuming.

Initially, the method can be carried out as follows. After the preliminary plan has been discussed, a number of possible simplifications or other improvements will be considered. Past usage figures provide the basis of the system. The following action should be taken.

1. Establish the lead time;

2. Divide the time span in respect of which the usage figures are known into periods equivalent to the lead time. It may happen that this cannot be done satisfactorily because, say, the lead time is six weeks whereas only monthly usage figures are given. Also, the lead time may not be the same in all cases. The time span should then be divided into equal periods in two or three different ways, for instance once into periods of one month and once into periods of two months (see Goudriaan and Cahen [Go 3], 1932);

3. Prepare a survey per article, in which the following data from one period invariably appear on the same line, and are afterwards interpolated.
— the expected usage of the particular article, or in other words the demand which existed at the beginning of the period. Sometimes a commercial forecast of this demand is available, or otherwise it may be known as a result of an 'explosion' of the assembly programme. In many cases, however, no such forecast has ever been made or, if it has, no record of it has been preserved. In

such cases, one of the following data should be adopted and used in lieu of the required forecast.

a. the 'moving annual total' of the demand, converted to a period of the given length;

b. the average demand per period over the calendar year. However, this value only becomes known after the event and was therefore not available as a forecast in the past. The error involved will be discussed later;

c. a value obtained by smoothing

— the real demand;

— the ratio of real to expected demand.

Each line now counts as an observation. By scheduling the real/expected ratio per article, we would obtain the frequency distribution shown on the right in Fig. 4. Given z, this would enable us to determine B_z directly for the product in question, by drawing a straight line l in the frequency distribution, so that

$$\frac{\text{hatched area}}{\text{total area}} = z \ (\text{Fig. 43})$$

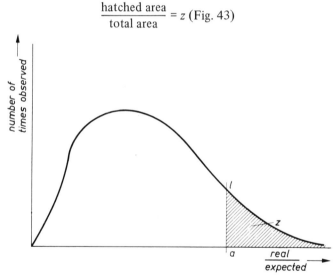

Fig. 43 Principle of graphical determination of the re-order level.

Thus the re-order level B_z can invariably be established as

$$(\text{expected demand during } t) \times a_z$$

where a_z is the factor real/expected associated with l.

Generally speaking, however, it is not necessary to make such frequency distributions separately for each code number (that is, each article). Instead, all the observations can be combined in one chart, as follows.

4. Plot the ratio real/expected for all the observations against the expected demand. This produces a concentration of dots as shown in Fig. 44.
Now draw freehand a curve defining the upper boundary of the concentration or 'cloud', so that

$$\frac{\text{number of points above the curve}}{\text{total number of points}} = z$$

Often, this procedure can be greatly simplified by employing double log paper; usually a straight line can then be drawn instead of a curve. A logarithmic scale will in any case be essential where the turnover varies widely throughout an assortment of products.

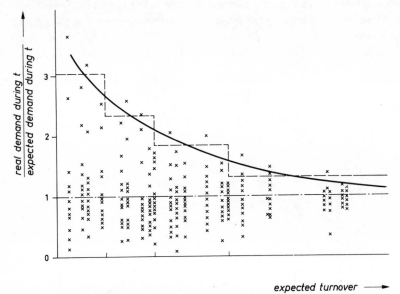

Fig. 44 'Cloud' of dots representing the ratio real/expected.

All this constitutes a major step forward. The re-order level is plotted against the forecast demand, on the assumption that a sufficiently significant relationship exists between annual demand and the maximum deviation which may reasonably be expected.

As the next step, the individual turnovers can be classified, after which an average factor a_z can be established for each class. This produces, say, the broken line in Fig. 44.

In some cases this 'stepped' line will be sufficient in itself. Alternatively, a point governed by the average demand and the average factor a_z can be established for each class and these individual points can then be joined by drawing a line through them.

In the check calculations which have to be carried out periodically (say once a year) in order to confirm the validity of the derived factors, the procedure can be simplified a number of times, as follows.

1. unchanged;

2. unchanged;

3. unchanged;

4. classify the observations according to the 'expected demand' in the manner previously indicated;

5. make a cumulative frequency distribution *per class* of the observations real/expected;

6. the factor a_z associated with z can be determined directly per class, whereby B_z is established as $B_z = a_z \times d_t$ (Fig. 45).

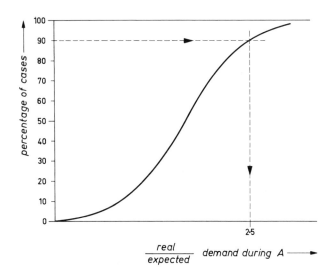

Fig. 45 Determination of factor *a* per changeover class, from the cumulative frequency distribution of real/expected. The factor *a* associated with a service function of 90%, that is with z = 10%, is 2·5.

So much for the initial outline of the graphical-empirical method, certain aspects of which will now be considered individually.

19.2 Labour saving

It will be evident that in reality there is no need to plot all the points in the graph, or to calculate the ratio real/expected for all the periods. All that we really need to know is the upper $100z\%$ of the observations.

The following method of approximation can be employed. Simply take the period of maximum demand per year and per article and use this as an observation. For instance, Goudriaan and Cahen invariably took the month of peak demand and drew through the observations thus obtained a line, above which lay 20% of the points; this means that the demand was above the line in one out of 5 x 12, that is in one out of sixty periods of one month, since each point represents the highest of 12 monthly values. The estimated ratio of one in seventy is somewhat on the low side, because it does not necessarily follow that all the other observations will be below the line. If the month of peak demand for a given article is well above the line, then it is by no means inconceivable that the point denoting the month of next highest demand is also above the line; this holds good, at any rate, for the articles most in demand throughout the year, in respect of which the standard deviation is usually relatively small.

Otherwise, the most effective labour-saving device is to study a random sample of the articles instead of all of them. Where there is reason to suspect that the articles do not constitute a homogeneous group, a subdivision must be made or the irregularity of demand must be established separately for each article, for example by smoothing. We shall come back to this later.

Other possibilities are: (1) to adopt, for each article, the maximum deviation which can occur as between the calculated re-order level and that which ultimately proves necessary; (2) to introduce another explanatory variable, for example the number of orders per year.

19.3 Periods of no demand

It may well happen, particularly in the case of products having a low annual turnover, that there was no demand whatever for them during a number of periods. In the present method of calculation, it is quite correct to count these 'nil observations' as observations; if a period of no demand commences after the re-order level is reached, then the replenishment order will arrive whilst the stock is still positive. With the demand behaving in this way, however, it is questionable whether it will be continuous enough to warrant the use of the graphical-empirical method described here (see following section).

19.4 Tacit assumptions

It should be borne in mind that the method described is based on the following assumptions.

1. That at the start of the lead time the economic stock equals the re-order level (or in other words that the last order from a customer has not taken the stock very far below the re-order level);
2. That in a period following the attainment of the re-order level, the demand is not systematically higher or lower than in any other period of the same length.
3. That the maximum deviation is significantly related to the annual turnover.

19.5 Goudriaan's and Cahen's classical study

Because the article in which Goudriaan and Cahen published their study [Go 3] of inventory control as applied to mass-produced articles has only had a very limited circulation, we shall now reproduce that portion of it which deals with the determination of re-order levels (or order levels as they call them).

'When is new stock to be ordered.'

It is general practice to order new stock when the existing stock has fallen below a certain level. This level, which we will call the *order level*, must be so high that the branch will not be without stock during the time of delivery of the order and it must therefore be sufficient to cover the probable sales during the time of delivery.
  The sales of a certain article are effected by
  1. general trend
  2. seasonal fluctuations
  3. incidental fluctuations.
The influence of the general trend apart from seasonal and incidental fluctuations is easily taken into account by basing the forecast of the probable sales on the moving annual total of the previous period.
  To take also the other two fluctuations into account the empirical statistical way has been chosen, i.e. for each article out of the 300 to 1500 stock articles in each country the maximum monthly and bimonthly sales of a previous year have been plotted in a diagram in relation to the total sales of that year.
  Fig. 46 shows the result of this operation for the monthly sales. Each vertical column represents a certain class of annual sales; each horizontal line represents a certain class of maximum monthly sales; the number in each square indicate the number of cases. The dispersion of the maximum monthly sales in each class of annual sales is considerable. Now it

was not considered necessary to take all the cases into account. It was decided to take a slight risk and to disregard 20% of the total number of cases in each class of annual sales.

At first glance it seems that this would mean that for 20% of the articles the order level would once a year be insufficient to cover the sales during the time of delivery. Further consideration, however, shows that in actual practice this percentage will be much lower, because a real danger will only occur when the beginning of the period of maximum sales

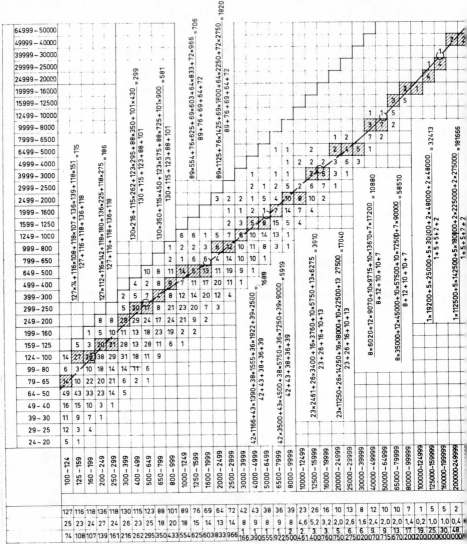

Fig. 46 Frequency diagram of maximum monthly sales as a
function of annual sales.

coincides more or less with the attainment of the order level. This combined probability can affect only a small fraction of the 20%.

Practice has in fact shown that we hardly ever run short of stocks as a result of disregarding these 20% of the cases. The figures of the bottom line of Fig. 46 (max. sales limits of 80% cases) indicate per class of annual sales the monthly sales level below which 80% of all cases remain and the trend of these figures is fairly regular. To eliminate hazardous influences we established weighted averages for groups of five classes of annual sales (see calculation in the graph). The circles indicate these weighted averages and the empirical curve determined by these circles is taken as the basic relationship between annual sales and maximum monthly sales. For the bimonthly sales the calculation has been effected exactly in the same manner.

In Fig. 47 the maximum monthly and bimonthly sales are represented as a percentage of the corresponding annual sales. The real order level corresponding in general with a time between one or two months, is determined by interpolation between these two curves. The remarkable fact is that the curves show a similar trend for all countries. They differ only in heights, owing to local circumstances. By establishing the curves for a certain country from the data of different years, the differences are found to be extremely small, thus indicating a high degree of invariability.

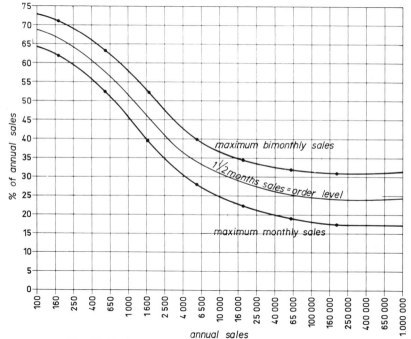

Fig. 47 Maximum monthly and bimonthly sales and order levels as a function of annual sales.

So we are entitled to formulate the general law:

'The maximum monthly and bimonthly sales for articles which are sold in small quantities are relatively much larger than for articles which are sold in large quantities. This fact is not at all surprising as articles of the first kind are generally bought by fewer customers and thus show more irregularities in their sales than articles of the second kind.'

19.6 Variants

As we said before, many variants of the above method are described in the literature. The following examples may serve to illustrate this point. It will be seen from the article by Goudriaan and Cahen that in the case of goods the demand for which is very much less stable than for mass-produced articles, they plot the sales in a given month against the sales in the preceding three months.

For a chemical product, Ackoff [Ac 1] established that the ratio between the demand per month and the peak demand in one of the preceding three months approximately followed a normal distribution and exceeded 2·0 in only 7·3% of the cases. Bluck, Smith and Thackray [Bl 1] constructed a chart, also for a chemical product, in which the relationship between the total demand per month and the peak demand on three consecutive days was represented, for each month, by a point (the lead time is three days). They then drew, by eye, a line above which only a certain percentage of the points appeared.

It is, of course, most unwise to adopt without question methods developed to deal with one specific case.

20 Analytical methods

20.1 Use of the Poisson distribution

A situation which is readily calculated occurs when theoretical considerations suggest, and practical tests confirm, that the demand follows a Poisson distribution, the average value of which can be forecast with reasonable accuracy.

Beginning with a given value for the multiple of the standard deviation to be adopted as a safety margin, the entire range of applications can be covered in one table (see Tables 21 and 22 borrowed from Goudriaan).

TABLE 21

UNILATERAL CHANCE OF SUCCESS FOR THE CASE OF THE POISSON
DISTRIBUTION AT THE 2s and 3s LIMITS

$\bar{n}$	$s = \sqrt{n}$	$\bar{n} + 2s$	$\bar{n} + 2s$ rounded	Unilateral chance of excess in %	$\bar{n} + 3s$	$\bar{n} + 3s$ rounded	Unilateral chance of excess in %
1	1·000	3·000	4	1·90	4·000	5	0·54
2	1·414	4·828	5	5·27	6·242	7	0·45
3	1·732	6·464	7	3·35	8·196	9	0·38
4	2·000	8·000	9	2·13	10·000	11	0·28
5	2·236	9·472	10	3·18	11·708	12	0·55
6	2·450	10·900	11	4·26	13·350	14	0·36
7	2·646	12·292	13	2·70	14·938	15	0·57
8	2·828	13·656	14	3·42	16·484	17	0·37
9	3·000	15·000	16	2·20	18·000	19	0·24
10	3·162	16·324	17	2·70	19·486	20	0·35
11	3·317	17·634	18	3·22	20·951	21	0·47
12	3·464	18·928	19	3·74	22·392	23	0·30
13	3·606	20·212	21	2·50	23·818	24	0·40
14	3·742	21·484	22	2·88	25·226	26	0·26
15	3·873	22·746	23	3·27	26·619	27	0·33
16	4·000	24·000	25	2·23	28·000	29	0·22

20.2 Goudriaan's formula

There are situations in which it is permissible to assume that the number of customers' orders follows a Poisson distribution whilst the batch size follows a different distribution independently. The formulae derived in 6.1.3 are then applicable

$$\mu_C = \mu_A \times \mu_B$$

$$\sigma_C{}^2 = \sigma_A{}^2 \, (\sigma_B{}^2 + \mu_B{}^2)$$

where

μ_A is the average number of orders per period

σ_A is the standard deviation in the number of orders per period

μ_B is the average size of a customer's order

σ_B is the standard deviation in the size of the customer's orders

μ_C is the average demand per period in terms of quantity of products

σ_C is the standard deviation in the demand per period, in terms of quantity of products.

The above formulae can be combined to give

$$\sigma_C{}^2 = \mu_A \mu_B{}^2 \left\{ 1 + \left(\frac{\sigma_B}{\mu_B}\right)^2 \right\}$$

This is the formula published by Goudriaan [Go 1] in 1962.

The buffer stock is now put at $k\sigma_c$, where k is usually fixed arbitrarily, possibly per group or class of products; k can be corrected if necessary when the actual results of applying the formula are known. Of course, there is nothing to prevent us from trying to match by trial and error some theoretical distribution of our own choosing.

This is discussed more fully in Section 20.5.

The next point to consider is how the values of μ_A, μ_B and σ_B/μ_B required per product can be established in practice.

Goudriaan suggests that this can be done as follows. Fixed tables should be used; it is best to omit μ_B (average customer's order) from the tables. A standard series can be used for the ratio σ_B/μ_B, for which $\sqrt{(1 + (\sigma_B/\mu_B)^2)}$ is tabulated.

In Table 23, taken from Goudriaan, series R80 is chosen for the radical form. It appears that, with practice, the magnitude of the coefficient of variation σ_B/μ_B can be estimated fairly accurately.

Apart from the turnover per period μ_C it is now necessary to know the number of orders μ_A; μ_B then follows directly from this.

A table similar to Table 23 can be constructed for every value of $\sqrt{(1 + (\sigma_B/\mu_B)^2)}$ which occurs.

RE-ORDER LEVEL FOR DIFFERENT LEAD TIMES AND ESTIMATED SALES IN QUANTITIES PER YEAR

(Lead time and sales increments according to R10; safety margin referred to 2s)

Estimated sales in quantities per year		Lead time in												
years		0·063	0·080	0·100	0·125	0·160	0·200	0·250	0·315	0·400	0·500	0·630	0·800	1·000
months		—	—	1·1–1·3	1·4–1·8	1·9–2·1	2·2–2·6	2·7–3·3	3·4–4·1	4·2–5·3	5·4–6·6	6·7–8·3	8·4–10·6	10·7–13·2
weeks		3–4	4–5	5–6	6–7	8–9	10–11	12–14	15–18	19–23	24–28	29–36	37–46	47–57
days		22–25	26–32	33–40	41–50	51–64	65–80	81–100	101–125					
nominal	Limits													
10	8·9–11·2	2	3	3	4	4	5	6	7	8	10	12	14	17
12·5	11·3–14·1	3	3	4	4	5	6	7	8	10	12	14	17	20
16	14·2–17·7	3	4	4	5	6	7	8	10	12	14	17	20	24
20	17·8–22·3	4	4	5	6	7	8	10	12	14	17	20	24	29
25	22·4–28·1	4	5	6	7	8	10	12	14	17	20	24	29	35
31·5	28·2–35·4	5	6	7	8	10	12	14	17	20	24	29	35	43
40	35·5–44·6	6	7	8	10	12	14	17	20	24	29	35	43	53
50	44·7–56·2	7	8	10	12	14	17	20	24	29	35	43	53	64
63	56·3–70·7	8	10	12	14	17	20	24	29	35	43	53	64	80
80	70·8–89·1	10	12	14	17	20	24	29	35	43	53	64	80	98
100	89·2–112	12	14	17	20	24	29	35	43	53	64	80	98	120
125	113 –141	14	17	20	24	29	35	43	53	64	80	98	120	147
160	142 –177	17	20	24	29	35	43	53	64	80	98	120	147	185
200	178 –223	20	24	29	35	43	53	64	80	98	120	147	185	228
250	224 –281	24	29	35	43	53	64	80	98	120	147	185	228	282
315	282 –354	29	35	43	53	64	80	98	120	147	185	228	282	356
400	355 –446	35	43	53	64	80	98	120	147	185	228	282	356	440
500	447 –562	43	53	64	80	98	120	147	185	228	282	356	440	544
630	563 –707	53	64	80	98	120	147	185	228	282	356	440	544	690
800	708 –891	64	80	98	120	147	185	228	282	356	440	544	690	856
1000	892–1122	80	98	120	147	185	228	282	356	440	544	690	856	1064
1250	1123–1412	98	120	147	185	228	282	356	440	544	690	856	1064	1320
1600	1413–1778	120	147	185	228	282	356	440	544	690	856	1064	1320	1680
2000	1779–2238	147	185	228	282	356	440	544	690	856	1064	1320	1680	2090
2500	2239–2818	185	228	282	356	440	544	690	856	1064	1320	1680	2090	2600

Hypothesis: demand follows Poisson distribution.

Warning:
This table can be used only if the demand per sale is for one single unit. Copied from: *T. Eff and Doc.* **32** (1962) no. 8.

Example:
For a lead time of 10–11 weeks, or 0·2 year, the estimated annual sales amount to 80; this produces $n = 16$; $\sqrt{n} = 4$; $n + 2\sqrt{n} = 24$.

TABLE 23

$$\sqrt{\left(1+\left(\frac{\sigma_B}{\mu_B}\right)^2\right)}$$ (according to Goudriaan)

$\sqrt{\left(1+\left(\frac{\sigma_B}{\mu_B}\right)^2\right)}$ nominal	Exact upper limit for		$\sqrt{\left(1+\left(\frac{\sigma_B}{\mu_B}\right)^2\right)}$ nominal	Exact upper limit for	
	$\sqrt{\left(1+\left(\frac{\sigma_B}{\mu_B}\right)^2\right)}$	$\frac{\sigma_B}{\mu_B}$		$\sqrt{\left(1+\left(\frac{\sigma_B}{\mu_B}\right)^2\right)}$	$\frac{\sigma_B}{\mu_B}$
1·00	1·029		2·12	2·175	
		0·243			1·934
1·06	1·090		2·24	2·304	
		0·435			2·080
1·12	1·155		2·36	2·441	
		0·577			2·23
1·18	1·223		2·50	2·585	
		0·705			2·40
1·25	1·296		2·65	2·738	
		0·824			2·55
1·32	1·373		2·80	2·901	
		0·940			2·72
1·40	1·454		3·00	3·703	
		1·054			2·90
1·50	1·540		3·15	3·103	
		1·171			3·08
1·60	1·631		3·35	3·255	
		1·288			3·29
1·70	1·728		3·55	3·448	
		1·411			3·51
1·80	1·830		3·75	3·652	
		1·535			3·74
1·90	1·939		4·00	3·868	
		1·665			3·98
2·00	2·054				
		1·797			

20.3 Determination of second moment by means of correlation calculation

To be able to determine the re-order level, we really need to know the first, second, third and higher moments of the frequency distribution of the difference between forecast and real demand. The forecast value of the first moment of the frequency distribution of the demand, that is the average demand, has been established by one of the methods discussed earlier. Experience has shown that within a range of articles there is often a relationship between average demand and standard deviation of the demand, which is reasonably reliable and reproducible from year to year. In many cases, this relationship is found to take the following form

$$\sigma = c\mu^p$$

$$\log \sigma = \log c + p \log \mu$$

Where this relationship exists, it provides a useful means of determining the standard deviation of the demand as a function of the expected demand. In such cases it is not necessary to employ separate formulae for each product or to estimate the standard deviation from past records.

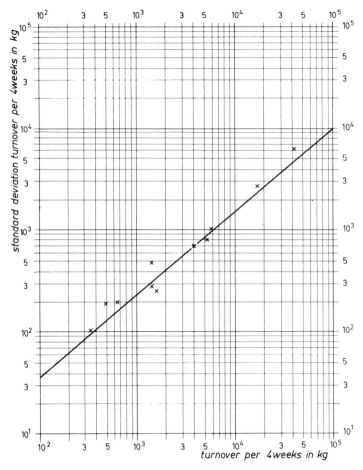

Fig. 48a.

One or two examples of correlation encountered in practice are given in Figs. 48a to c inclusive. In the correlation diagram, each article is represented by a dot.

Would it not be possible to reason out beforehand whether a relationship $\sigma = c\mu^p$ exists in a given case and whether the values of c and p can be calculated from more fundamental data? Although some work has been done on these lines, there is still much to be done. Hence we shall merely demonstrate that such a relationship may occur. Note, therefore, that the following does not provide direct evidence of the existence of the relationship $\sigma = c\mu^p$, but

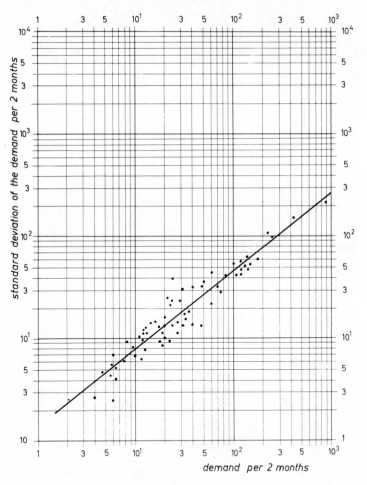

Fig. 48b.

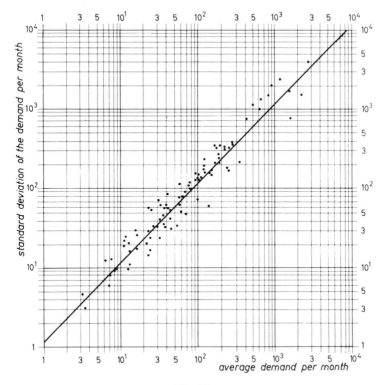

Fig. 48c.

merely implies that this relationship has been detected empirically in several cases. Having noted this, we shall simply try to find a possible explanation for it.

Assume that for each product of a uniform assortment, the frequency distribution of the total demand per period t (having a mean μ and a standard deviation σ) is governed by the frequency distribution of the number of orders per period (μ_A, σ_A) and the frequency distribution of the order quantity (μ_B, σ_B), whereby the following applies

$$\mu = \mu_A \mu_B$$

$$\sigma^2 = \mu_A \sigma_B^2 + \mu_B^2 \sigma_A^2$$

(these formulae were discussed in section 6.1.3).

If one article within a uniform assortment of articles has a higher turnover than another, this will *usually* be partly due to a relatively larger number of orders for the former article and partly due to the fact that these orders are relatively larger individually. It is a generally accepted hypothesis that the average number of orders increases proportionately with μ^a and that the average order quantity increases with μ^b. If we also assume that the sales are independent of one another and that the frequency distribution of the order quantities retains the same coefficient of variation, we may write

$$\mu_A = C_1\mu^a, \quad \sigma_A = C_2\mu^{a/2}$$
$$\mu_B = C_3\mu^b, \quad \sigma_B = C_4\mu^b$$

Since $\mu = \mu_A\mu_B$, we have

$$C_1 = \frac{1}{C_3}$$

and

$$a + b = 1$$

By employing formulae from the foregoing we now find

$$\sigma = \text{constant } \sqrt{(\mu^{2-a})}$$

or $\qquad \sigma = \text{constant } \mu^{1-a/2}$

This relationship can also be expressed as

$$\sigma = c\mu^p$$

in which, evidently, $p = 1 - (a/2)$.

Three specific cases illustrate the occurrence of special forms of the equation $\sigma = c\mu^p$ more clearly.

Case 1. If the increased turnover is brought about exclusively by an increase in the number of orders (standard packing, low ordering costs), then $a = 1$ and $p = 0.5$.

Case 2. If the increased turnover is brought about exclusively by an increase in the order quantity, then $a = 0$ and $p = 1.0$ (not inconceivable where the circle of customers is fixed and the same for each article).

Case 3. Assume that the number of customers is the same for each article; for example, a number of wholesalers order the articles concerned from a central store. Also assume that the customers base their orders upon the formula for the optimum order quantity (without discount). An increase in turnover distributed evenly amongst the customers, for example by a factor of four, then results in twice as many orders which on average are twice the original size. In this case, $a = 0.5$ and $p = 0.75$.

If the regression line found is to have any practical value, the correlation coefficient for the relationship between μ and σ will have to be very high.

Suppose the following regression line is found

$$\sigma_1 = c\mu^p$$

Then with a change of excess of about 2% on both sides it follows that

$$\frac{\sigma_1}{f} < \sigma < f\sigma_1$$

The value of f is determined by the calculated correlation coefficient r for $\log \sigma$ and $\log \mu$ and also by the quotient between the largest value and the smallest value of σ, that appear in the correlation diagram.

TABLE 24

TABLE OF f VALUES

	ratio σ_{max} to σ_{min}									
r	10	20	50	100	200	500	1000	2000	5000	10 000
0·7	2·28	2·91	4·04	5·18	6·63	9·20	11·8	15·1	20·9	26·8
0·8	2·00	2·46	3·23	3·98	4·90	6·45	7·94	9·78	12·9	15·8
0·85	1·83	2·20	2·80	3·36	4·04	5·14	6·17	7·41	9·43	11·3
0·9	1·65	1·92	2·34	2·73	3·17	3·88	4·51	5·24	6·40	7·44
0·95	1·43	1·60	1·84	2·05	2·29	2·64	2·94	3·28	3·78	4·21
0·96	1·38	1·52	1·73	1·90	2·10	2·39	2·63	2·90	3·29	3·63
0·97	1·32	1·44	1·61	1·75	1·90	2·13	2·32	2·52	2·82	3·06
0·98	1·26	1·35	1·48	1·58	1·69	1·86	1·99	2·13	2·33	2·50
0·99	1·18	1·24	1·32	1·38	1·45	1·55	1·63	1·71	1·82	1·91
1·00	1·00	1·00	1·00	1·00	1·00	1·00	1·00	1·00	1·00	1·00

Example

If in a group of pairs the quantities (μ, σ) the extreme values of σ are given by

$$\sigma_{max} = 1\ 234\ 000 \text{ and } \sigma_{min} = 2468, \text{ then } \frac{\sigma_{max}}{\sigma_{min}} = 500$$

Assuming that we find $\sigma_1 = 10\mu^{0·7}$ with $r = 0·96$, then $f = 2·39$, so that the confidence limits for σ are

$$\frac{10}{2·39}\mu^{0·7} < \sigma < 2·39\mu^{0·7}$$

It will be evident that unless r assumes a very high value, the confidence limits are too wide.

Another point which is certainly worth mentioning, although no definite statement concerning it can be made at this juncture, is as follows. In the literature, little or no attention has been given to the fact that turnover and standard deviation for each article are determined from only a small number of observations. In many cases each individual point in the correlation diagram is merely

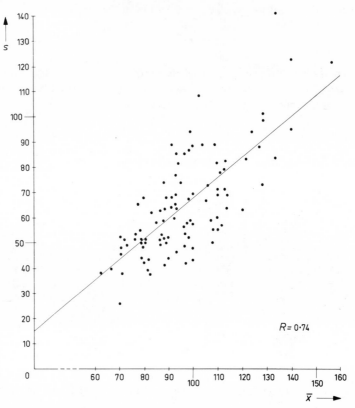

Fig. 49*a* Each point is calculated from a series of 12 samples from a gamma distribution with two degrees of freedom.

deduced from 12 monthly demand figures. Accordingly, the points in the correlation diagram do not reflect μ and σ themselves, but instead merely represent relatively rough estimates of them. In general, this has the effect of putting the correlation coefficient found on the low side. The calculation is hampered by the fact that the mean and the standard deviation of a sample of n individual draws from a given probability distribution are not distributed independently of one another. Fig. 49*a* illustrates this.

To get an idea of the effect of the test sample upon the correlation coefficient found, despite this drawback, one or two 'Monte Carlo' calculations† were carried out. They were based upon a range of products with full correlation between μ and σ, namely $\sigma = 0.71\mu^{1.00}$. Throughout them, a gamma distribution with two degrees of freedom was adopted as the frequency distribution of the demand. Table 25 is a survey of the results of the 'Monte Carlo' calculations. Two examples of results are given in Fig. 50.

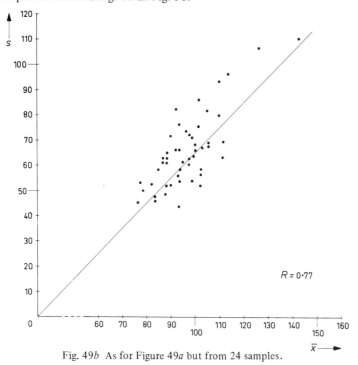

Fig. 49*b* As for Figure 49*a* but from 24 samples.

The table provides the best estimate of the correlation coefficient found in the event of a 100% correlation between μ and σ. The apparent conclusion is that with samples of the size employed, the effect of the test sample is barely perceptible in the case of assortments of articles having a range of 10^3 or more. However, there is no reason to expect a high correlation coefficient in the case of a range in the region of 10. It will also be evident that we should try to obtain a longer series of demand figures, although this will not always be possible.

One or two examples of results obtained are given in Table 26 and in Fig. 48.

In anticipation of the change which will have to be made later from demand

† See Chapter 36.

TABLE 25*a*

SOME DATA CONCERNING THE EFFECT OF THE TEST
SAMPLE UPON THE CORRELATION COEFFICIENT OF
THE RELATIONSHIP $\sigma = c\mu^p$

Single point calculated from twelve monthly figures		
Number of articles in the sample	Range	
	10^1	10^3
10	0·92	0·989
20	–	0·992
30	0·93	0·993

TABLE 25*b*

Each point calculated from twenty-four monthly figures

Number of articles in the sample	Range	
	10^1	10^3
10	0·96	0·994
20	–	0·995
30	–	0·997

per time unit (week, month) to demand per lead time, we should point out that it is well worth while to determine the relationship between σ and μ not only in terms of the demand per month (available in the form of monthly figures), but also for the bimonthly demand. Thus it is possible to ascertain whether the demand figures in two successive periods are sufficiently independent of each other to warrant the assumption that $\sigma_2 = \sigma_1\sqrt{2}$.

Table 26 gives a survey of the constants c, p and r in a number of cases covered by the calculations so far.

Even if, in the first instance, the correlation coefficient proves to be on the low side, there are one or two possible alternatives which nevertheless produce satisfactory results in some cases. Firstly, we can try to divide the assortment in one way or another into still more homogeneous subgroups. Secondly, we can try to introduce one other significant variable in addition to the turnover itself.

From what we have seen so far, the number of orders is the obvious choice. An example of this method is given in Fig. 51. At first glance the result appears unsatisfactory, but by noting the number of orders per year at each point we find distinct evidence that in this case the number of orders is highly significant.

We can now resort to the method mentioned a moment ago and divide the assortment into classes based upon the number of orders per year, or in other

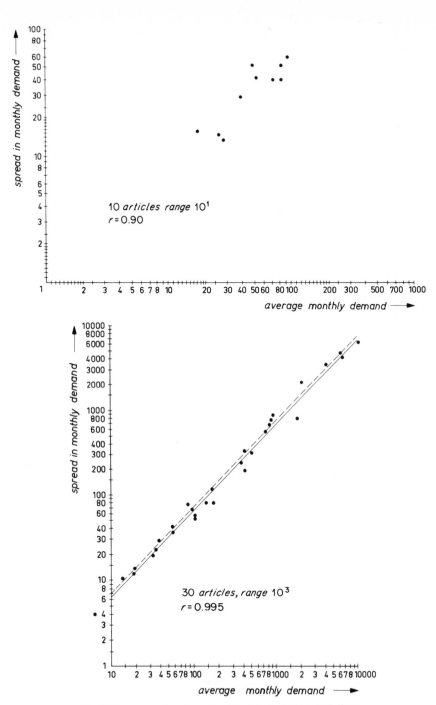

Fig. 50 Two examples of results of the Monte Carlo calculations.

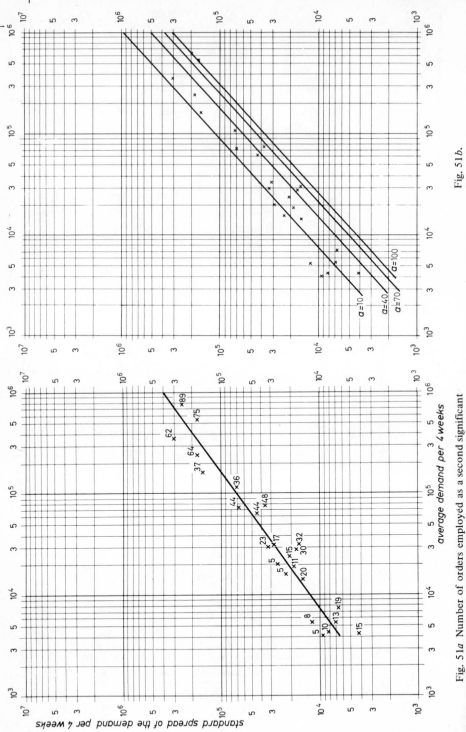

Fig. 51a Number of orders employed as a second significant

Fig. 51b.

TABLE 26

Type of Product	c	p	r
material 1	2·39	0·93	0·961
material 2	8·84	0·81	0·984
material 3	6·83	0·82	0·990
material 4	1·44	0·74	0·964
chemicals	2·42	0·73	0·953
component 1	48·15	0·46	0·863
component 2	1·16	0·81	0·930
component 3	98·01	0·27	0·585
component 4	17·44	0·55	0·954
component 5	7·63	0·76	0·975
packing 1	3·06	0·78	0·963
packing 2	13·05	0·70	0·970
end product 1	1·31	0·91	0·936
end product 2	1·49	0·83	0·910
end product 3	1·35	0·84	0·906
end product 4	2·86	0·82	0·975
end product 5	2·24	0·88	0·961
end product 6	4·73	0·68	0·911
end product 7	3·48	0·69	0·932
end product 8	3·25	0·67	0·915
end product 9	4·49	0·67	0·965
end product 10	4·08	0·67	0·918

words carry out a multiple regression calculation in which σ is explained by correlation with μ and with the number of orders. The variance of σ is made up of the variance of μ and the variance of the number of orders per year; the calculated relationship can then be plotted for a series of values of the number of orders.

Last but not least it is sometimes worthwhile to divide the overall range in two. This is useful only if the relationship proves to fall short of exact linearity in a wide range; the object of the division into two subranges is then to find an approximation with two different straight lines.

20.3.1 *The calculation of mean and standard deviation per article*

There are one or two further points worth noting concerning the determination of the average demand and the standard deviation per article. The method of calculation which will now be discussed can be used for the majority of problems involving estimation of the standard deviation of the demand. The basic premise is that the average demand value does not vary, or at any rate varies only gradually.

If this is so, it will invariably be possible to evolve a method of forecasting the average demand with reasonable accuracy. (See Section III, Forecasting p. 57.)

At the same time there are situations in which the following method of calculation does not apply: assume that we are considering the usage of a component employed in the assembly of certain end products. If the quantities assembled fluctuate appreciably from one period to another, as sometimes happens, then the usage of the particular component will likewise fluctuate from one period to another. However, these fluctuations were predictable; 'explosion' of the programme of end products reveals how many components will be required. In this case there should also be pairs of figures available, representing the forecast and real demand or usage for each period; at the same time it often happens that the forecasts have not been preserved. As a general rule, also, records of the actual usage figures cover only a few periods in the past.

When the series of demand figures available for each article are studied, it is a matter of some importance that instead of merely taking these figures at face value and introducing them into a calculation procedure, we should study them in order to ascertain whether there are any incidental effects which would be best left out.

Large orders which are known well beforehand and therefore do not have to be delivered from stock sometimes occur incidentally. The average and standard deviation of the demand figures can now be established in the manner already described.

Where there is reason to suspect a trend or a slight cyclic effect, it is advisable to estimate the standard deviation about this trend or cyclic effect as follows. Assume that the consecutive demand figures are not drawn from a stationary distribution and that in the absence of any incidental effect, three consecutive demand figures would form a straight line.

For every three consecutive demand figures, then, we assume that

$$x_1 = a + u_1$$
$$x_2 = a + b + u_2$$
$$x_3 = a + 2b + u_3$$

where a and b are constants, u_1, u_2 and u_3 are independent samples from a stationary probability distribution. Our problem now is to determine the standard deviation of u from known values of x_1, x_2 and x_3.

Now $x_2 - x_1 = b + u_2 - u_1$

and $x_3 - x_2 = b + u_3 - u_2$

It then follows that

$$\Delta_2 = (x_3 - x_2) - (x_2 - x_1) = u_3 - u_2 - u_2 + u_1$$

or $\Delta_2 = x_3 - 2x_2 + x_1 = u_3 - 2u_2 + u_1$

Bear in mind that in the graphical representation of points x_1, x_2 and x_3 the distance from x_2 to x_1x_3 is given by $\frac{1}{2}(x_1 - 2x_2 + x_3)$ (Fig. 52).

Hence we have

$$\text{var}(\Delta_2) = \text{var}(u_3) + \text{var}(2u_2) + \text{var}(u_1) = \text{var}(\underline{u}) + 4\,\text{var}(\underline{u}) + \text{var}(\underline{u}) = 6\,\text{var}(\underline{u})$$

$$\text{var}(\Delta_2) = \frac{\displaystyle\sum_{i=1}^{i=n-2} (x_i + x_{i+2} - 2x_{i+1})^2}{n-2}$$

therefore $\sigma = \sqrt{\text{var}(\underline{u})} = \sqrt{\left(\dfrac{\displaystyle\sum_{i=1}^{i=n-2} (x_i + x_{i+2} - 2x_{i+1})^2}{6(n-2)}\right)}$

where n is the number of demand values.

(var $(2u_2) = 4\,\text{var}(\underline{u})$, since $\underline{u}$ has a standard deviation σ; the variable $2\underline{u}$ has a standard deviation 2σ and therefore a variation var $(2\underline{u}) = (2\sigma)^2 = 4\sigma^2$.)

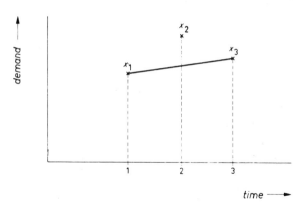

Fig. 52 Determination of the standard deviation in the case where incidental effects occur.

20.4 Changeover from demand per time unit to demand per lead time

The method described in the previous paragraph enables us to estimate the second moment of the frequency distribution of the demand during a given time unit, for example one month.

To be able to determine the re-order levels, however, we must change over to the frequency distribution of the demand during a period equivalent to the lead time.

It is usually assumed that the deviations in two successive periods are not correlated, so that

$$\sigma_t = \sigma_1 \sqrt{t}$$

where
σ_1 is the standard deviation of the demand per time unit;
σ_t is the standard deviation of the demand during the lead time t;
t is the lead time in terms of time units.

As we have seen, the validity of the assumption that the deviations are independent is readily tested by determining the relationship between μ and σ not only for μ and σ_1, but also for μ and σ_2 and possibly for μ and σ_3 as well. If autocorrelation is shown to exist, it is necessary to resort to a method of interpolation.

We should again point out that none of these methods need be particularly exact, since we are not concerned with irrevocable decisions, but rather with decisions which can be modified in the light of differences which emerge as between the real and expected numbers of stockouts.

20.5 The shape of the frequency distribution of the demand during the lead time

When the first and second moments of the frequency distribution of the demand during the lead time are known, a further assumption concerning the shape of the frequency distribution has to be made, to enable the re-order level to be calculated.

It was assumed in paragraph 20.1 that the demand follows a Poisson distribution. If the demand per time unit follows a Poisson distribution, then the demand per lead time will do likewise. (The relevant tables have already been discussed.)

Let us return to the Poisson distribution with modified scale, based upon the package unit or upon some other demand unit established artificially by calculation. This distribution can be matched very accurately in some cases, as Bosch, Marshall/Boggess and Goudriaan have shown (1962).

Goudriaan demonstrated that in circumstances in which the number of orders follows a Poisson distribution, the third moment of the matched Poisson distribution is closer to the real third moment than that of the gamma distribution which will be discussed shortly, provided that:

— the order quantity is distributed symmetrically;
— or the order quantity is distributed asymmetrically, but results in a skewness smaller than 2. This is so in very many cases.

Practical experience has shown that often a gamma distribution also constitutes an acceptable approximation of the frequency distribution of the demand. So far, neither the possibility that the number of orders follows a Poisson distribution, nor the skewness of the order quantity distribution, has been investigated systematically. Attention has been focused exclusively upon the frequency distribution of the demand per time unit or per lead time. As explained in

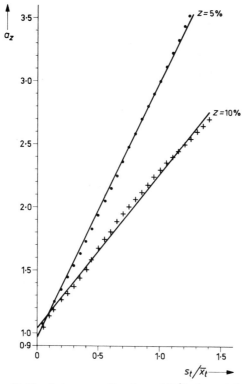

Fig. 53 The factor a_z as function of $S_t/\bar{x}_t$ determining the re-order level B_z.

paragraph 5.2, the sum of a number of individually independent gamma-distributed quantities itself also follows a gamma distribution.

The procedure for matching a gamma distribution to test sample results whose standard deviation S and mean $\bar{x}$ have been established (in one way or another) is as follows. As we saw in paragraph 5.2, a gamma distribution having its origin at zero is governed by two parameters, namely:

– the scale parameter a;
– the number of degrees of freedom n.

TABLE 27

TABLE FOR DETERMINING THE RE-ORDER LEVEL BY MEANS OF THE FORMULA $B_z = a_z \bar{x}_t$ BASED UPON THE ASSUMPTION THAT THE DEMAND FOLLOWS A GAMMA DISTRIBUTION

R = range for sample size N;
$\bar{x}$ = mean demand for sample size 4;
d = conversion factor for calculating the standard deviation from the range;

S_t = standard deviation of the demand during the lead time;
n = shape parameter of the gamma distribution;
$\bar{x}_t$ = mean demand during the lead time.

Sample size $N=4$		Sample size $N=6$		$\dfrac{S_t}{\bar{x}_t}$	$n = \left(\dfrac{\bar{x}_t}{S_t}\right)^2$	values of a_z						
$\dfrac{R}{\bar{x}}$	$d=\dfrac{S}{R}$	$\dfrac{R}{\bar{x}}$	$d=\dfrac{S}{R}$			$z=25\%$	$z=10\%$	$z=5\%$	$z=2.5\%$	$z=1\%$	$z=0.5\%$	$z=0.1\%$
2·31	0·61	2·93	0·48	1·40	0·51	1·43	2·70	3·83	5·00	6·60	7·85	10·80
2·28	0·60	2·88	0·47	1·35	0·55	1·43	2·65	3·73	4·85	6·35	7·55	10·40
2·21	0·59	2·80	0·47	1·30	0·59	1·42	2·60	3·63	4·70	6·10	7·25	9·80
2·16	0·58	2·71	0·46	1·25	0·64	1·42	2·55	3·53	4·55	5·89	6·90	9·30
2·11	0·57	2·65	0·45	1·20	0·69	1·41	2·50	3·43	4·40	5·60	6·60	8·80
2·04	0·56	2·55	0·45	1·15	0·76	1·41	2·45	3·32	4·20	5·35	6·30	8·30
1·97	0·56	2·46	0·45	1·10	0·83	1·40	2·40	3·22	4·00	5·10	6·00	7·80
1·91	0·55	2·38	0·44	1·05	0·91	1·40	2·35	3·11	3·85	4·85	5·65	7·35
1·83	0·55	2·28	0·44	1·00	1·00	1·39	2·30	3·00	3·70	4·60	5·30	6·90
1·76	0·54	2·19	0·43	0·95	1·11	1·39	2·24	2·90	3·55	4·35	5·00	6·60
1·69	0·53	2·09	0·43	0·90	1·24	1·38	2·18	2·80	3·40	4·10	4·75	6·10
1·60	0·53	1·99	0·43	0·85	1·38	1·37	2·12	2·70	3·25	3·90	4·50	5·70
1·53	0·52	1·89	0·42	0·80	1·56	1·37	2·06	2·59	3·10	3·70	4·25	5·30
1·45	0·52	1·79	0·42	0·75	1·78	1·36	2·01	2·48	2·95	3·50	4·00	4·95
1·36	0·51	1·68	0·42	0·70	2·04	1·35	1·95	2·37	2·80	3·30	3·75	4·60
1·27	0·51	1·57	0·41	0·65	2·37	1·33	1·88	2·26	2·65	3·10	3·50	4·25
1·18	0·51	1·46	0·41	0·60	2·78	1·31	1·80	2·15	2·50	2·90	3·25	3·90
1·09	0·50	1·35	0·41	0·55	3·31	1·30	1·74	2·05	2·35	2·70	3·00	3·60
1·00	0·50	1·23	0·41	0·50	4·00	1·28	1·67	1·94	2·20	2·50	2·75	3·39
0·90	0·50	1·12	0·40	0·45	4·94	1·25	1·59	1·84	2·07	2·35	2·55	3·05
0·81	0·49	1·00	0·40	0·40	6·25	1·23	1·51	1·74	1·95	2·20	2·40	2·80
0·71	0·49	0·87	0·40	0·35	8·16	1·20	1·44	1·64	1·85	2·05	2·20	2·55
0·61	0·49	0·75	0·40	0·30	11·11	1·18	1·37	1·54	1·75	1·90	2·05	2·30
0·51	0·49	0·63	0·40	0·25	16·0	1·15	1·31	1·45	1·60	1·70	1·80	2·00
0·41	0·49	0·50	0·40	0·20	25·0	1·13	1·26	1·35	1·43	1·50	1·60	1·70
0·31	0·48	0·38	0·40	0·15	44·0	1·10	1·19	1·26	1·35	1·35	1·45	1·55
0·21	0·48	0·25	0·40	0·10	100·0	1·07	1·13	1·17	1·20	1·25	1·27	1·33
0·10	0·48	0·13	0·40	0·05	400·0	1·03	1·06	1·06	1·10	1·12	1·13	1·16

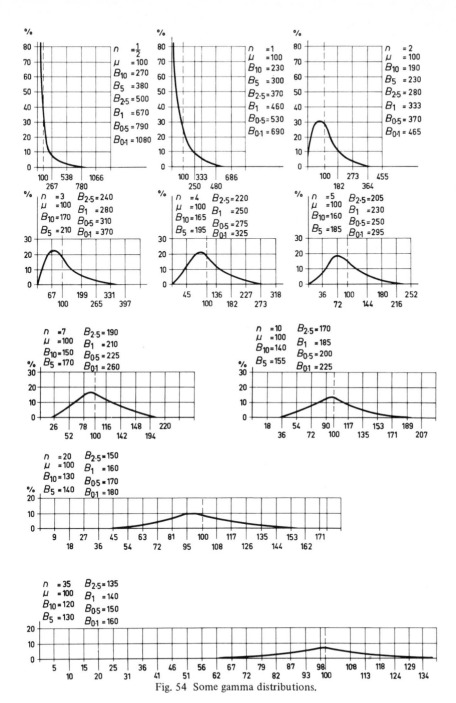

Fig. 54 Some gamma distributions.

They are estimated by means of the following two equations

$$n = \left(\frac{\overline{x}}{S}\right)^2 \qquad \text{and} \qquad a = \left(\frac{\overline{x}}{n}\right)$$

To determine the re-order levels associated with a given chance of excess, we can either employ tables, or make use of a computer programme.

The data required to determine the re-order level B_z directly as

$$B_z = a_z x_t$$

will be found in Table 27.

In this table, a_z is given with z and the ratio S_t/x_t as entries.

The first column of the Table can be used as entry when the same available comprises only four demand values: the range R can then be calculated and R/x can be determined. To illustrate matters, the conversion factor d, with the aid of which S can be estimated when R is known, is given in column 2. Columns 3 and 4 are constructed in the same way as columns 1 and 2.

There are two simple solutions to the problem of incorporating the results of Table 27 in a computer programme. The first is to incorporate the table itself in the programme and employ a classification. The second is to approximate the values of the table via a simple analytical relationship; in this way, all the values of the column $z = 5\%$ can be approximated reasonably accurately to a linear function of $S_t/\overline{x}_t$ (Fig. 53).

Fig. 54 shows a number of gamma distributions.

21 Standard deviation in the lead time

21.1 The need to find a suitable calculation procedure

The possibility of variation in the lead time t itself has been ignored in the calculations so far. It was argued in paragraph 18.2 that this method of calculation is usually justified. At the same time, there are two possible situations requiring a calculation procedure which takes account of a standard deviation in the delivery time.

1. A major variation in the lead time is sometimes unavoidable.
2. As we shall see, the level s in a (s, S) system can be calculated approximately as if it were a level B in a (B, Q) system with stochastic lead time.

The following will now be discussed one after another:

– a general approach;
– a numerical method;

for the calculation of B in a (B, Q) system in which the lead time t is a stochastic variable.

21.2 A general approach

In the first place, the following general formula can be employed

$$V_{dt}^2 = V_d^2 + V_t^2 \tag{1}$$

where
V_t is the coefficient of variation (σ/μ) of the lead time t;
V_d is the coefficient of variation of the demand during a period equivalent to the expected value of the lead time $E(t)$;
V_{dt} is the coefficient of variation of the demand during the lead time.

This formula is based upon a formula in paragraph 6.1.3, namely

$$\sigma_{dt}^2 = E(t) \times \sigma_{d1}^2 + \{E(d1)\}^2 \times \sigma_t^2 \tag{2}$$

where $d1$ is demand during unit of time (the 'number of orders' is interpreted as 'length of the lead time' in terms of the number of periods and 'order quantity' is interpreted as 'demand per period').

Further we can write

$$V_t = \frac{\sigma_t}{E(t)}$$

$$V_d = \frac{\sigma_{d1}\sqrt{E(t)}}{E(t) \times E(d1)}$$

$$V_{dt} = \frac{\sigma_{dt}}{E(t) \times E(d1)}$$

By substituting the last three results in formula (2), we obtain formula (1) which gives proof of the first formula. Note that this derivation is based on the assumption that the demand figures *do not* exhibit autocorrelation.

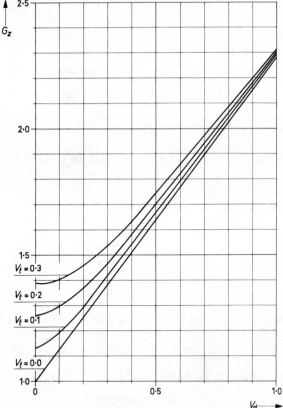

Fig. 55 The multiplication factor to determine the re-order level G_t as a function of V_t and V_d.

The following proposition holds good in many cases:

If the demand per period follows a gamma distribution and the lead time a normal distribution, then the demand during the lead time will likewise follow closely a gamma distribution (albeit with a different form parameter).

By combining this proposition with the above formula, re-order levels for a very wide range of applications can be calculated according to the method described earlier.

Proof of the proposition is provided by H. J. M. Moonen [Mo 2], who also suggests the following method of calculation based on the sole assumption that the lead time follows a normal distribution and the demand a gamma distribution. The re-order level B_z can then be calculated as

$$B_z = G_z E(d1) \times E(t)$$

The values of G_z can be read from Table 28 or Fig. 55.

TABLE 28

MULTIPLICATION FACTOR G_z FOR DETERMINING THE RE-ORDER LEVEL
WHEN THE COEFFICIENT OF VARIATION OF THE LEAD TIME IS V_t AND
THE COEFFICIENT OF VARIATION OF THE DEMAND IN THE AVERAGE
LEAD TIME IS V_a

V_t \ V_a	0·0	0·1	0·2	0·3
0·00	1·00	1·13	1·26	1·38
0·05	1·06	1:16	1·27	1·39
0·10	1·13	1·19	1·29	1·40
0·15	1·20	1·24	1·32	1·43
0·20	1·26	1·30	1·36	1·46
0·25	1·32	1·36	1·41	1·50
0·30	1·39	1·42	1·47	1·55
0·35	1·46	1·48	1·53	1·60
0·40	1·52	1·55	1·59	1·65
0·45	1·58	1·61	1·65	1·70
0·50	1·65	1·68	1·71	1·75
0·55	1·72	1·74	1·77	1·81
0·60	1·78	1·80	1·83	1·86
0·65	1·84	1·86	1·89	1·92
0·70	1·91	1·92	1·95	1·97
0·75	1·98	1·99	2·01	2·03
0·80	2·04	2·05	2·07	2·09
0·85	2·10	2·11	2·13	2·14
0·90	2·17	2·18	2·19	2·20
0·95	2·24	2·24	2·25	2·25
1·00	2·30	2·30	2·31	2·31

Moonen demonstrates that the results obtained from this table or graph are very little different from those obtained by applying the above proposition on the assumption that the demand during the lead time also follows a gamma distribution.

21.3 Numerical method

The following will be taken as a numerical example:

— demand per week follows a normal distribution with $E(d) = 10$ products and $\sigma = 3$ products;
— lead time t follows a rectangular distribution with upper and lower limits of 3 and 4 weeks, respectively.

For this situation there exists an exact method of calculation which has been adapted for use as a routine by Harling and Bramson [Ha 2]. For this purpose, the frequency distribution of the lead time is divided into a number of classes. The fidelity with which the result of the calculation reflects the exact outcome increases with the number of classes. Given 5 classes and a value of $B = 50$ for the re-order level, the calculation in the case which we have adopted as a numerical example will be as follows.

TABLE 29

CALCULATION OF THE PROBABILITY OF STOCKOUT IN A SPECIFIC CASE

(1)	(2)	(3)	(4)	(5)	(6)	(7)	(8)	(9)
Class lead time in weeks	Class midpoint M in weeks	Buffer stock in number of products	Sales of σ during M in number of products	$\dfrac{(3)}{(4)}$	Unilateral chance of excess	Proba-bility of M	(6) × (7)	Overall probabil-ity of stockout per order
3·01–3·20	3·105	19	5·29	3·60	0·0002	0·2	0·0000	
3·21–3·40	3·305	17	5·45	3·13	0·0009	0·2	0·0002	0·0096
3·41–3·60	3·505	15	5·61	2·68	0·0037	0·2	0·0007	d.i. =
3·61–3·80	3·705	13	5·76	2·26	0·0119	0·2	0·0024	1%
3·81–4·00	3·905	11	5·92	1·86	0·0314	0·2	0·0063	

Explanation

Calculate, for each line, what the probability of stockout would be if the lead time were exactly M, without fluctuation.

Buffer stock = re-order level B − expected demand during
    lead time M
Expected demand during lead time $M = 10M$

Standard deviation of the demand during $M = 3\sqrt{M}$ (standard deviation of sales in one week is 3, sales follow normal distribution, sales in successive weeks uncorrelated).

The resultant probability that the stock will be negative when a replenishment order Q arrives is given in column (9).

22 The re-order level in the case of fixed-interval re-ordering

22.1 A method of approximating s in (s, S)

If the interval $(S - s)$ in an (s, S) system is large in relation to the demand per re-order interval and if the lead time t is constant, then the following will hold good to a reasonable approximation (see Fig. 56).

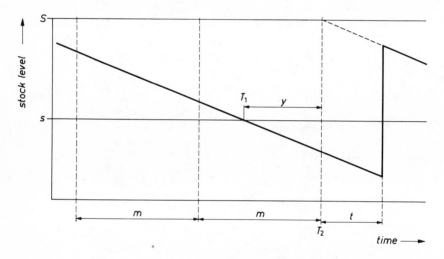

Fig. 56 Calculation of the re-order level (s) in the case of fixed-interval re-ordering.

Let us assume that the stock variation is continuous. If the stock has fallen below s at time T_2, then the level s has been passed somewhere in the preceding interval at time T_1. If the distance $T_1 T_2$ is y, then y follows a rectangular frequency distribution between 0 and m (length of the interval), since there is no apparent reason why any specific value of y should be preferred. In other words, s may be regarded as referring to the re-order level B in a (B, Q) system with a lead time which follows a rectangular distribution between t and $t + m$. On average, then, a period $(t + m/2)$ has to be bridged.

Now, the calculation procedure described earlier (paragraph 21.2) under the heading of 'A general approach' can be used in this case, provided that $t > 1.25\ m$. The following then applies to the rectangular distribution

$$\sigma = \tfrac{1}{6}\,m\sqrt{3} = 0.29$$

In other cases the numerical method described in the previous paragraph can be employed; an arithmetical example of this will be given later.

The following is sometimes used as a rough indication: calculate s as if it referred to a level B in a (B, Q) system with a constant lead time $(t + 0.7\ m)$. That this constitutes a rough approximation will be seen amongst other things from the following survey relating to the example given in Section 21.3.

TABLE 30

Re-order level s	Percentage stockout calculated according to the numerical method with 5 classes	Rule of thumb
50	1·0	1·2
45	5·9	8·2
40	21·2	30·1

When periodic re-ordering is made necessary by a production cycle in which the position of a product in the cycle is not determined, the lead time may be between t and $(t + m)$. The interval to be bridged is then between t and $(t + 2m)$ and follows a triangular distribution with an average $(t + m)$.

22.2 Determination of s by the numerical method; example

To elucidate matters, the numerical method will now be demonstrated once more for the following case.

Given
$$s = 500$$
$$S = 2100$$
$$E(\underline{d}) = 200$$
$$t = 0.5\ m$$

The demand per period $\underline{d}$ follows a gamma distribution with the form parameter $n = 2$.

TABLE 31

(1)	(2)	(3)	(4)	(5)	(6)	(7)	(8)
Lead time class	Class mid-point	Proba-bility of lead time in this class	Expected demand	Demand follows gamma distribu-tion with $n =$	$\sigma^1(d)$ ————— (4)	500 ——— (4)	Chance of excess
$(0\cdot5 \div 0\cdot7)\,m$	$0\cdot6\,m$	$0\cdot2$	120	$1\cdot2$	$0\cdot91$	$4\cdot17$	$1\cdot0\%$
$(0\cdot7 \div 0\cdot9)\,m$	$0\cdot8\,m$	$0\cdot2$	160	$1\cdot6$	$0\cdot79$	$3\cdot12$	$2\cdot5\%$
$(0\cdot9 \div 1\cdot1)\,m$	$1\cdot0\,m$	$0\cdot2$	200	$2\cdot0$	$0\cdot71$	$2\cdot50$	$4\cdot3\%$
$(1\cdot1 \div 1\cdot3)\,m$	$1\cdot2\,m$	$0\cdot2$	240	$2\cdot4$	$0\cdot64$	$2\cdot08$	$7\cdot2\%$
$(1\cdot3 \div 1\cdot5)\,m$	$1\cdot4\,m$	$0\cdot2$	280	$2\cdot8$	$0\cdot60$	$1\cdot78$	$10\cdot3\%$
						total (3) x (8) = **5·1%**	

Explanation of the first line

Assume that the lead time is constant at $0\cdot6\,m$. The expected demand will then be $0\cdot6 \times E(\underline{d}) = 120$. For the gamma distribution of the demand per period, we have $n = 2$, therefore

$$\sigma_1(d) = \frac{E(\underline{d})}{\sqrt{2}}$$

In the absence of autocorrelation, the following applies to a period of $0\cdot6\,m$

$$\sigma^1(d) = \sigma_1(d)\sqrt{0\cdot6}$$

It follows that the value of n for the gamma distribution of the demand during $0\cdot6\,m$ is

$$n = 1\cdot2 \text{ (see paragraph 5.2)}$$

To establish the entry in a table giving the coefficient of variation, we must calculate $1/\sqrt{1\cdot2} = 0\cdot91$.

It is also necessary to know the ratio

$$a = \frac{\text{re-order level}}{E(\underline{d})} = \frac{500}{120} = 4\cdot17$$

In the table for determining the re-order level (see Table 27) which is based on the assumption that the demand follows a gamma distribution, we find a $1\cdot0\%$ chance of excess.

As the final result of the calculation we find that the probability of stockout is $5\cdot1\%$. This calculation was verified by means of a simulation, from which it emerged that the stock was negative in 10 out of 1000 periods.

On average, one order was placed every $\dfrac{1700}{200} = 8.5$ periods, since the average order will amount to

$$S - s + 0.5E(\underline{d}) = 2100 - 500 + 100 = 1700$$

In the simulation, we might reasonably have expected the number of periods with negative stock to be

$$0.051 \times \frac{1}{8.5} \times 1000 = 6$$

The difference between the expected value 6 and the value found 10 may have been brought about by chance deviations.

23 Calculation of optimum B and Q for a (B, Q) system

Calculation of optimum B and Q for a (B, Q) system

Notation: as usual D, Q, K, F, B, and in addition:

δK = inventory costs per individual product per year;

t = lead time;

$\underline{d}$ = demand during lead time, in terms of quantity of products;

$\hat{d}$ = forecast demand during the lead time;

R = costs per stockout, regardless of the actual quantitative shortage;

π = costs per product not supplied from stock;

σ_t = standard deviation of the distribution of $(\underline{d} - \hat{d})$, $\sigma_t = \sigma_1 \sqrt{t}$;†

$\underline{x}$ = the standardised deviation = $(\underline{d} - \hat{d})/\sigma_1 \sqrt{t}$;

$f(x)$ = probability density of $\underline{x}$;

w = safety factor.

So far, B^* and Q^* have been calculated separately by taking into account individually the effects of B and Q upon the variable costs. In fact, however, the total variable costs per year C can be formulated as $C(B, Q)$ and the optimum values of B and Q have then to be calculated from

$$\frac{\delta C}{\delta B} = \frac{\delta C}{\delta Q} = 0$$

This calculation will now be demonstrated for different situations.

23.1 Loss per stockout

Let us first proceed on the assumption that each stockout owing to late arrival of a replenishment order results in a loss R. Instead of regarding the re-order level B itself as a variable in this calculation, we shall define the buffer stock as $w\sigma_1\sqrt{t}$, where w is the variable to be chosen. Given w, B can be calculated. Also, $\sigma_1\sqrt{t}$ is substituted for σ_t, where σ_t is the standard deviation of the frequency distribution of $\underline{d} - \hat{d}$.

† Consecutive values of $(\underline{d} - \hat{d})$ are assumed to be independent.

As before,

$\underline{d}$ is the demand during the lead time, in quantitative terms

$\hat{d}$ is the forecast demand in the lead time, likewise in quantitative terms

Finally, the variable $\underline{x}$ is introduced

$$\underline{x} = \frac{\underline{d} - \hat{d}}{\sigma_1 \sqrt{t}}$$

The probability density function of $\underline{x}$ is indicated by $f(x)$.

The above situation arises amongst other things if, in the event of impending stockout, delivery of the orders already placed is speeded up. The result is that although actual stockout is avoided, the rush delivery costs an amount R.

In this situation:

– the ordering costs amount to $(D/Q)F$ per year;
– the stockout costs per year amount to (number of orders per year) x (expected costs per order).

The number of orders per year is D/Q.

Stockout occurs during a lead time if (demand during L) $> B$.

Therefore if $\qquad\qquad \underline{d} > \hat{d} + w\sigma_1\sqrt{t}$

or if $(\underline{d} - \hat{d})/\sigma_1\sqrt{t} > w$, that is if $\underline{x} > w$.

Per replenishment order, then, the probability that costs R will be incurred is

$$P[\underline{x} > w] = \int_{w}^{0} f(x)\,dx$$

At a rough estimate, the average stock is

$$\frac{Q}{2} + w\sigma_1\sqrt{t}$$

The total variable costs per year thus amount to

$$C = \frac{D}{Q}F + \frac{Q}{2}\delta K + w\sigma_1\sqrt{t}\,\delta K + \frac{D}{Q}R \int_{w}^{\infty} f(x)\,dx$$

where w and Q are the independent variables.

We now take $\dfrac{\partial C}{\partial Q} = 0$, from which it follows that

$$0 = \frac{-DF}{Q^2} + \frac{\delta K}{2} - \frac{DR}{Q^2} \int_{w}^{\infty} f(x)\,dx$$

so that

$$Q^* = \sqrt{\left(\frac{2D\left(F + R \int\limits_{w}^{\infty} f(x)\,dx\right)}{\delta K}\right)} \tag{1}$$

Note: In this formula, $R \int\limits_{w}^{\infty} f(x)\,dx$ represents the expected costs per stockout.

We now take $\dfrac{\partial C}{\partial w} = 0$, from which it follows that

$$0 = \sigma\sqrt{(t)}\delta K + \frac{DR}{Q}\{-f(w)\} \quad \text{so that}$$

$$f(w^*) = \frac{\delta K \sigma\sqrt{(t)}Q}{DR} \tag{2}$$

Formulae (1) and (2) cannot be reduced to a convenient and explicit solution of Q and w. At the same time, Q and w can be established by iteration. As we have seen: the difficulty lies in determining first, second and higher moments of the frequency distribution of $\underline{x}$ for each of the products.

Example

The following numerical values are given

$\hat{d} = 72$, $t = 3{\cdot}6$ weeks, $D = 1000$
$\underline{d}$ follows from a normal distribution with $\sigma_1\sqrt{t} = 13{\cdot}3$

$\underline{x} = \dfrac{\underline{d} - \hat{d}}{13{\cdot}3}$ follows a normal distribution with $\mu = 0$ and $\sigma = 1$.

$R = £4$, $F = £5$, $\delta K = 40\text{p}$

The equations (1) and (2) are then as follows:

$$Q^* = 158\sqrt{\left(1 + 0{\cdot}8 \int\limits_{w}^{\infty} f(x)\,dx\right)} \tag{1a}$$

$$f(w^*) = 0{\cdot}00133\,Q^* \tag{2a}$$

As a first approximation we take the batch size according to Camp, that is $Q^* = 158$.
It then follows from (2a) that $f(w^*) = 0{\cdot}210$.

The associated values of $w = 1.13$ and

$$\int_{w}^{\infty} f(x) \, dx = 0.129$$

are found in a table of the normal distribution.

From (1a) we have $Q* = 168$, and the following values are then established in the same way

$$f(w*) = 0.224$$

$$w* = 1.07 \qquad \int_{w*}^{\infty} f(x) \, dx = 0.142 \qquad Q = 169$$

$$f(w*) = 0.225$$

$$w* = 1.07 \qquad \int_{w*}^{\infty} f(x) \, dx = 0.142 \qquad Q = 169$$

The speed of iteration attained by this method of calculation can be demonstrated by plotting the various processes involved in a chart.

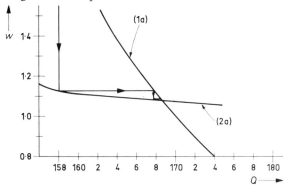

Fig. 57 The iteration process when calculating the values of
Q and w.

This derivation also explains the shape of the curves of Fig. 54 in 'An Introduction to Production and Inventory Control'.

23.2 Loss incurred on each product which is late in arriving. Subsequent delivery permitted

Let us now assume that the costs depend upon the number of products in arrears. Instead of sales being forfeited in the event of stockout, orders are accepted for subsequent delivery. This situation is encountered in assembly departments which draw components from stock. Here, the loss incurred through a shortage of components may depend upon the number involved, or in other words upon the number of end products whose completion is delayed.

The ordering costs are again $(D/Q)F$.

The inventory costs are approximately $(Q/2 + w\sigma\sqrt{t})\,\delta\,K$.

The following then holds good for each order:

if $\underline{d} - \hat{d} > w\sigma\sqrt{t}$, subsequent deliveries amount to $\underline{d} - \hat{d} - w\sigma\sqrt{t}$ products; this can also be formulated as

$$\left(\frac{\underline{d} - \hat{d}}{\sigma\sqrt{t}} - w\right)\sigma\sqrt{t} = (\underline{x} - w)\sigma\sqrt{t}$$

The expected costs of stock shortage per replenishment order are

$$\pi\sigma\sqrt{t}\int_w^\infty (\underline{x} - w)f(x)\,dx$$

Accordingly, we have

$$C = \frac{D}{Q}F + \frac{Q}{2}\delta K + w\sigma\sqrt{(t)}\delta K + \frac{D}{Q}\pi\sigma\sqrt{t}\int_w^\infty (\underline{x} - w)f(x)\,dx$$

From $\dfrac{\partial C}{\partial Q} = 0$, it follows that

$$Q^* = \sqrt{\left(\frac{2D\,F + \pi\sigma\sqrt{t}\displaystyle\int_w^\infty (\underline{x} - w)f(x)\,dx}{\delta K}\right)} \tag{3}$$

Note: As before, the numerator is $2D$ (expected costs of ordering and stockout per batch).

From $\dfrac{\partial C}{\partial w} = 0$ we have

$$\int_w^\infty f(x)\,dx = \frac{\delta KQ}{\pi D} \tag{4}$$

In this case also, a solution can be found by iteration.

23.3 Sales forfeited, loss π per product

In the event of stockout, sales are forfeited, whereby a loss π is incurred on each product which would otherwise have been sold. Thus the demand D is not fully met.

Hadley and Whitin [Ha 1] have shown that in this case

$$Q^* = \text{see (3)}$$

$$\int_{w}^{\infty} f(x)\, dx = \frac{\delta KQ}{\pi D + \delta KQ} \tag{5}$$

23.4 Costs as a function of average negative stock

In some cases, the costs of stockout depend not only upon the number of products in arrears, but also upon the time for which customers are kept waiting; to put it in another way, the stockout costs are proportional to the average backlog. A set of equations covering this situation is to be found in the book by Holt and Modigliani [Ho 1].

24 Determination of the levels s and S by dynamic programming

The levels s and S in a (s, S) system can be established relatively simply for two extreme cases, namely:
1 $s = S$, the system of fixed-interval replenishment;
2 $(S - s) \geqslant d$, or in other words, where the need to place an order only arises infrequently (less than once per 5 periods).
In other cases dynamic programming (DP) may provide a solution.

In the present chapter, a simple re-ordering problem will be solved numerically by means of dynamic programming†. Both the methods discussed in Chapter 9 will be employed. Some typical advantages and drawbacks of dynamic programming are worth mentioning again, namely:

a. The arithmetic involved is considerable. At the same time, the entire procedure is readily programmable for a computer.
b. The optimum type of order policy follows automatically from the calculation. It is not necessary to choose *a priori* from the possibilities available. In the example given here, the (s, S) method does in fact prove to be best.
c. In this example the average demand is assumed to be stable and the costs of inventory and backlog are assumed to be linear, in order to simplify matters. However, these assumptions do not constitute essential conditions for the method of calculation employed.

The optimum strategy for each costs definition and demand series given can be found by the method indicated.

24.1 Definition of the problem
The weekly demand $\underline{d}$ for a certain component follows the following frequency distribution.

The demand is 0, 1, 2 or 3 products. The probabilities of same are 0·4; 0·3; 0·2 and 0·1, respectively.

$\underline{d} =$	0	1	2	3
$p(\underline{d}) =$	0·4	0·3	0·2	0·1

† The program has been written by A. R. W. Muyen.

It is easily verified that the mean and the standard deviation of this distribution are both unity.

The component concerned is held in stock. An order to replenish the stock can be placed if necessary at the end of a week. In so doing it is necessary to take the lead time into account. This is about $2\frac{1}{2}$ weeks.

The following costs have to be taken into account in solving the problem:

ordering costs: £10p per order;

inventory costs: 1p per item per week;

costs of late delivery: 10p per item per week.

At the end of the week the inventory is checked and the results of this check are used to calculate the inventory costs. Expressed in units of 1p, the costs for a given week are: (i = inventory and x = order)

$$i \text{ if } i \geq 0$$
$$10i \text{ if } i < 0$$

possibly increased by 10 if $x > 0$.

The problem is to find the strategy which will eventually cut the costs to a minimum.

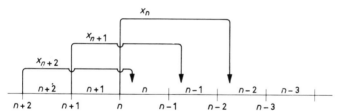

Fig. 58 The extra system of numbering periods and times employed.

24.2 Further analysis

Employing a system of subtraction similar to that used at a rocket launching, we shall number periods and times back to front (see Fig. 58). At the end of a week, for example week $(n + 1)$, we must decide whether to order, and if so, how much to order. The effect of this order upon the stock will not be felt until week $(n - 2)$. The final stock for that week is

$$i_{n-3} = i_n + x_{n+2} + x_{n+1} + x_n - d_n - d_{n-1} - d_{n-2}$$

where i_n is the final stock for week $(n + 1)$;

x_n is the order placed at the end of week $(n + 1)$ and arriving in week $(n - 2)$;

d_n is the demand in week n.

To determine x_n at the end of week $(n + 1)$, the above expression can be divided into three components:

a. the fixed component $e_n = i_n + x_{n+1}$, that is stock on hand and on the way (economical stock);
b. the decision component x_n;
c. the stochastic component $D3 = d_n + d_{n-1} + d_{n-2}$

$$i_{n-3} = e_n + x_n - D3$$

so that

Consecutive values of e are related in accordance with

$$e_{n-1} = e_n + x_n - d_n$$

The criterion which we use to determine the optimum ordering strategy for time n is whatever variable costs we expect up to a time T very far in the future.

The quantity e_n provides the necessary information as to the consequences of a given choice of x_n, namely:

a. the directly variable costs to be expected, or in other words the costs related to i_{n-3} and x_n;
b. the probability distribution of e_{n-1}.

Because it has these two characteristics, e_n is called the *state* of the system. Given the costs expectations for all the states e_{n-1}, it is possible to determine the costs expectations for a particular e_n and therefore also the optimum decisions together with the associated expected costs.

As in Chapter 8, the given numerical example will now be calculated 'from back to front':

Assume that we are at a time T, which we shall call the 'end'. No further costs will be incurred after this time. Given the state at that time, then, we can specify all the associated costs directly, since:
if the technical stock $i \geqslant 0$, then $V_0 = i$, and
if the technical stock $i < 0$, then $V_0 = 10i$.

As in Chapter 8 V indicates the value.

Bear in mind that we are at present concerned only with the technical stock. Although goods still on order at the 'end' time (time T, or time 0 as we shall call it from now on) *have* cost us money (ordering costs) they will be of no use to us after that time.

It will therefore be evident that *no* orders should be placed at the times 'one period before the end' or 'two periods before the end'. We therefore go straight back to the time: 'three periods before the end'. Before doing so, however, let us consider the situation immediately *after* the order is placed. Moreover, we shall consider only the inventory costs over period 1, not those over periods 2 and 3 since they are governed partly by decisions taken before time 3. Remember that the expected costs over period 1 are governed exclusively by the economic stock at time 3, immediately after the order is placed. We can calculate the expected costs over period 1 without necessarily knowing how they are divided as between technical stock and 'stock on the way'. The simple fact is that anything on order at time 3 will arrive before time 0 and anything ordered after time 3 is bound to arrive after time 0.

We shall therefore call the economic stock at time 3 the state e_3. Let state $e_3 = 5$ *after* the placing of a possible last order. Also, let $f(5)$ represent the expected costs in period 1.

3   2   1   0

3   2   1

Fig. 59 The last periods.

Of course, the final, or end stock at time 0 is governed by the demand in periods 3, 2 and 1. Thus it will be necessary for us to know the probability distribution of $D3$ = the demand in three periods.

It is by no means difficult to calculate this distribution.

$D3$	Probability
0	0·064
1	0·144
2	0·204
3	0·219
4	0·174
5	0·111
6	0·056
7	0·021
8	0·006
9	0·001

Next, the expected costs are found as in Table 32.

In this way, the function $f(e)$ can be calculated for every value of e. The probability of a negative value of $(e - D3)$ is 0 for $e \geqslant 9$ and the probability of a positive value of $(e - D3)$ is 0 for $e \leqslant 0$. In these cases the expected costs of $(e - D3)$ equal the costs of $(e - E(D3))$, therefore

$$\text{with } e \leqslant 0, \quad f(e) = -10(e - 3)$$
$$\text{and with } e \geqslant 9, \quad f(e) = e - 3$$

The function $f(e)$ is plotted in Fig. 60, whilst the calculation of $f(e)$ is repeated more fully in Appendix 6.

TABLE 32

D3	(e − D3)	Costs	Probability	Costs x Probability
0	5	5	0·064	0·320
1	4	4	0·144	0·576
2	5	3	0·204	0·612
3	2	2	0·219	0·438
4	1	1	0·174	0·174
5	0	0	0·111	0·000
6	−1	10	0·056	0·560
7	−2	20	0·021	0·420
8	−3	30	0·006	0·180
9	−4	40	0·001	0·040

$f(5) = 3·320$

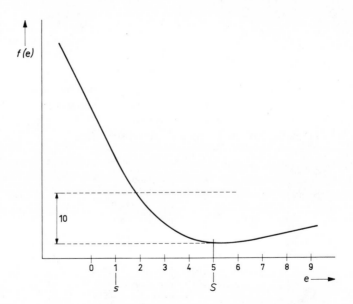

Fig. 60 Calculation of S and s with dynamic programming.

What we have calculated so far is the value of the state immediately after the (possible) placing of an order. This is not enough in itself, however. We now have to determine the value associated with a given state *before* the placing of an order, assuming that the optimum ordering strategy is employed.

Assume that the economic stock $e = 8$ and that no order has yet been placed. There is obviously no point in placing an order which would cost 10p, or 10 units of 1p, and would merely add to $f(e)$.

The same applies to $e = 5$. ·

Not so when $e = 3$, however. Here, the placing of an order can reduce $f(e)$; it will be evident that there is nothing to be gained by ordering more than the quantity required to make $e = 5$. The value of e consistent with the minimum $f(e)$ is therefore the level S. Nevertheless, there is no profit in placing an order in this case, since the ordering costs outweigh the reduction in $f(e)$ achieved.

Only when $e = 1$ or less does the placing of an order improve the situation, a fact which is illustrated once more by the table (Table 35).

TABLE 33

e before order is placed	$f(e)$	e after order is placed bringing level to S	Ordering costs	W on ordering	W when no order is placed	Decision	$V_3 =$ value for optimum decision
7	4·1				4·1	–	4·1
6	3·4				3·4	–	3·4
5	3·3				3·3	–	3·3
4	4·5	5	10	3·3 + 10 = 13·3	4·5	–	4·5
3	7·5	5	10	3·3 + 10 = 13·3	7·5	–	7·5
2	13·0	5	10	13·3	13·0	–	13·0
1	20·7	5	10	13·3	20·7	order	13·3
0	30·0		10	13·3	30·0	order	13·3

In Table 33, V_3 is shown against e before the placing of an order. The optimum strategy can be found by working backwards through the calculation in the manner described in Chapter 9, using the value-determination method.

We shall demonstrate one step in this process fully in view of the fact that it involves one or two problems.

Firstly, we calculate the value $W_4(e)$ immediately *after* the placing of an order.

Let $e_4 = 7$. What are the expected costs up to the 'end'? To answer this, consider the inventory costs over the periods 1 and 2. The costs over period 1 are known if the state at time 3 is known; this is based on the assumption that an order is placed at time 3 in accordance with the optimum strategy. The first step is to ascertain what the state at time 3 will be. This involves the following calculation.

TABLE 34

	Possible values of e_3	Obtained if $d =$	Probability of this	$V(e_3)$	Probability x $V(e_3)$
$e_4 = 7$	7	0	0·4	4·1	1·64
	6	1	0·3	3·4	1·02
	5	2	0·2	3·3	0·66
	4	3	0·1	4·5	0·45

expected value $V(e_3) = 3·77$

The same method can be used to determine amongst other things:

e_4	Expected value of $V(e_3)$
9	5·06
8	4·24
7	3·77
6	4·00
5	5·47
4	7·98

The costs over period 2 are again defined by $f(e)$, and in the present case therefore $f(e_4)$.

In this way the following survey is obtained:

TABLE 35

e_4 prior to ordering	$f(e)$	Expected value $V_3(e)$	$W_4(e)$ prior to ordering	W if order is placed	Decision	V_4 = value for optimum decision
9	6·0	5·1	11·1		—	11·1
8	5·0	4·2	9·2		—	9·2
7	4·1	3·8	7·9		—	7·9
6	3·4	4·0	7·4		—	7·4
5	3·3	5·5	8·8	7·4 + 10 = 17·4	—	8·8
4	4·5	8·0	12·5	17·4	—	12·5
3	7·5	10·9	18·4	17·4	order	17·4

The level S is now 6, since 7·4 is the lowest value in the column $W_4(e)$.

The calculations are continued on these lines until the value function no longer changes perceptibly, where the definition of value is slightly different from that employed hitherto. The value was originally defined as the costs expectation up to a time T in the remote future. Since it obviously makes no difference exactly how far ahead T lies, provided that it is far enough, it is immaterial if a similar amount is subtracted from all the values for a given week. What really has to be decided is how much more or less in the way of costs is expected in one case than in another and from this point of view it makes no difference whether we mean the costs for the next 500, or the next 1000, weeks.

Definition: The value $V_n(e_n)$ associated with a *state* e_n is the increased costs expected (up to a time T in the future) over and above those associated with the optimum state S_n. According to this definition the minimum value in a certain week will be zero, namely $V_n(S_n) = 0$.

The procedure can now be formulated.

Given the value function

$$V_{n-1}(e_{n-1})$$

for all the e_{n-1}, the procedure for establishing the strategy and values for week n is as follows

Phase 1

For all the e_n, calculate

$$W_n(e_n) = f(e_n) + <V_{n-1}(e_n - d_n)> d$$

where

$W_n(e_n)$ is the provisional value of e_n when no order is placed;

$f(e_n)$ is the expected costs associated with $i_{n-3} = e_n - D_n$ where the probability distribution of D_n is known and is independent of n.

$<V_{n-1}(e_n - d_n)> d$ is the weighted average of the values $V_{n-1}(e_{n-1})$ with $e_{n-1} = e_n - d_n$.

With the given distribution of d we have

$$
\begin{aligned}
<V_{n-1}(e_n - d_n)> d = \quad & 0\cdot4\ V_{n-1}(e_n) \\
& + 0\cdot3\ V_{n-1}(e_n - 1) \\
& + 0\cdot2\ V_{n-1}(e_n - 2) \\
& + 0\cdot1\ V_{n-1}(e_n - 3)
\end{aligned}
$$

For the problem involved, the function $W_n(e_n)$ will have a convex form, or in other words the function is minimal for a certain S_n, diminishes in the range $e_n < S_n$ and rises when $e_n > S_n$. When we come to consider placing an order x_n at a given state e_n, then the provisional value will be

$$W_n^1(e_n) = 100 + W_n(e_n + x_n)$$

where 100 represents the ordering costs.

This equivalence can be verified by substituting $e_n + x_n$ for e_n in the above description of $W_n^1(e_n)$.

Phase 2

For all the e_n, calculate the optimum order quantity x_n as a function of e_n and the associated provisional value $W_n^1(e_n)$.

We have to determine the minimum of

$$W_n^1(e_n) = W_n(e_n) \qquad \text{and}$$
$$W_n^1(e_n) = 100 + W_n(e_n + x_n)$$

with x_n still to be determined $(x_n > 0)$.

With $e_n \geqslant S_n$, the following holds good for every x_n

$$W_n(e_n) < W_n(e_n + x_n)$$

so that with $e_n \geqslant S_n$ the optimum order is nil and $W_n^1(e_n) = W_n(e_n)$.

With $e_n < S_n$, assuming that an order is placed, the quantity to be ordered can be deduced from $e_n + x_n = S_n$, since this condition minimises the second expression for $W_n^1(e_n)$.

Still to be determined are the minima of $W_n(e_n)$ and $100 + W_n(S_n)$, the second of these quantities being a constant.

Now there is a certain quantity s_n for which

$$W_n(e_n) > 100 + W_n(S_n) \text{ when } e_n < s_n \text{ and}$$
$$W_n(e_n) < 100 + W_n(S_n) \text{ when } e_n \geqslant s_n$$

whence it follows that

with $e_n < s_n$ $\qquad W_n^1(e_n) = 100 + W_n(S_n)$

(order quantity $x_n = S_n - e_n$)

whilst with $e_n \geqslant s_n$ $\qquad W_n^1(e_n) = W(e_n)$

(no order).

Phase 3

For all the e_n, determine the value function

$$V_n(e_n) = W_n^1(e_n) - g_n$$

where $g_n = W_n(S_n)$

and the value function becomes

with $e_n < s_n$ $\qquad V_n(e_n) = 100$ $\qquad$ (order quantity $x_n = S_n - e_n$)
with $e_n \geqslant s_n$ $\qquad V_n(e_n) = W_n(e_n) - W_n(S_n)$ $\qquad$ (no order).

The above procedure will have to be repeated a number of times in order to reduce the differences between the value function $V_n(e_n)$ and $V_{n-1}(e_{n-1})$ to negligible proportions. Of course the strategy then becomes constant.

The process is then in the stationary state, or in other words the strategy and the value function are those associated with a continuous process of infinite length. The stationary value of g_n is equivalent in meaning to the average costs per week.

In carrying out the calculation process it is not necessary to keep the time index n. The value function $V_n(e_n)$ emerging from an iteration holds good for the following iteration as $V_{n-1}(e_{n-1})$. Any function can be employed as function $V_{n-1}(e_{n-1})$ for the first iteration. The better the choice, the fewer iterations will be required. It is simplest to take $V_{n-1}(e_{n-1}) = 0$ for all the e_{n-1}.

The calculation procedure for the value-determination method will now be briefly outlined with the aid of a simplified notation.

a. Initialization: $V(e) = 0$ for all the e's.
Calculate $f(e)$ (see above).
Establish a (not unduly restricted) range for e, within which s and S should lie.
b. Iteration:

Phase 1

Calculate $W(e)$ for all the e's.

$$W_e = f(e) + 0 \cdot 4 \ V(e) + 0 \cdot 3 \ V(e-1) + 0 \cdot 2 \ V(e-2) + 0 \cdot 1 \ V(e-3)$$

Phase 2

Determine the minimum of $W(e)$.
Use S to denote the appropriate e, and g to denote the associated function value $W(S)$.
Establish s so that $W(s) < g + 100$
and $W(s-1) > g + 100$

Phase 3

Calculate $V^1(e)$ from

$$V^1(e) = 100 \text{ for } e < s$$
$$V^1(e) = W(e) - g \text{ for } e \geqslant s$$

Phase 4

Compare $V^1(e)$ with $V(e)$.
If there are undue differences, repeat the iteration, after substituting $V^1(e)$ for $V(e)$.
c. The last results found for s, S, g and $V(e)$ then constitute the solution to the problem. Here, s and S are the known order quantities, g represents the average

costs per week. The value function $V(e)$ represents the extra costs to be expected in a given state, over and above those associated with state S.

The arithmetical results of the 1st to 5th (inclusive), the 20th, the 59th and the 60th iteration are given in the appendix. The levels s and S for each iteration are indicated by asterisks between the columns $W(e)$ and $V(e)$. In this calculation, however, we have taken $F = £1$. The levels s and S which emerge from the 60th iteration are 2 and 16 and the optimum costs 14·376p per week.

24.3 The strategy iteration method

In the case of the solution to the problem discussed so far, the process was halted after the 60th iteration because the value functions of the 59th and 60th iterations corresponded 'fairly exactly'. What 'fairly exactly' means in this context is difficult to define. What is certain is that the consecutive value functions resemble each other more and more, the longer the process is continued.

The principle of methods involving strategy iteration is that the generating and generated value functions are identical. This enables a number of equations to be constructed with these values as unknown quantities, provided that an assumption is made concerning the strategy parameters s and S. By resolving the equations we find the value function in the stationary state, associated with the assumed parameters. To ascertain whether they are the optimum parameters, one iteration is carried out in keeping with the previous solution. If it is found that this does not cause a change of strategy then this means, in terms of the previous method, that an infinite number of iterations have been passed over in finding the optimum solution. On the other hand, a change of strategy means that we have to begin all over again with the modified strategy, that is, construct equations expressing the self-generating value function, resolve them, and so on.

Scheduled, the method is then as follows.

a. Estimate the strategy parameters s and S.
b. Construct the equations for the values $V(e)$ and resolve them.
c. Try to improve the strategy according to the methods employed in Phase 1 and Phase 2 of the iteration in the system discussed earlier.
d. If the strategy has changed, return to b. If not, the strategy and the values found constitute the optimum attainable.

The construction and resolution of the equations will now be discussed more fully. Consider a complete iteration according to the previous method, but with

$W(e)$ superseded by $V(e)$ and with the parameters s and S as constants. The results are as follows

for $e < s$, $V(e) = 100$

for $e \geqslant s$, $V(e) = f(e) + 0\cdot4 V(e) + 0\cdot3 V(e-1) + 0\cdot2 V(e-2) + 0\cdot1 V(e-3) - g$

where $V(S) = g$.

The simple structure of these equations leads to a simple algorithm without any complications such as matrix inversions etc.

This algorithm is then as follows:

Expand a series $A(e)$ as follows

for $e < s$ $A(e) = 100$

for $e \geqslant s$ $A(e) = \dfrac{f(e) + 0\cdot3 A(e-1) + 0\cdot2 A(e-2) + 0\cdot1 A(e-3)}{1 - 0\cdot4}$

Expand a series $B(e)$ as follows

for $e < s$ $B(e) = 0$

for $e \geqslant s$ $B(e) = \dfrac{1 + 0\cdot3 B(e-1) + 0\cdot2 B(e-2) + 0\cdot1 B(e-3)}{1 - 0\cdot4}$

When these series have been expanded far enough, all that remains is to calcu-calculate

$$g = \frac{A(S)}{B(S)}$$

and $V(e) = A(e) - gB(e)$.

To complete the picture, the further development of the iteration is as follows. Calculate the following for all the e's.

$$W(e) = f(e) + 0\cdot4 V(e) + 0\cdot3 V(e-1) + 0\cdot2 V(e-2) + 0\cdot1 V(e-3)$$

Calculate S^1 as the value of e concomitant with the minimum $W(e)$.

Calculate s^1 as the lowest value of e whereby $W(e) < W(S) + 100$.

Verify that (s^1, S^1) is identical with (s, S). If it is not, substitute (s^1, S^1) for (s, S) and repeat the iteration.

Of course, the number of iterations required depends upon the first estimate of s and S. The first estimate can be obtained by means of the methods of approximation described earlier. The numerical results based on a first estimate of $s = 1$, $S = 25$ are as follows.

number of iterations	s	S
1	4	18
2	2	17
3	2	16
4	2	16

25 One article; several parallel inventory points

25.1 General introduction

The 'classical' inventory studies are planned for 1 article, held in stock at one point. This applies not only to Camp's publication (1922), but equally also to that of Galliher, Morse and Simon (1959).

The usual object of the study is to minimize the total variable costs per year. It is assumed that the different kinds of costs and the behaviour of the demand are fully established.

However, the problem at once becomes very much more complex when chain effects are involved, since a decision concerning one link in the chain may affect the costs in one or more of the other links. Also there are many more alternative solutions and the criteria for choosing amongst them are not always very precise.

A full analytical study of all the chain problems is not likely to become available at the present time. What is possible, and what we shall therefore do here, is to:

— draw attention to certain hazards;
— analyse certain principles;
— give some hints on how to construct ordering systems.

As explained in 'An Introduction to Production and Inventory Control', chain problems can be divided into the following categories:

— parallel grouping, intermittent flow;
— series grouping, intermittent flow;
— series grouping, continuous flow.

The first two categories will be analysed more fully in the present section as follows:

— one article
  ● number of inventory points parallel; Chapter 25;
  ● number of inventory points in series; Chapter 26;
— several articles, interacting; Chapter 27.

Problem

To begin with, then, we shall consider the situation in which parallel stocks of one particular article are held in stock at a number of inventory points; for example stocks of a given car component are held by dealers throughout the British Isles.

25.2 Ordering policy

Assume that these parallel stock points are replenished from a central warehouse or direct from the production line; what effect will this have upon the choice of ordering policy?

This subject is touched upon in Section 17.1 of 'An Introduction to Production and Inventory Control', where it is shown that there are two extremes of ordering policy, which are self-explanatory:

a. Proceed as though the overall stock of all the parallel points combined may be regarded as one. To do so is in fact to ignore certain costs, namely the costs of transporting goods from one stock point to another in order to make up shortages where necessary. The time required for this transport is also ignored. This may be an acceptable solution for expensive articles, such as spare motors.
b. Ignore the interaction altogether and consider each of the parallel points as an entirely independent case. This is feasible for inexpensive articles and where ordering costs at the central point are low, in which case the extra inventory costs are relatively low.

In all other cases, it is worth while to consider two situations separately, namely delivery from a central warehouse or ordering direct from a factory.

25.3 Delivery from a central warehouse

In general this does not affect the choice of the ordering system very much. Rather, the policy for ordering an article from a given store will be related to that of ordering articles in this store, which have to be obtained from the same supplier (see Chapter 27).

To promote a smooth flow of orders to the central point, it will sometimes be necessary to organize matters from this point so that, say, each customer is allotted a given day of the week on which he can place an order.

25.4 Ordering direct from a factory

It is, of course, assumed that the factory itself does not deliver from stock, otherwise the situation would be no different from the previous one. When the changeover costs in production are substantial as compared with the other ordering costs, it will be advisable to arrange matters so that the parallel stock points place orders at the same time. A combined order can be placed in one of the following ways:

- at fixed intervals which are the same for each point (analogous to (s, S) or (s, Q) system);
- as and when the stock situation requires it (analogous to (B, Q) or (B, S) system).

A method of calculation which can sometimes be used in the latter case is described by Winters [Wi 1]. It is based upon the following assumptions:

- n stock points have a common supplier, who does not himself deliver from stock;
- the possible interaction between order levels and batch sizes is ignored;
- the stock points invariably place an order together when the overall stock position warrants this;
- costs of stockout are calculated as being proportional to the average delivery arrears;

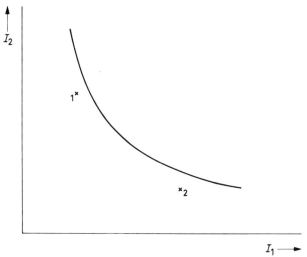

Fig. 61 An ordering curve with two stockpoints. I_i = economical stock in stockpoint i.

— any exchange of stock between the individual stock points is out of the question.

As a result of the calculation there are no re-order levels for the different stockpoints, but a re-order function is established which depends upon each of the individual stock levels. When this function becomes negative, an order must be placed. When only two stock points are involved, the situation can be clearly depicted in a chart. See Fig. 61.

If the point governed by the economic stock, for example point 1 or point 2, falls below the ordering curves, an order must be placed.

Winter emphasizes that he planned the calculations with infrequent shipments in mind. Otherwise, the re-ordering frequency should be chosen, with a view to practical considerations, at, say, once a week or once a fortnight, or in other words the calculation is rounded so that it does not have to be very accurate.

25.5 Allocation problem

The problem of allocation often arises in connection with parallel stocks. What happens is this. A certain number of products become available and have to be distributed amongst a number of stock points so as to minimize the total costs of stock holding and stockout over the coming period T. A solution to this problem of allocation is given by Simpson [Si 1]. The principal features of his article will now be discussed.

n　is the number of parallel stock points for one article;
T　is the period which must elapse before the next quantity becomes available for allocation;
Q　is the total quantity available;
Q_i　is the quantity allocated to stock point i;
S_i　is the demand during T in warehouse i;
　　The frequency distribution of S_i is known.
　　Each store has an initial stock zero.
E_i　is an abbreviation of $E(S_i)$.

Two assumptions are made concerning the costs of stockout and a calculation is carried out for each of them.

25.5.1 Rush deliveries

If the stock level in warehouse i falls below the action level a_i, a rush replenishment of the stock is delivered, either from the central store or from one of the other warehouses. The costs of this emergency action are p_i. We may assume, as an approximation, that not more than one rush replenishment will be necessary for a given stockpoint per period.

The costs of stock holding are the same for each stock point.

The problem is how to minimize the costs of emergency replenishments of all the warehouse stocks in period T.

$P[S_i \geqslant Q_i - a_i]$ = probability that warehouse i will be compelled to place a rush order.

The total expected costs during T are

$$\sum_{1}^{n} i p_i P[S_i \geqslant Q_i - a_i]$$

with $Q_i \geqslant 0$ and $\sum_{1}^{n} i Q_i = Q$.

Now, Simpson shows that:

In order to minimize the costs, matters must be so arranged that the value of $p_i P[S_i = Q_i - a_i]$ is the same for all the stock points.†

If the value of p_i is the same for all the stock points and if $a_i = 0$, then, the value of $P[S_i = Q_i]$ must be the same for all the stock points.

It is assumed that all the stocks were zero prior to the allocation. This is not usually so in practice. However, we can then add the existing stocks to Q and allocate the difference between Q_i and the stock already present to each stock point. If this difference proves to be negative for one or more of the stock points, then it is excluded from the allocation and the calculation is repeated.

Similar allocation problems have also been studied (in a different context) by van Hees and van der Meerendonk [He 1].

The problem can also be solved by dynamic programming. We shall not go into this, but instead we shall develop Simpson's method as applied to a relatively simple situation since, to quote Simpson himself: 'if the number of items is large, the job of storing and looking up the probability density functions is too big even for a large data processing machine'.

If the frequency distribution of $x = \dfrac{\text{forecast error}}{\text{standard deviation}}$ is *the same $f(x)$* for all the stock points and has the following characteristics (applicable, say, to the Gauss distribution):

− steadily increasing between $-\infty$ and 0;
− steadily decreasing between 0 and $+\infty$;
− $f(0) \leqslant 0.5$;

then the following applies.

† Note that this formula contains $P[S_i = Q_i - a_i]$, not $P[S_i \geqslant Q_i - a_i]$; for proof, see Simpson.

It can be shown that the requirement

$$\left(\frac{p_i}{\sigma_i}\right) f\left(\frac{Q_i - E_i}{T_i}\right) = k, \text{ that is independently of } i,$$

is not only essential, but also sufficient for an optimum allocation. Since this result may not seem feasible at first glance, we shall try to put it more clearly with the aid of an example relating to a discrete problem. Assume that there are only two stock points. At both, the demand in period T follows a normal distribution. However, $\mu_1 = 20$, $\sigma_1 = 7$, whilst $\mu_2 = 20$, $\sigma_2 = 3$. There are 48 products to be distributed. Also $p_1 = p_2$ and $a_1 = a_2 = 0$.

Now Q_1 and Q_2 should be so chosen that the two values of

$$\left(\frac{p_i}{\sigma_i}\right) f\left(\frac{Q_i - E_i}{Q_i}\right)$$

are as nearly as possible alike. The calculation is reproduced in the following table, from which it emerges that $Q_1 = Q_2 = 24$ is the solution, whilst the validity of this result is also verified.

TABLE 36

	Solution 1		Solution 2		Solution 3	
	Q_1 23	Q_2 25	Q_1 24	Q_2 24	Q_1 25	Q_2 23
$u_i = \dfrac{Q_i - E_i}{\sigma_1}$	0·430	1·67	0·572	1·33	0·715	1·00
$f(u_i)$	0·364	0·099	0·338	0·165		
$\dfrac{f(u_i)}{\sigma_i}$	0·052	0·033	0·048	0·055		
$\dfrac{f(u_1)}{\sigma_1} - \dfrac{f(u_2)}{\sigma_2}$	+0·019		−0·007		less than −0·007	
Probability of a rush order	0·333	0·048	0·283	0·092	0·237	0·159
Sum of probabilities of a rush order	0·381		0·375		0·396	

The reader can acquire a better understanding of Simpson's proposition by recalculating this sum himself. The proof is to be found in the original article.

Only one frequency distribution need now be employed instead of n distributions. In these circumstances an iterative routine can be worked out for a computer. However, if the following also applies: p_i/σ_i has approximately the same value for each of the stock points, then, and only then, there applies the rule that

$$Q_i = E_i + \left(\frac{\sigma_i}{\Sigma \sigma_i}\right)(Q - \Sigma E_i) = E_i + k\sigma_i$$

where $E_i = E(S)$ for stock point i.

Accordingly, the following allocation rule holds good where subject to the above simplifications:

– give the expected demand to each stock point;
– divide the remainder, that is $(Q - \Sigma E_i)$, in proportion to the standard deviations σ_i.

All that has been said so far concerns the 'rush deliveries' situation. Other hypothetical situations will now be discussed.

25.5.2 No rush deliveries

If the stock is not replenished by emergency action in case of need, then stockout will sometimes occur. It is reasonable to suppose that the costs of stockout will then be proportional to the number of items short. The costs, which now have to be minimized, are

$$C = \sum_{i=1}^{n} w_i \int_{Q_i}^{\infty} (S - Q_i) g_i(S)\, dS$$

where
w_i is the loss owing to sales forfeited for stock point i;
(S) is the probability density function of the demand S, here regarded as a continuous distribution.

Simpson demonstrates that the following is an essential condition for obtaining the optimum

$$w_i P[\underline{S}_i \geqslant Q_i] = k \qquad\qquad k = \text{constant}$$

If in this case the value of w_i is the same for all the stock points, then, the essential condition will be

make $P[\underline{S}_i \geqslant Q_i]$ the same for all the stock points.

On the further assumption that in this situation the frequency distribution of forecast error$/\sigma_i$ is likewise the same for each of the stock points, we again have as the optimum allocation

$$Q_i = E_i + \frac{\sigma_i}{\Sigma \sigma_i}(Q - \Sigma E_i) = E_i + k\sigma_i$$

Summary of the article by Simpson

The allocation procedure

$$Q_i = E_i + k\sigma_i$$

is not only a convenient instruction but also an exact solution in the following circumstances:

a. *Rush deliveries*

Costs proportional to number of emergency actions. The probability that two rush deliveries to the same stock point will be necessary within the period T is negligible. The same frequency distribution

$$\frac{S_i - E(S_i)}{\sigma_i}$$

holds for all the stock points.

Other characteristics of this distribution are: steady rise between $-\infty$ and 0, steady fall between 0 and $+\infty$, $f(0) \leqslant 0.5$.

The value of p_i/σ_i is the same for all the stock points.

b. *No rush deliveries*

Costs proportional to number of sales forfeited. All the stock points have the same distribution for $(S_i - E(S_i))/\sigma_i$, which also has the above three characteristic features.

26 One article; a number of stock points in series

26.1 Examples

This situation is also described in 'An Introduction to Production and Inventory Control', paragraph 17.2.

There is an important distinction here between:

— stationary situations; the frequency distribution of the demand from the ultimate customer invariably remains the same;
— non-stationary situations; the ultimate demand has an average value which varies in time.

It is particularly in the non-stationary, or supposedly non-stationary, situation that chains present serious problems.

The special problems associated with series grouping will be illustrated by means of examples. Before doing so, however, we shall give three examples of the stationary situation to supplement what has been said about this in paragraph 17.2 of 'An Introduction to Production and Inventory Control'.

Example 1

An outline of a system involving one factory, one factory store and four sales outlets is given on pages 181, etc. of the book by Magee [Ma 1]. The demand at each sales outlet follows a Poisson distribution with an average of 25 items per week. The lead time is two weeks. Accordingly, the following applies to the total demand per fortnight

$$\mu = 200, \sigma = \sqrt{200} \approx 14$$

According to the tables of the normal distribution, which may be used as an approximation here, the total demand in a fortnight will only exceed ≈ 235 in $\approx 1\%$ of all cases. Each of the sales outlets employs a (B, Q) system with $Q = 100$. On average, each sales outlet (stock point) will place a replenishment order with the factory store once every four weeks. Accordingly, the following continues to hold for the order flow from the sales outlets

$$\mu = \tfrac{1}{4} \times 4 \times 2 \times 100 = 200$$

In reality, however, σ is appreciably greater. The probability that two orders will be received from the same sales outlet within a fortnight can safely be ignored (hence the Tables 8.6 and 8.7 on page 185 of Magee's book must be wrong); it will be evident that the probability that the demand at one sales outlet will exceed 100 in a fortnight is negligible. This demand follows a normal distribution with $\mu = 50$ and $\sigma = \sqrt{50} = 7 \cdot 1$.

The number of orders received by the factory store during a period of two weeks therefore follows a binomial distribution with $p = 0 \cdot 5$ and $n = 4$.

Probability of	0 orders	1 order	2 orders	3 orders	4 orders
amounts to	6·25%	25%	37·5%	25%	6·25%

Note: Each order is for 100 items.

Now $\sigma = 100\sqrt{np(1 - p)} = 100\sqrt{4 \times 0 \cdot 5 \times 0 \cdot 5} = 100$ instead of 14.

The use of separate (B, Q) systems in each individual link has therefore added considerably to the irregularity of the demand in the last link.

In fact the factory store is no longer able to place any reliance on the demand. This handicap tends to raise the level of the buffer stock in the factory store unduly. As a rule, the factory store stocks a wide variety of articles and the result is that the load on the production capacity fluctuates dangerously. The demand made on the factory fluctuates more than the actual demand from the customers.

Example 2

Brown [Br 1] demonstrates the same effect still more clearly for a longer chain. Take the case of a certain spare part used on board 125 ocean-going ships. Groups of five ships are provisioned by one depot ship, there is one shore depot for every five depot ships and five shore depots in all are supplied from the main warehouse. The main warehouse orders direct from the factory. The demand, as reflected by the orders to the factory, has a $\sigma = 75$, whereas the actual usage, for all the ships combined, only has a $\sigma = 4 \cdot 5$.

Brown demonstrates this effect as evidence that it is very difficult for the manufacturer to forecast the demand from the orders he receives. Ultimately, the entire provisioning system may be regarded as a pipeline, with the factory pumping goods into one end and the demand sucking goods from the other end. 'It may be cheaper in the long run to pay for a watermeter at the far end than to try elaborate techniques of forecasting from poor data'.

The results of a simulation, mentioned by Brown, can be displayed as in Figs 62, 63 and 64.

		undergoes σ	used Q
	1 *factory*	75	241
	1 *main warehouse*	34	241
	5 *shore stations*	14	51
	25 *depot ships*	6·7	11
	125 *ships*	4·5	2

Fig. 62 A chain of stocks.

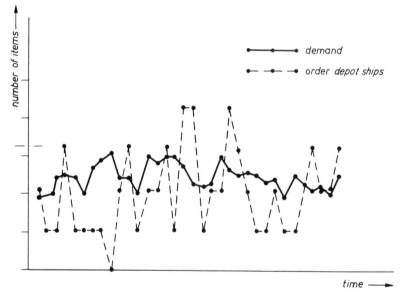

Fig. 63 The chain effect.

The effect demonstrated can be calculated as follows.
Assume that the demand per ship per period comprises:

p = probability of demand for 1 product;
$q = 1 - p$ = probability that demand will be zero.

The probability that the demand will be 2 or more products is negligible.

There are n ships, ordering from one depot ship. If the ships use $Q = 1$, then the demand x from the depot ship follows a binomial distribution with

$$E(x) = pn$$
$$\sigma_1(x) = \sqrt{(n \times pq)} = \sqrt{(np\,(1-p))}$$

If the ships handle a batch size Q, however, the number of *orders* follows a binomial distribution in which $p' = p/Q$.

Although a certain amount of negative autocorrelation takes place, we may nevertheless employ

$$E(y) = n\left(\frac{p}{Q}\right)$$

$$\sigma(y) = \sqrt{\left(n\left(\frac{p}{Q}\right)\left(1 - \left(\frac{p}{Q}\right)\right)\right)}$$

as characteristics of the distribution of the number of *orders* y to the depot ship.

For the frequency distribution of the number of *items* x ordered by the depot ship, we now have

$$E(x) = n\frac{p}{Q} \times Q = np$$

but
$$\sigma_2(x) = Q\sigma(y) = \sqrt{(np\,(Q-p))}$$

The 'amplification factor' σ_2/σ_1 resulting from the use of the batch size Q then becomes

$$\frac{\sigma_2}{\sigma_1} = \sqrt{\left(\frac{Q-p}{1-p}\right)}$$

Note: This effect is independent of n.

TABLE 37

SOME VALUES OF THE AMPLIFICATION FACTOR

	$p = 0.1$	$p = 0.5$
$Q = 2$	1.4	1.7
$Q = 3$	1.8	2.2
$Q = 10$	3.3	4.3
$Q = 100$	10.5	14.1

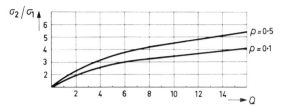

Fig. 64 The amplification factor σ_2/σ_1 as function of batch size and probability distribution of the demand, $p = 0\cdot1$, $0\cdot5$ respectively.

Example 3

The situation is as follows. The products A, B and C are made from the same material G. Each of these products contains an element of material G. Material G is held in stock and replenished by orders placed with an outside supplier.

Products A, B and C are also held in stock; they are ordered in accordance with a (B, Q) system, subject to a lead time of $2\frac{1}{2}$ weeks (mainly production time). Material G can be ordered once in three weeks; the 'periodic replenishment' system (that is an s, S system where $s = S$ is employed).

Assume that the demand for A, B and C over a given period follows the pattern depicted in Table 38 (demand already in terms of quantity of G required).

TABLE 38

DEMAND FIGURES

Week number	A	B	C	Week number	A	B	C
1	4	16	66	14	10	31	24
2	5	9	9	15	4	11	33
3	6	8	14	16	5	45	7
4	3	11	14	17	3	20	19
5	8	8	13	18	4	15	32
6	3	27	27	19	1	6	22
7	10	7	40	20	8	16	12
8	17	6	9	21	8	11	44
9	2	6	58	22	2	8	37
10	4	8	46	23	1	10	17
11	2	10	28	24	16	2	10
12	5	6	13	25	0	19	13
13	8	34	10	26	3	8	6
				27	4	11	30

The following are also given:	A	B	C
Re-order level B	20	45	75
Batch size Q	48	66	105
Initial stock	25	46	70

The reader can easily verify for himself that the results of the ordering system described are in fact presented in Table 39. A very good example is also given on page 195 in the book of van Ackoff and Sasieni [Ac 2].

TABLE 39

ORIGINAL AND DERIVED DEMAND

Interval	Original requirement for G in the form of demand for A, B and C	Derived orders for G
1–3	137	114
4–6	114	171
7–9	155	153
10–12	122	105
13–15	165	66
16–18	150	285
19–21	128	105
22–24	103	0
25–27	94	171
Difference highest–lowest	71	285

There now follow two examples to show that the consequences of linking simple ordering systems into a chain are if anything still worse when the behaviour of the demand is non-stationary than when this is stationary.

Example 4

Brown's simulation in the equilibrium state has already been discussed in Example 2. The initial behaviour of the system described here was even wilder. The re-order level employed was

$$B = \text{demand over the last four months.}$$

Following the initial run-in, the main store re-ordered only after 100 periods (100 months, or nearly ten years) at rest. No orders were received by the main store for 34 months, although the demand continued steadily with $\mu = 25$ and $\sigma = 4\cdot47$ throughout that time.

Example 5

Dr R. F. Meyer (at present at Harvard University) once carried out the following calculation. To ascertain how far fluctuations or abrupt changes in demand are propagated in an amplified form, he studied the behaviour of a single stock point and calculated the amplification factor, which in this case is

$$\frac{\text{amplitude of outgoing order}}{\text{amplitude of incoming demand}}$$

The stock point studied is a warehouse which is permitted to place an order once a month with the main store. The ordering procedure for the warehouse is as follows: order a quantity sufficient to restore the economic stock to the desired level. This level is determined by multiplying the forecast demand during (interval between orders and lead time) by a fixed factor k. It is assumed that the forecast demand has been established by 'double smoothing'.

The demand from the warehouse is assumed to follow a sinusoidal pattern.

The amplification factor then proves to depend mainly upon:

— the safety factor used in determining the desired stock level;
— the smoothing factor α;
— the lead time t.

This relationship is depicted in Fig. 65.

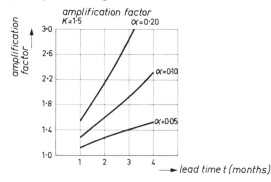

Fig. 65 Amplification factors associated with a frequency of once a year; safety factor $k = 1\cdot5$.

26.2 Methods of combating 'upsweep effect'

What can be done to prevent the so-called 'upsweep effect'? There are four more or less effective methods, which will now be discussed one after another.

1. the 'base-stock' system;
2. a fixed-interval system with an order after each interval;
3. corrected method of calculating the batch size;
4. variants such as the 'three-bin' system.

In view of the risks associated with the non-stationary state, methods 2, 3 and 4 also involve making every effort to limit the stock in the remote warehouses, which can be accomplished by ensuring fast, reliable delivery from the main store (see 'An Introduction to Production and Inventory Control', *Principal laws of planning*).

26.2.1 *The base-stock system*

As far as we know, the original idea of the 'base-stock' system came from Kimball and was defined in an internal memorandum by Arthur D. Little. The system is strongly recommended by Magee (1958).

The base-stock system can be defined in two different ways although in essence the two definitions are entirely equivalent:

a. The information concerning the demand is forwarded systematically to each link in the chain. In the extreme case every individual sale is reported. Periodic reporting is also possible.

In a manufacturing company the information concerning the demand will in fact have to be deduced, for example by 'explosion', or in other words by translation into terms of components by means of part lists, whilst some departments prefer to have the information classified per capacity group. This can be done by means of a computer.

b. Each stock point bases its orders not only upon its own existing stock, but also upon the overall stock throughout the system, 'downstream' from the particular stock point.

It will be evident that a and b are merely two different ways of saying the same thing, since the overall stock can only change as a result of the real demand. At the same time, method b may be preferable in practice to method a, where rejects and scrap have to be taken into account as well.

Examples of the practical application of the base-stock system are given by Magee (1958), page 191, and in 'An Introduction to Production and Inventory Control', page 135.

The effect of the base-stock system can be clearly illustrated with the aid of a cumulative chart. The adoption of a base-stock system at a given stock point means that the supply *to* that stock point is based on the ultimate demand and all 'upsweep' effects are eliminated from it.

In all probability it will therefore be possible to stabilize the behaviour of a chain by adopting a base-stock system at a few strategic points, or in other words the information concerning the ultimate demand need not be propagated throughout the entire chain.

Clark and Scarf [Cl 1] have shown that a base-stock system is in fact the optimum, at any rate subject to certain assumptions.

26.2.2 The fixed-interval re-ordering system

In the example discussed by Magee, a periodic (or fixed-interval) system constitutes a considerable improvement as compared with a (B, Q) system as regards the costs of the system as a whole. In this particular example, it does not matter that the orders arrive all at once instead of being distributed over a period.

A periodic system implies that the information concerning the demand in the period just ended is forwarded periodically in the form of an order to the next stock point. As a result, the demand at this next stock point is then indeed very much more regular than with a (B, Q) system. In Magee's example, moreover, the average order quantity is appreciably smaller than the optimum order quantity as calculated for the (B, Q) system by means of the uncorrected formula of Camp.

26.2.3 Corrected calculation of batch size

In the case of very cheap products, for which methods 1 and 2 would be too expensive, the calculation of Q must still take account of the effect upon buffer stocks at the 'upstream' stock points.

However, this is more easily said than done. A general formula to cover this situation has yet to be worked out.

26.2.4 Variants such as the 'three-bin' system

A variant of the base-stock system which may be described as the 'three-bin' system and is already in use or under consideration in various places, is available for cheap products having a long optimum cycle.

The gist of the three-bin system is as follows. As soon as the stock has been replenished it is divided into three portions (accommodated if necessary in 3 bins). When the second bin is broached, a warning signal is sent to the supplier and when the third bin is broached the actual order is sent. To the best of our knowledge the effects of this system as compared with the base-stock system have not been investigated so far.

26.3 Where should the stock be located in a base-stock system?

In a chain consisting of operations and transport movements, it is possible in principle to locate a stock between two successive phases.

Simpson [Si 2] has described a method of calculation for determining where buffer stocks should be located in a base-stock system.

To begin with, let us assume that there are stocks at all the points. As soon as

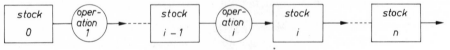

Fig. 66 A stock chain.

one product is withdrawn from stock n, this information is propagated as an order throughout the entire chain. Each operation involves the processing of one product.

One product, ordered from stock point i, is delivered within a time S_i† (guaranteed supplier's lead time, or delivery time).

One product, ordered at operation i, is delivered within the time $S_{i-1} + T_i$, where T_i is the guaranteed throughput time for operation i.

We note $L_i = S_{i-1} + T_i$.

The demand at stock point i has a mean $\bar{x}_i(A)$ and a standard deviation $\sigma_i(A)$. So far the demand is the same at each of the stock points.

The stock at stock point i must be sufficient to cover the demand which may reasonably be expected during the time $A = L_i - S_i$, since L_i is the time which elapses between the sending of the order and the arrival of the product ordered at stock point i; stock i is served by operation i and L_i is the lead time of operation i. If the required delivery time from stock i is not 0, but S_i, however, then it is only necessary to cover the time $A = L_i - S_i$.

Simpson also proceeds on the assumption that the material is held in stock, therefore $S_0 = 0$, and that delivery from the last warehouse to the final customer is from stock, therefore $S_n = 0$.

The average buffer stock at stock point i is then calculated as

$$I_i = k_i \sigma_i(A) = k_i \sigma_i(1) \sqrt{A} = k_i \sigma_i(1) \sqrt{(L_i - S_i)} = k_i \sigma_i(1) \sqrt{(S_{i-1} - S_i + T_i)}$$

where k_i is a constant which does not depend on A.

The inventory costs at stock point i are calculated as $c_i + p_i I_i$, where p_i is the inventory cost per piece and c_i is the inventory cost per stock point (does not depend on I_i).

The total inventory costs can now be formulated and are a function of $S_1, S_2 \ldots, S_{n-1}$.

Now all the values of S are limited, since S_i cannot be less than 0 and cannot exceed $T_1 + T_2 + \ldots + T_i$.

† In the following chapters we use Simpson's notation which is different from the notation in the other chapters of this book.

Next, Simpson demonstrates that in the optimum solution the following applies to each of the intermediate stock points: either $S_i = 0$ or the stock is completely eliminated, therefore $S_i = S_{i-1} + T_i$.

To put it in another way: if there are n operations, therefore $(n-1)$ possible intermediate stock points, only the costs of 2^{n-1} alternatives need be compared.

Example of Simpson's unbranched chain

Let us assume that there are three operations and therefore two end stocks plus two possible intermediate stocks. It will therefore be necessary to compare $2^2 = 4$ possibilities. The level of the stocks 1, 2 and 3 is at stake.

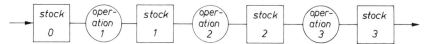

Fig. 67a An unbranched stock chain.

To simplify matters c_1 and c_2, the *fixed* costs of holding stock at 1 and 2, respectively, are ignored.

The *variable* inventory costs are then

$$C = p_1 k_1 \sigma_1 \sqrt{(-S_1 + T_1)} + p_2 k_2 \sigma_2 \sqrt{(S_1 - S_2 + T_2)} + p_3 k_3 \sigma_3 \sqrt{(S_2 + T_3)}$$

In this case $\sigma_1 = \sigma_2 = \sigma_3 = \sigma$.

According to Simpson, the following four solutions merit consideration:

TABLE 40

	Solution 1	Solution 2	Solution 3	Solution 4
Stock 1	Affirmative	Affirmative	Negative	Negative
Stock 2	Affirmative	Negative	Affirmative	Negative
	$S_1 = 0$	$S_1 = 0$	$S_1 = T_1$	$S_1 = T_1$
	$S_2 = 0$	$S_2 = T_2$	$S_2 = 0$	$S_2 = T_1 + T_2$

Solution 1 → $C = p_1 k_1 \sigma \sqrt{T_1} + p_2 k_2 \sigma \sqrt{T_2} + p_3 k_3 \sigma \sqrt{T_3}$

Solution 2 → $C = p_1 k_1 \sigma \sqrt{T_1} \qquad\qquad + p_3 k_3 \sigma \sqrt{(T_2 + T_3)}$

Solution 3 → $C = \qquad\qquad + p_2 k_2 \sigma \sqrt{(T_1 + T_2)} + p_3 k_3 \sigma \sqrt{T_3}$

Solution 4 → $C = \qquad\qquad\qquad + p_3 k_3 \sigma \sqrt{(T_1 + T_2 + T_3)}$

In order to provide an example of a numerical result, it is also assumed that

$p_2 = a p_1$ and $p_3 = b p_1$ and $T_1 = T_2 = T_3 = 1$ and $k\sigma = 1$

The costs then amount to: solution $1 \rightarrow 1 + a + b$

solution $2 \rightarrow 1 + b\sqrt{2}$

solution $3 \rightarrow a\sqrt{2} + b$

solution $4 \rightarrow b\sqrt{3}$

An optimum solution is then obtained, which depends upon the values of a and b and can be depicted in a chart (Fig. 67b).

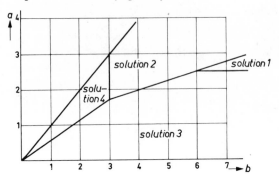

Fig. 67b Solution as a function of the cost ratio.

Example of Simpson's branched chain

Bear in mind the assumption that a 'base-stock' system is employed.

There are n ultimate sales outlets, for each of which the demand has a standard deviation σ.

There are now only two alternatives:

no stock at point 1: $S_1 = T_1$; $S_2 = 0$

$$C = np_2k_2\sigma\sqrt{(T_1 + T_2)}$$

stock at point 1: $S_1 = 0$; $S_2 = 0$

$$C = c + p_1k_1\sigma\sqrt{n}\sqrt{T_1} + np_2k_2\sigma\sqrt{T_2}$$

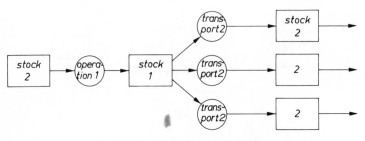

Fig. 68 A branched stock chain.

Ignoring c, this means that there *should* be stock at 1 (central inventory) if

$$n > n^*, \qquad n^* = \left[\frac{p_1 k_1}{p_2 k_2} \times \frac{\sqrt{T_1}}{\sqrt{(T_1 + T_2)} - \sqrt{T_2}} \right]^2$$

The higher p_2, then, the sooner a central inventory will be necessary (that is: at a relatively lower n).

The higher k_2, or in other words the greater the margin of safety required, the sooner a central inventory will be desirable.

With $k_1 = k_2$ and with $p_1/p_2 = 0.7$, the following values of n^* apply

T_2/T_1	5	1	0.2
n^*	11	3	1

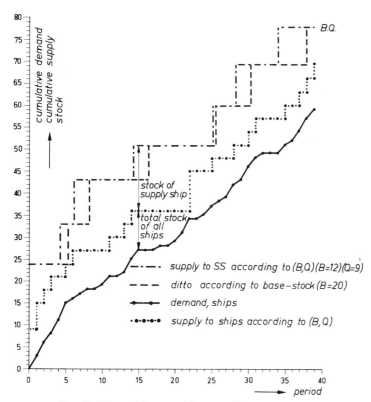

Fig. 69 Effect of 'base-stock' system. For example 2, Section 26.1.

Some additional, miscellaneous remarks concerning the base-stock system

1. In the base-stock system, the goods flow, order flow and information flow are separate. The information flow has a very important part to play.
2. The base-stock system is more expensive in practice than, say, the (B, Q) system. At the same time, it enables $\approx 80\%$ of the capacity to be controlled by applying it to 20% of the code numbers. A three-bin system, perhaps, for the other code numbers?
3. The base-stock system can also be carried out according to one of the methods $(B, Q), (B, S), (s, S)$ or (s, Q).
4. In several existing systems, 'upsweep' apparently does not present much of a problem. This may be due to negative correlation in the demand, Q taken temporarily on the low side (divided shipments) or to the fact that Q is sometimes taken less than Q^*.

27 Several articles; stock points parallel

The situation 'several articles; stock points parallel' has a number of features in common with the situation 'one article; stock points parallel' discussed earlier, but is more prone to complications.

The present discussion will be confined to the situation in which a variety of articles are held in stock in the same warehouse. There are two major complications which may occur, as compared with the situation involving only one stock point:

a. costs are incurred through interaction;
b. there are common limiting factors (money, space, capacity, number of orders).

These two cases will be discussed separately.

27.1 Complex costs pattern

When several different products which have to be ordered from the same supplier and/or brought by the same means of transport are stored in one warehouse, the principal question which arises is: should the orders be placed for each product individually, or would it be better to place a collective order from time to time?

So far we have simply talked about 'the ordering costs'; in the present situation there are fixed costs per order (regardless of the number of articles and of the quantity per article) and in addition there are fixed costs per article ordered (regardless of the quantity ordered).

To simplify matters, assume that the ordering costs per article may be left out of account as being negligible in relation to the ordering costs per order. In this case Camp's formula may be applied to all the articles, regarded as a single unit. To this end, the formula can best be couched as follows

$$Q = \sqrt{\left(\frac{2\,FD}{\delta}\right)}$$

where
D is the annual turnover in terms of money;
Q is the batch size in terms of money.

In these circumstances, the allocation problem solved in Chapter 25 may arise.

Now assume that the ordering costs per article are such that they cannot be ignored. Also that the demand per article is known *and constant*. The following line of reasoning then leads to a solution, albeit not necessarily optimal: assume that all the articles are invariably ordered collectively. Now seek the optimum ordering cycle. In these circumstances Camp's formula cannot be applied to each article individually, since this would result in a wide variety of ordering frequencies. However, the reasoning employed is exactly the same as that which led to Camp's formula: that is the weighting of inventory costs and ordering costs.

Let F_1 = ordering costs per order;
  F_2 = ordering costs per article;
  D_i = annual demand for article i in terms of quantity;
  K_i = cost of each article i;
  δ = required % profitability per year;
  n = number of different articles.

For convenience, the space costs are ignored or incorporated in δ.

Now let m = the length of the ordering cycle, in months.

The total variable costs are

$$C_{tot} = \frac{12}{m}(F_1 + nF_2) + \frac{1}{2}\frac{m}{12}\delta \sum_{i=1}^{i=n} D_i K_i$$

It follows that

$$m^* = \sqrt{\left(\frac{288(F_1 + nF_2)}{\delta \sum_i D_i K_i}\right)}$$

The formula can also be converted to another form representing the optimum number of orders per year g

$$g^* = \frac{12}{m^*}\sqrt{\left(\frac{\delta \sum_i D_i K_i}{2(F_1 + nF_2)}\right)}$$

As we have seen, this value of g^* is not necessarily optimal in fact, since the calculation was based on the assumption that all the articles are invariably ordered collectively. However, it is worth while to calculate the 'individual frequencies' also for the different articles

$$g_i^* = \sqrt{\left(\frac{\delta D_i K_i}{2F_2}\right)}$$

If g_i is less than $0.5\, g^*$ for a given article, then it will probably be more profitable to refrain from ordering that article on every occasion; this is the advice given by Magee because 'there is no simple way of arriving at the best cycle variation of this sort other than by trial'.

Another complication which can be taken into account is that the demand is stochastic. This means that longer ordering intervals necessitate relatively higher buffer stock levels.

Last but not least there is the situation, which will be discussed by way of example, in which a manufacturer produces a number of articles in his own factory, whereby there are differences in some of the changeover costs and the demand is stochastic. The problem is to determine the re-order interval and the batch size per article.

The changeover costs matrix is of the kind illustrated in Table 3 of 'An Introduction to Production and Inventory Control'. Thus the articles are preferably brought together in groups. If a number of machines are arranged in parallel in the factory, the most costly conversions can be avoided altogether in the allocation of article groups to machines.

Assume that, following such an allocation, the main groups of articles indicated in Table 41 have to be made on one machine.

TABLE 41

MAIN GROUPS OF ARTICLES ALLOCATED, FOR PRODUCTION,
TO THE SAME MACHINE

Number of subgroup	Serial number article	Numbering per subgroup i	Costs of changeover to the article mentioned on the next line
$j = 1$	1	$i = 1$	OK
	2	$i = 2$	F
	3	$i = 3$	F
			F
			F
		$i = N_1$	OK
$j = 2$		$i = 1$	F
			F
		$i = N_2$	OK
$j = 3$			F
			F
			OK
$j = 4$			F
			OK
$j = 5$			F
			OK
R	n	N_R	

Note that there are main groups and subgroups. Changeovers from one subgroup to another cost an amount OK.

It is assumed that a periodic re-ordering system is employed, so that the opportunity to order each article occurs at intervals. Also, the following notation will be employed:

m = ordering cycle, in months;
f_i = the number of cycles in which, on average, article i is made once. So, if
    $m = 2$ and $f_i = 3$, an article i is on average made once per six months.

The following types of costs now have to be taken into account:

— the costs of the batch size stock;
— the changeover costs;
— the costs of the buffer stock;
— the costs of stockout.

As we shall see later, m^* and f_i^* cannot readily be calculated analytically from the variable costs equation yet to be compiled. In practice, moreover, m can only assume a very limited number of values, for example one week, two weeks, one month, two months. For this reason it is better to simply calculate the expected value of the variable costs for a number of values of m.

Changeover costs

Every time article i is made, changeover costs amounting to at least F are incurred. Per year, this amounts to

$$\left(\frac{12}{mf_i}\right) F \text{ (m given, f_i still to be determined)}$$

Changeover costs are also incurred in the event of a change to subgroup j. The probability that the subgroup j will also become involved within a given cycle is governed by the probability that at least one of the articles in subgroup j will be ordered within that time.

The probability that article i will be ordered within a given cycle is $1/f_i$.

The probability that one or more articles in subgroup j will be ordered is, for each *cycle*

$$1 - \left\{\left(1 - \frac{1}{f_1}\right)\left(1 - \frac{1}{f_2}\right)\dots\left(1 - \frac{1}{f_{N_j}}\right)\right\} = 1 - \prod_{i=1}^{i=N_j}\left(1 - \frac{1}{f_i}\right)$$

The expected changeover costs F_j for subgroup j per cycle therefore amount to

$$F_j = \left\{1 - \prod_{i=1}^{i=N_j}\left(1 - \frac{1}{f_i}\right)\right\}(OK - F) + F\sum_{i=1}^{i=N_j}\frac{1}{f_i}$$

The changeover costs per *month* for *j* are found to be

$$\frac{1}{m} F_j$$

Accordingly, the total changeover costs for all the groups per year are

$$FM = \sum_{j=1}^{j=R} \left(\frac{12}{m}\right) F_j$$

Given m, the optimum value of f_i can be determined for each article. In so doing, we leave the costs term including the factor $(OK - F)$ out of account; the error involved is small. Per article, the costs affected by the choice of f_i are

$$\left(\frac{12}{mf_i}\right) F + \left(\frac{mf_i}{2 \times 12}\right) D_i K_i \delta$$

It follows that the optimum f_i is

$$f_i^* = \sqrt{\left(\frac{12^2 \times F \times 2}{m^2 D_i K_i \delta}\right)} = \sqrt{\left(\frac{288 F}{D_i K_i \delta m^2}\right)}$$

Only the integral positive values of f_i can be used, however.

Now find a value of p such that the above costs function, represented by sented by

$$\frac{C_1}{f_i} + C_2 f_i$$

assumes the same value for $f_i = p$ and for $f_i = p + 1$; f_i^* is then the integral number between p and $p + 1$.

From the equation $$\frac{C_1}{p} + C_2 p = \frac{C_1}{p + 1} + C_2 (p + 1)$$

we have $$p^2 + p = \frac{C_1}{C_2}$$

whence it follows that $$p + 1 = \frac{1}{2} + \sqrt{\left(\frac{1}{4} + \frac{288 F}{\delta D_i K_i m^2}\right)}$$

and $f_i^* = (p + 1$, rounded downwards)

Batch size stock

For article i, made once per mf_i months, the batch size is $Q_1 = (mf_i/12)D_i$.
The costs of the batch size stock are

$$\frac{mf_i}{2 \times 12} D_i K_i \delta$$

The total batch size inventory costs per year for all the groups are found to be

$$SK = \sum_{i=1}^{i=n} \frac{mf_i}{2 \times 12} D_i K_i \delta$$

Buffer stock

Here it is best to base the calculation on a given probability of stockout z, which can if necessary be made dependent upon, say, the class of turnover. Assume that the re-order level s for article i may be formulated as follows

$$s_i = C_{zi} \frac{D_i}{12} t$$

where t is the delivery time, and C_{zi} is a constant depending upon z, D_i and $\sigma_i \sqrt{t}$, in which σ_i represents the standard deviation of the monthly demand for article i. We then have to determine t as a function of m and afterwards calculate the buffer stock.

As a rough estimate, the delivery time may be regarded as the sum of

- the time required to prepare for the production, a constant t_v;
- the interval m, since if a decision not to order is taken at a given moment, then there will be no further opportunity to place an order until a time m has elapsed;
- a time between 0 and m, because the duration of the production cycle is m and we do not know beforehand at what point in the production cycle article i will occur (although there are some applications in which this period *is* known *and* constant).

The calculation need not necessarily be very exact, since our object is to show the effect of the choice of m upon the buffer stock, not to determine actual re-order levels. Taking the assumptions made in Chapters 20 and 21 into account, we take $t = t_v + 1.75 m$. The re-order level s is calculated as

$$s_i = C_{zi} \frac{D_i}{12} (t_v + 1.75\ m)$$

The next step is to determine the expected buffer stock. By the time the new order arrives, the stock will have fallen, on average, an amount

$$0.5\ m + t_v + 0.5\ m = m + t_v$$

below the re-order level.

The expected buffer stock is

$$b_i = C_{zi} \frac{D_i}{12} (t_v + 1 \cdot 75\,m) - \frac{D_i}{12} (m + t_v)$$

$$= \frac{D_i}{12} [C_{zi}(t_v + 1 \cdot 75\,m) - (m + t_v)]$$

The annual costs of the total buffer stock then become

$$VV = \sum_{i=1}^{i=n} \delta K_i \frac{D_i}{12} [C_{zi}(t_v + 1 \cdot 75\,m) - (m + t_v)]$$

Final result

The total variable costs associated with a given value of m correspond to

$$C_m = FM + SK + VV$$

This does not take into account the costs of determining the order, which has to be done once per cycle. Table 42 shows the best way to display the results.

For these calculations a computer is almost indispensible, since the problem often involves numerous articles and a number of values of m have to be covered. We also have to consider how far the result may be influenced by, say, the level of the changeover costs. This is soon answered when a computer programme has been established (Table 43).

Interpretation of the result

The above programme can be used to find an optimum cycle and the associated optimum batch size for each article. Practical hints on interpretation are given in 'An Introduction to Production and Inventory Control', Chapter 15.

27.2 Common limiting factors

27.2.1 Limited capital

The batch size for each article is calculated separately by means of a suitable formula, say, for convenience, Camp's formula. The result shows that on average the investment required would be

$$\sum_{i=1}^{i=n} \frac{Q_i}{2} K_i$$

However, the amount G available is less than the capital required. The calculation must now be repeated subject to this limitation; this can be done very neatly by means of the Lagrange multiplier. The reasoning here is as follows.

TABLE 42

RESULTS OF CALCULATION OF OPTIMUM CYCLE AND ORDERING FREQUENCIES

Sub-group no.	Arti-cle no.	Annual turnover items D_i	Price per item K_i	Batch size according to Camp	$m = \frac{1}{2}$ month		$m = 1$ month		$m = 2$ months	
					f_i	s_i	f_i	s_i	f_i	s_i
1	1	32 000	1·8p	11 000	8	11 000	4	15 000	2	19 000
	12	16 000	1·8p	7 500	11	5 700	6	8 000	3	9 700
2	1	48 000	2·0p	13 000	7	12 000	3	18 000	2	23 000
4	4	38 000	1·8p	12 000	8	11 500	4	16 500	2	21 000
per month	total changeover costs					1 343		1 157		914
	total costs batch size stock					500		520		580
	total costs buffer stock					658		1 045		1 346
				total cost		2 501		2 722		2 840

Assumed probability of stockout: 20%

TABLE 43

SENSITIVITY OF RESULTS TO LEVEL OF CHANGEOVER COSTS PER CHANGEOVER

Main group	Assumed change-over costs	Total variable costs			
		$m = \frac{1}{2}$ month	$m = 1$ month	$m = 1\frac{1}{2}$ months	$m = 2$ months
1	$F = 85, OK = 160$	7 514	8 896	9 725	10 698
	$F = 120, OK = 210$	8 272	9 311	10 013	10 919
2	$F = 85, OK = 160$	2 366	3 008	3 614	4 318
	$F = 120, OK = 210$	3 621	3 693	4 071	4 660
3	$F = 85, OK = 160$	1 970	1 970	2 218	2 266
	$F = 120, OK = 210$	1 980	1 975	2 132	2 269

Conclusion: choice of m^* is not affected very much by the above differences in changeover costs.

The problem is to minimize†

$$C = \sum_{i=1}^{i=n} \frac{D_i}{Q_i} F + \sum_{i=1}^{i=n} \tfrac{1}{2} Q_i \delta K_i$$

subject to the limitation

$$\sum_{i=1}^{i=n} \tfrac{1}{2} Q_i K_i = G$$

It can be shown that this problem is identical with the following.
Minimize

$$C' = \sum_i \frac{D_i}{Q_i} F + \sum_i \frac{Q_i}{2} \times \delta K_i + h \left(\sum_i \frac{Q_i K_i}{2} - G \right)$$

where h is the Lagrange multiplier. C' must be minimized as a function of Q_i and h. By taking $\partial C'/\partial Q_i = 0$, we find that

$$Q_i^* = \sqrt{\left(\frac{2 D_i F}{(\delta + h) K_i} \right)}$$

And with $\partial C'/\partial h = 0$, we have

$$G = \sum_i \frac{Q_i K_i}{2}$$

By substituting the value of Q_i^* in the last result, we obtain

$$G = \sqrt{\left(\frac{F}{\delta + h} \right)} \sum_i \sqrt{\left(\frac{D_i K_i}{2} \right)}$$

From this, h can be deduced as

$$h = \frac{F}{2} \left(\frac{\sum \sqrt{(D_i K_i)}}{G} \right)^2 - \delta$$

and with it all the values of Q. It will be evident from the form of the equation that h here constitutes a necessary additional profit on the capital invested.

27.2.2 Limited space

If the space available M is less than the space which would be needed, on average, according to Comp's formula, the problem can be solved by following the same line of reasoning.

The problem is as follows.
Minimize

$$C' = \sum_i \frac{D_i}{Q_i} F + \sum_i \frac{Q_i}{2} (K_i \delta + s p_i)$$

† To simplify matters the space costs are ignored or assumed to be discounted in δ.

where sp_i represents the space costs per item per year for product i, subject to the limitation

$$\sum_i \frac{Q_i}{2} x_i = M$$

where x_i represents the number of cubic metres required for one product i.
    Take instead the equivalent problem of minimizing.

$$C' = \sum_i \frac{D_i}{Q_i} F + \sum_i \frac{Q_i}{2} (K_i \delta + sp_i) + h \left(\sum_i \frac{Q_i}{2} x_i - M \right)$$

We now have

$$\frac{\partial C}{\partial Q_i} = 0, \quad \text{or} \quad Q_i = \sqrt{\left(\frac{2 D_i F}{\delta K_i + sp_i + hx_i} \right)}$$

$$\frac{\partial C}{\partial h} = 0, \quad \text{or} \quad \sum_i \frac{Q_i}{2} x_i = M$$

By substituting the first result in the second one we obtain

$$\sqrt{\left(\frac{F}{2} \right)} \sum_i \sqrt{\left(\frac{D_i}{\delta K_i + sp_i + hx_i} \right)} = M$$

The simplest way to solve the problem is to first calculate the value of the left-hand term for one or two values of h and then plot the required value h^* in a graph. For more elaborate methods of determining h^*, see Holt and others, [Ho 1], page 189, etc.

27.2.3 Limited number of changeovers

By employing the method already demonstrated in two examples, it is also possible to deal with the problem which arises when the number of changeovers per year must not exceed a certain limit Z. The result will now be given direct

$$Q_i = \sqrt{\left(\frac{2 D_i (F + h)}{\delta K_i} \right)}$$

$$h = \frac{\delta}{2} \left(\frac{\sum \sqrt{(D_i K_i)}}{Z} \right)^2 - F$$

where h therefore constitutes the additional changeover costs involved.

Calculations when F and δ are unknown

The theory so far provides us with a means of improving matters even when no information is available concerning F and $δ$. This can be done in two ways:

— keep the number of changeovers per year constant and minimize the variable costs (which is equivalent to minimizing the stock);
— keep the capital investment in batch stocks constant and minimize the variable costs.

Starr and Miller [St 1] give an interesting proposition for this situation.
If the optimum batch size per article can be calculated according to

$$Q_i^* = \sqrt{\left(\frac{2D_iF}{δK_i}\right)} \qquad (δ \text{ and } F \text{ independent of } i)$$

(leaving limitations of money, space and changeovers out of account) then the following holds for the optimum situation, for the entire assortment of goods and for every value of $F/δ$:

$$(TV)(TO) = \text{constant} = \tfrac{1}{2}\sum_i \sqrt{(D_iK_i)}^2$$

where TV is the total stock = $\Sigma(Q_iK_i)/2$
          TO is the total number of orders per year = $\sum_i(D_i/Q_i)$

The proof of this proposition is trivial. At the same time it is interesting to note that in a chart depicting the relationship between TV and TO, the optimum situation *must* lie on the hyperbola indicated above. No situation represented by a point above the curve can be optimum.

28 Norms in inventory control

28.1 Control

Inventory control in the true sense of the term involves making a regular comparison between 1, the actual stock on hand and 2, the norm to which this stock must conform. It is not easy to determine the actual stock on hand at any given moment and, if anything, still more difficult to establish norms. In order to provide norms which are in any way realistic, the first essential is to make a careful study of what the practical application of inventory control really involves.

Theoretical estimates of stock norms for a re-ordering system with a re-order level and an optimum batch size have already appeared in several books† and articles. Often, however, it will be necessary to introduce such norms in advance of an entirely new and optimum re-ordering system.

The proper course is therefore to define the entire process from an 'uncontrolled state' to an optimum re-ordering system, including stock norms, in phases.

Phase 1. Analysis of the existing re-ordering system or stock replenishing system and formulation of 'rules for stock norms' based upon the *existing* procedures. This provides stock norms for the existing situation (not yet optimum), enabling this to be brought into some form of order.

Phase 2. Introduction of improved decision rules in the system of stock replenishment. Training of responsible officials in the use of the new decision rules.

Phase 3. Adaptation of the 'rule-of-thumb norms' to make them fully consistent with the improved decision rules introduced in Phase 2.

Phase 4. Revision of the methods of calculating the norms and elaboration of those aspects which are important to the norms.

Usually, only the methods of calculation mentioned in Phase 4 are dealt with in the literature.

These methods of calculation are intended to cover all the cost components and other factors. It is characteristic of inventory problems that they have numerous aspects and involve several types of costs; allowance must be made for

† Brown, R. G. Statistical Forecasting for Inventory Control, McGraw-Hill (New York), 1959.

conversion costs of the production process, ordering costs, inventory (carrying) costs, profit-earning capacity of the capital investment, risk of obsolescence and costs of delay. Moreover, some of the quantities involved are in the nature of random variables, such as market forecasts and production plans derived from these, percentages defective, illness, tempo and in many cases, even lead times. The task of evolving standards to cover all these aspects is very complex indeed.

28.2 A practical starting point

A practical and at the same time logical step towards a controlled inventory situation, also giving scope for the successful completion of Phases 2 and 3, is to divide the whole article assortment into product categories, whereby the same decision rules govern the re-order level and the order quantity per category.

Although arbitrary in principle, the choice of these categories can be supported by one or two theoretical criteria. Since those costs which can be swayed in establishing the order quantity do not increase very much in response to substantial deviations from the optimum order quantity, this approach can still produce good results.

For example, a method of inventory control evolved by the Philips company for components is described briefly in the following paragraph.

28.3 The A.B.C. system of inventory control†

This approach stems from the well-proved proposition that many articles represent only a very small fraction and a few articles the bulk of the total monetary value.

In the A.B.C. system of inventory control articles are classified as A, B or C, namely:

A-articles; the small group of articles representing much of the total turnover.
B-articles; the middle group.
C-articles; the wide range of articles whose share of the total turnover is small.

Within this system a suitable choice of order frequency (or order quantity) and re-order level will have to be made.

Practical considerations restrict the range of possible re-order frequencies to, for instance

$$f = \tfrac{1}{4}, \tfrac{1}{2}, 1, 2, 3, 4, 5 \text{ or } 6 \text{ months}$$

† 'The A.B.C. system of inventory control' by R. Borgnana; memorandum issued internally by the Philips company in October 1968.

The re-order frequency is here expressed in months, thereby indicating that an order quantity covers the demand for a period such that re-ordering becomes necessary after f months.

The buffer stock, also expressed in months of demand, is similarly restricted.

$$tv = \tfrac{1}{4}, \tfrac{1}{2}, 1 \text{ month}$$

An important parameter for the classification of articles is the monthly turnover. Each article must be assigned to that category where its costs of acquisition and carrying costs are lowest.

The following formula can be used to establish the limits between two categories

$$G_{i,\,i+1} = \frac{C}{f_i f_{i+1}}$$

where $G_{i,i+1}$ is the limit such that articles with a turnover above it are assigned to the category with re-order frequency f_{i+1} whilst those with a turnover at or below it come into the category with f_i.

The factor C is equal to $24F/\delta$. (F = ordering costs or costs of acquisition; δ = carrying costs percentage per year.) With $\delta = 0\cdot24$ and $F = £1$ it follows that $C = 100$.

Assuming the value of f_i to be limited to $f_A = \tfrac{1}{2}$; $f_B = 1$; $f_C = 3$ months, it follows that

$$G_{A,B} = \frac{100}{\tfrac{1}{2} \times 1} = £200 \text{ per month}$$

$$G_{B,C} = \frac{100}{1 \times 3} \approx £30 \text{ per month}$$

This implies that articles whose monthly turnover exceeds £200 fall into category A. B includes all the articles with a turnover between £200 and £30; the remainder fall into category C.
remainder fall into category C.

It will be evident that costs can be reduced by extending the range of values of f_i, although on the other hand this adds to the administrative costs of implementing the system. A similar limitation is now imposed on the buffer stock.

The proof of formula

$$G_{i,\,i+1} = \frac{C}{f_i f_{i+1}}$$

is as follows.

The monthly ordering and carrying costs of article x with a turnover W_x in category i are

$$K_{x,i} = \tfrac{1}{2}Q_x \frac{x}{12} + N_i F$$

where N_i is the number of batches received per month $= 1/f_i$.
Now $Q_x = f_i W_x$ and so

$$K_{x,i} = \frac{\delta}{24} f_i W_x + \frac{F}{f_i}$$

Article x must be assigned to the category where the total costs K_x are smallest.
The border between categories i and $i+1$ is where the costs of article x are the same in both categories, that is

$$K_{x,i} = K_{x,i+1}$$

$$\frac{\delta}{24} f_i x + W \frac{F}{f_i} = \frac{x}{24} f_{i+1} W_x + \frac{F}{f_{i+1}}$$

The value of W_x thus formulated is the border between categories i and $i+1$.

$$W_x \frac{\delta}{24}(f_i - f_{i+1}) = F\left(\frac{1}{f_{i+1}} - \frac{1}{f_i}\right)$$

With $C = 24F/\delta$ we then have

$$W_x = C \times \frac{1}{f_i f_{i+1}} = G_{i,i+1}$$

28.4 Application of A.B.C. inventory control

The method outlined here leads to inventory control through simple procedures.
A description of this system as applied to a concrete case involving a total of
1320 articles with a monthly turnover of £111 400 is given in the above brochure.
Table 44 shows the results.

Example of A.B.C. – inventory control

$f_a = \tfrac{1}{2}, f_b = 1, f_c = 3$ months; $tv_a = \tfrac{1}{2}, tv_b = \tfrac{1}{2}, tv_c = 1$ month.
$F = £1, \delta = 0.24$.

TABLE 44

Category	Limits £	Number of items	%	Demand value £100 units	%	Inventory in £100 units			Inventory in months			Number of lots received	Lots received per item per month
						Total	*LSS*	*BS*	Total	*LSS*	*BS*		
A	> 200	112	8	813	71	610	203	406	0·75	0·25	0·5	224	2
B	< 200 > 33	274	21	249	22	249	125	125	1	0·5	0·5	274	1
C	< 33	934	71	84	7	210	126	84	2·5	1·5	1	311	0·33
Total	−	1320	100	1146	100	1069	454	615	0·93	0·40	0·53	809	0·6

LSS = Lot-size stock
BS = buffer stock (safety stock)

28.5 The lognormal distribution and the Lorenz curve

Starting point

So far, stock norms have been established for groups of articles on the assumption that the articles within a group are dealt with uniformly. On this assumption it was necessary to seek a classification covering articles ordered in the same quantities and having the same buffer stocks (both expressed in terms of time, for example weeks or months). We can dispense with this necessity amongst other things by applying a natural law widely exploited in industry, physics and economics, namely that the *logarithm of a variable* is normally distributed.

This is the case with the distribution of incomes, hotel prices, post-office savings, the sales of industrial products, to mention but a few. It can be explained by the fact that the particular variable is subject to numerous influences which act upon it entirely independently and fortuitously. This is a characteristic which can be exploited to good effect in dealing with problems of inventory control.

When the relationship between the number of articles and the turnover of these articles is plotted on lognormal graph paper, the line representing the fraction of the number of articles is found to run parallel to that representing the fraction of the total turnover. This can be seen in Fig. 70a, from which can be read the percentage of the turnover associated with each percentage of the total number of articles.

In the case illustrated, the variance of the lognormal distribution is $\sigma^2 = 3\cdot2$ and $\sigma = 1\cdot78$. For *this* value of the variance, the 20–80 rule applies; but the 35–90 rule, etc., can also be derived from the graph.

Certain relationships can also be deduced for other values of the variance. The nomogram in Fig. 70b can be used for this purpose. Wallis and Roberts mention the Lorenz curve in this connection. The Lorenz curve depicts the relationship between the percentage of the total turnover and the percentage of the total number of articles [Wa 1].

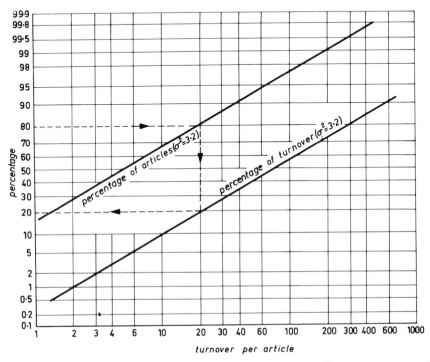

Fig. 70a The Lorenz curve of articles and turnover with $\sigma^2 = 3 \cdot 2$.

An important point to remember is that if the logarithm of the variable is normally distributed, the same variable raised to a given power also follows a lognormal distribution. Further information on this point is given in studies by R. G. Brown.

The following characteristic can be deduced from this

$$\overline{x^k} = \frac{1}{2} \overline{x}^k \, e^{k(k-1)\,\sigma^2}$$

where x is a variable whose logarithm is normally distributed and σ is the standard deviation of the lognormal distribution.

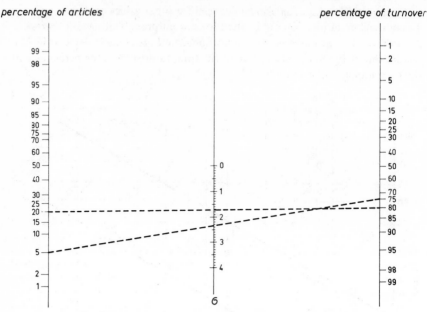

percentage of articles

percentage of turnover

Fig. 70b The relationship between the percentage of articles
and the percentage of turnover as a function of spread in
turnover of articles.

This characteristic is of importance in inventory control because the optimum
order quantity $Q = \sqrt{(2DF/C_i)} = qD^{1/2}$ and the buffer stock can be written as
$VV = CD^p$, where p is usually between 0·5 and 1. The sum of Q and VV can
therefore be expressed as a function of D^t.

Given the turnover D for each article and $\overline{D}$ for the average of the entire article
group, the batch size and the buffer stock for the entire assortment can be
calculated, namely $Q = qD^{1/2}$.

namely $Q = qD^{1/2}$.

N = total number of articles in the group

$$\frac{N}{2}\overline{Q} = \frac{N}{2}q\overline{D}^{1/2} = \frac{N}{2}q(\overline{D})^{1/2}e^{-\sigma 2/8}$$

With $p = 0·75$, the following applies to the buffer stock

$$\frac{N}{2}(\overline{VV}) = \frac{N}{2}C(\overline{D^p}) = \frac{N}{2}C(\overline{D})^{3/4}e^{-3\sigma^2/32}$$

Given only the *relationship* between buffer stock or batch size and turnover
per article (D), then, the average stock level for the entire assortment can be

deduced from the average turnover for the *entire* group ($\bar{D}$) of articles. The latter is usually known or is readily calculated.

The above principles are employed in the chart which will now be discussed.

28.6 Stock norms for a group of articles; calculation chart

The calculation chart which will now be discussed is based upon the widely applicable natural law previously mentioned, that the demand per article in a group of articles follows a lognormal distribution. A. R. W. Muyen has evolved a comparatively simple method of calculation based upon this law, the principle of which will be demonstrated with the aid of an example.

We saw in the previous paragraph that if the average demand per article (D) follows a lognormal distribution, then each function containing D to a given power is likewise lognormally distributed. They are functions of the form $y = cD^p$. The mean values and variances of the demand, the average stock level, the number of orders and the order quantity are often functions of this kind or sums of them.

For example: the order quantity $= q_1 D^{1/2}$
  the buffer stock $= q_2 D^p (0.5 \leqslant p \leqslant 1)$
  the number of orders per time unit $= q_3 D^{-1/2}$

For the stock level we have:
The average of the total = total of the averages = N x expected average
(N = number of articles).
The variance of the total = total of the variances = N x expected variance.
The expected average and the expected variance of the stock level, number of orders, etc., per article are therefore the average values of lognormal distributions.

The essence of the method of calculation is as follows.

a. Take a random sample from the whole article group and determine the average demand D for each article in this sample.
b. Plot the values thus established on logarithmic probability paper.
c. Calculate or read from this the 50% and 99% points.
d. Calculate for these two points the functions whose total data are required. The values thus calculated now constitute the 50% and 99% of the derived distributions.
e. With the aid of the two calculated percentages, the expected average value of the particular function can be read from a nomogram (see Fig. 71).
f. Multiplying this by N produces the required total expectation.

The example given here is based upon the following information:

Number of articles = 200

$x(50\%) = 50$ ⎫ deduced from a graphical representation of the test sample
$x(99\%) = 10\,000$ ⎰ values on lognormal probability paper.

$Q = 120\sqrt{2D}$

D = the average demand per month

Buffer stock = $20D^{2/3}$

Batch size stock = $\frac{1}{2}Q$

Number of orders per month = D/Q

‚The values of σ and $\bar{x}$ can be read from Fig. 71

Stock replenishment is carried out according to the (B, Q) system, as it is called.

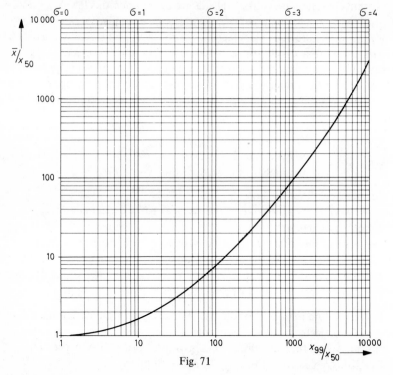

Fig. 71

The calculation is carried out in Table 45; a sample totalling 200 articles has been taken and the distribution of this has been plotted on lognormal probability paper, from which the values at the 50% and 99% points have been read. The values of batch size stock, buffer stock and number of orders associated with this value of D can be calculated on the basis of x_{50} and x_{99}. This has been done on the lines beyond x_{50} and x_{99}. Next, the ratio x_{50}/x_{99} is calculated as a measure of the ratio $\bar{x}/x_{50}$ (the skewness) and of σ, as will be seen in Fig. 71.

TABLE 45

CALCULATION OF THE TOTAL AVERAGES

Number of articles $N = 200$	Demand per month	Batch size	Buffer stock	Batch size stock	Number of orders per month
	D	$120\sqrt{2D}$	$20D^{2/3}$	$\frac{1}{2}Q$	D/Q
x_{50}	50	1 200	272	600	0·042
x_{99}	10 000	17 000	9 250	8 500	0·59
x_{99}/x_{50}	200		34	14	14
* σ	2·3		1·5	1·15	1·15
* $\bar{x}/x_{50}$	14		3·2	1·9	1·9
$\bar{x}$	700		870	1 150	0·08
Total average $N\bar{x}$	140 000		174 000 230 000		16·0
Total stock			404 000		

* Can be read from Fig. 71.

TABLE 46*

CALCULATION OF TOTAL VARIANCES

Number of code numbers $N = 200$	Demand per month	Batch size	Quantity ordered per month	Number of orders per month
Variance per article	$6 \cdot 25 D^{3/2}$ $\sigma = 2 \cdot 5 D^{3/4}$	$\frac{1}{12}Q^2$	$6 \cdot 25 D^{3/2} + \frac{1}{6}Q^2$	$\dfrac{6 \cdot 25 D^{3/2}}{Q^2} + \frac{1}{6}$
x_{50}	2 209	120 000	2 209 + 240 000	$0 \cdot 00153 + \frac{1}{6}$
x_{90}	6·25 × 10⁶	24 × 10⁶	6·25 × 10⁶ + 48 × 10⁶	$0 \cdot 0216 + \frac{1}{6}$
x_{99}/x_{50}	2 830	200	2 830 200	14 1
σ	3·5	2·3	3·5 2·5	1·15 0
$\bar{x}/x_{50}$	385	14	385 14	1·9 1
$\bar{x}$	850 000	1 680 000	850 000 + 3 360 000	$0 \cdot 0029 + \frac{1}{6}$
Total variance $N\bar{x}$	170 × 10⁶	336 × 10⁶	170 × 10⁶ + 672 × 10⁶ = 842 × 10⁶	0·58 + 33·3 33·9
Standard deviation	13 000	18 300	29 000	5·8

* By means of Fig. 71.

We can then calculate $\bar{x}$ for the two stock components and for the number of orders per month. The total average is then obtained by multiplying by $N\bar{x}$.

In practice the real stock never coincides exactly with the average thus calculated, but varies about this within certain limits owing to the stochastic nature of the demand. In order to assess the correctness of the real stock level, it is necessary to know within what limits the stock level can be permitted to vary. To establish these limits we must determine the variance of the stock level.

The standard deviation of the demand, the batch size stock, the quantity ordered per month and the number of orders per month is determined in Table 46. The methods of determining the variances of these quantities will now be explained one by one.

The standard deviation of the demand is given as $2 \cdot 5 D^{3/4}$.

The variance is then

$$(2 \cdot 5 D^{3/4})^2 = 6 \cdot 25 D^{3/2}$$

The batch size stock varies per article between 0 and Q; the variance is then $\frac{1}{12} Q^2$ (rectangular distribution).

On average, the quantity per month equals the demand per month; the demand is greater due to the discontinuous nature of the ordering system. The extra variance may be assumed to be approximately $\frac{1}{6} Q^2$ (two rectangular distributions). The variance of the quantity ordered per month therefore becomes $6 \cdot 25 D^{3/2} + \frac{1}{6} Q^2$.

The variance of the number of orders per month can be derived from the above by dividing this by Q^2.

The result of the calculations in Tables 45 and 46 can be summarized as follows.

TABLE 47

	Number of articles	Demand per month	Buffer stock	Batch size stock	Quantity ordered per month	Number of orders per month
Average	200	140 000	174 000	230 000	140 000	16·0
Standard deviation	—	13 000	—	18 300	29 000	5·8

The upper and lower limits for the above quantities can be established with the aid of the average and the standard deviations.

Section V: Calculation of Production Level (Continuous Supply)

29 Determination of production level

(Freely adapted from an article by R. F. Meyer and A. R. W. Muyen entitled, 'The production planning of many-product assembly operations').†

29.1 Introduction

Given an assembly plant comprising a number of small, independent assembly lines, each assembly group operating such a line can produce one complete article. A plant might consist of, say, a hundred or more of such groups.

The production level of a given product can be varied by varying the number of groups engaged in assembling that product. This can be done by operating an assembly line on a two or three shift basis or by converting another assembly line to the production of the particular article. The object of the present chapter is to define a system of production control suitable for this kind of manufacturing operation.

Formulation of the problem

We shall consider those cases in which components (or subassemblies) are produced continuously on the basis of forecasts of future demand. In other words this constitutes production to stock. The end product into which these components are ultimately assembled may be made either to stock or to order, depending upon the type of product.

Instead of discussing general theory in this chapter, we shall deal with a specific problem.

Assume that certain components (of which there are several different types) are produced in a number of factories throughout Europe. The components are required partly for use within the company owning the factories and partly for sale to other companies. They are produced to forecasts and a fair amount is known about the frequency distribution of the forecast error.

Take the case of a plant comprising about two hundred assembly groups and producing ten different types of component. The production level of a given

† Published in *The International Journal of Production Research*, 5 (1966), 1, 61.

type of component can be raised by retraining a group of workers to make this type. The retraining has two initial effects; a drop in output owing to the relatively low work rate during start-up (or schooling), and a relatively high percentage of rejects during this period.

A stock is maintained for each type of component and the demand is normally satisfied from stock. The occurrence of a stock-out will usually cause a hold-up in another plant, where the particular component is required for the assembly of an end product. The work force in the other plant will not normally be left idle, however, but instead they will, if possible, be assigned to the assembly of a different end product. At the same time, in-process stocks of other components or half completed assemblies for use in the end product whose assembly is slowed down will build up. In other words, a shortage of (relatively inexpensive) components will cause additional and very much more expensive in-process stocks to build up at a later stage.

In the short term, the above retraining of an assembly group is the only way to vary the production level of a given type of component; however, the total number of groups available is limited. Although this total can be adapted in the long run, we shall not consider that possibility in the present chapter. What can be done, in Europe, is to ship stock from one plant in the concern to supplement a low stock level at another plant.

29.2 The simplified problem

In order to give an insight into these matters, we begin by abstracting from the complex situation the simplest model which still appears relevant to this. We shall therefore focus our attention upon the production of one type of component at one particular plant. At the end of each period† a decision must be made as to whether to raise, lower or maintain the production level of this type at this plant.

The following information, which we require in order to make this decision, is available.

a. Long-term and short-term forecasts of demand, together with a knowledge of the frequency distribution of the forecast error;
b. The current production level and stock level;
c. Assembly groups can be obtained from, or released to, a central labour pool. The cost of adding or withdrawing one such group (or shift) is made up of the costs of retraining, of the additional initial rejects and possibly of production

† We shall assume for the time being that the length of the period is known; in fact, it is
  also a variable which can be chosen to suit the circumstances.

forfeited. Half of this cost is ascribed to the type of component whose production level is raised and half to the type whose production level is lowered.† Let A represent the cost of lowering the rate of production by one component per week;

d. The inventory carrying charge (r) per component and per period is known. The cost of a backlog existing may be regarded as comparable to the cost of carrying a negative inventory of one component throughout one period, but at a much higher rate. This is in keeping with the fact that backlogs of components cause a build-up of in-process stocks of far more expensive end products at a later stage in the production process. If certain components cannot be delivered on time and therefore create a backlog, they will have to be supplied eventually; backlog demand is not lost;

e. At the end of the period a decision is made as to the production rate for the coming period; the time required for planning, preparation and so on will be ignored, and the production lost during the retraining period will not be deducted from the quantity produced (but will be taken into account only as regards its effect upon the costs).

As a further simplification we shall assume initially that the forecasts of future demand are constant at F components per period, whilst the forecast errors are independent of one another and follow a stationary distribution with variance σ_s^2.

Under these greatly simplified conditions we shall seek a planning policy enabling us to establish a new level of production for each period, so as to minimize the expected total costs in the long term. These total costs are the sum of inventory carrying charges, backlog costs and initial schooling costs. More precisely, suppose that the inventory at the end of period $i-1$ is I_{i-1} (which may be either positive or negative) and the production level is P_{i-1}; the schooling (or production changeover) costs then incurred will be $A|P_i - P_{i-1}|$.

Furthermore, if sales reach a value S during period i, we shall be assessed an inventory carrying charge (or backlog charge) on the inventory

$$I_i = I_{i-1} + P_i + S_i$$

remaining at the end of the period.

This charge (or costs) will be

$$\begin{array}{lll} rI_i & \text{if} & I_i \geqslant 0 \\ -RI_i & \text{if} & I_i \leqslant 0 \end{array}$$

Each period, a new P_i has to be chosen and the production changeover costs, inventory costs and backlog costs resulting from this decision are calculated. In this simple form, the decision problem clearly lends itself to being played as a

† As we have seen, the total labour force is assumed to be constant.

game by human planners; also, systematic optimum decision rules can be calculated as a means of resolving the problem. Several such games are played; an example will be given later.

Our long-term objective is to minimize the average value per period of C_i

$$C_i = A|P_i - P_{i-1}| + \begin{cases} rI_i & \text{if } I_i \geqslant 0 \\ -RI_i & \text{if } I_i \leqslant 0 \end{cases}$$

All the terms on the right-hand side of the equation are now divided by r, leaving only the cost ratios A/r and R/r as important factors.

The following specific example has been chosen.

a. One group (or shift) produces 5000 components per period;
b. Retraining costs for an assembly shift amount to £2000, that is £1000 for the component whose production level rises and £1000 for the component whose

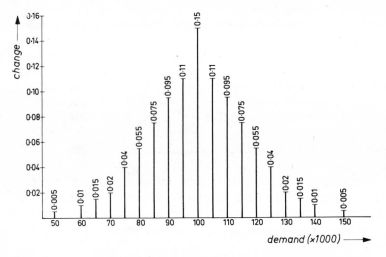

Fig. 72 Probability distribution of demand.

production level falls ('receiving' and 'giving' types as they are called). As a result $A = 1000/5000 = 0.2$;
c. The inventory costs (carrying charge) are approximately £0·02 per period per component;
d. The backlog costs are approximately £0·40 per period per component;
e. The forecast demand is 100 000 components per period; the probability distribution of the forecast error is plotted in Fig. 72; the standard deviation of this distribution is $\sigma_s = 17\,500$.

The linear decision rule

The first systematic rule tried in the case described was based upon the theory of linear decision rules for production planning formulated by Holt, Modigliani, Muth and Simon [Ho 1]. In essence, they regard the (constant) expected demand *F* as an 'ideal' production level, select a similar ideal level of inventory and then establish a new level of production equal to the ideal level of production *F* plus corrections proportional to the deviations of the actual levels of production and inventory from the ideal levels. A suggested new production level is calculated according to

$$P_i = F + k_1(P_{i-1} - F) + k_2(I^* - I_{i-1})$$

and P_i is then rounded to the nearest integral number of shifts.

An appendix in the original article shows how optimum values of k_1, k_2 and I^* can be chosen, for given values of A, r, R and σ_s. For the special case described above ($A = 0.2, r = £0.02, R = £0.40, F = 100\,000, \sigma_s = 17\,500$) we find that the optimum parameters for the linear decision rule are $I^* = 49\,500$; $k_1 = 0.58$; $k_2 = 0.11$.

The resulting costs per period are

inventory carrying charges	£997
backlog charges	£232
production changeover charges	£389
total per period	£1618

A point to be borne in mind is that these costs are based on the possibility of continuous rather than discrete production levels. Rounding to the nearest integral number of full shifts probably causes some additional costs which would make the real costs somewhat higher than indicated above.

The dynamic programming decision rule

It turned out that the linear decision rule did not improve substantially on the performance of the better human planners. By means of dynamic programming we can obtain the *optimum* rule for the decision problem posed above. The essentials of this approach will now be outlined.

Each period, a new production level P_i for the coming period *i* has to be chosen on the basis of the current production level P_{i-1} and the current stock level I_{i-1}, taking into account the constant quantities r, R, A and the distribution of forecast errors. What is needed, then, is a decision rule which enables a definite new production level P_i to be calculated for any existing state (P_{i-1}, I_{i-1}) of the system.

As usual in dynamic programming (DP), a future time $t = T$ is chosen far enough ahead to ensure that any decision taken at the present time will have a negligible effect on the outcome at time $t = T$, which also means that the level of demand forecast for the period around $t = T$ is of no importance for the current decisions regarding the production level for the period just about to begin.

Again, as usual in dynamic programming, it is necessary to define the value function.

Let $V(P, I)$ be the expected value of all the expenditure in terms of inventory carrying and backlog charges and for production changeovers, assuming the system to be in the state (P, I) at time i and if the optimum policy is followed from this time on until time $t = T$. By definition, the value function at time $t = T$ is zero for every state (P, I). In the original article it is demonstrated how the value function at time $T - 1$, $T - 2$, etc., can be calculated, using the known methods.

The determination of the value function at time i involves assigning an optimum P_i to each state (P_{i-1}, I_{i-1}).

The general structure of the resultant decision rule is shown in Fig. 73 (see also 'An Introduction to Production and Inventory Control', paragraphs 10.4 and 10.5). Once this simple structure has been found, it soon becomes evident that this must in fact be the structure of the *optimum* decision rule. The explanation of Fig. 73 is as follows.

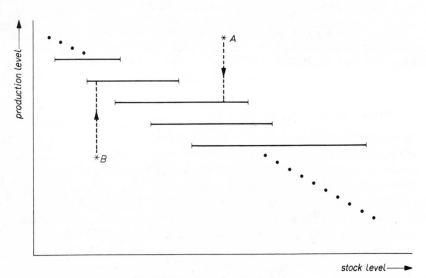

Fig. 73 Structure of optimal strategy.

There is a discrete number of possible production levels (or rates), correspond-ing to the employment of an integral number of production teams. For any given rate of production P, there is a range of inventory levels, indicated by a solid line. If $P_{i-1} = P$ is the current production level and if the current stock level I_{i-1} falls within the range indicated, then the production level P will have to be main-tained throughout the following period as well. Fig. 73 therefore shows the ranges of inventory level which require no change in the level of production.

Supposing the system to be in a state (P_{i-1}, I_{i-1}) which does not lie on one of the horizontal line segments in Fig. 73, a change of production level is called for; such a change is of course indicated in the diagram as a vertical move away from the current state. If the current state is that shown, say, as point A, then the production level will have to be lowered. Similarly, the production level would have to be raised if B were to be the current state. It will be evident that the vertical motion in the diagram should stop as soon as a level of production permissible at the particular stock level is reached.

Once the structure of the optimum strategy is known, there remains only the problem of determining the left-hand and right-hand endpoints of the inventory ranges shown in Fig. 73. The value function at time i will have a minimum value at some particular values I^* and P^* of the inventory and production levels, respectively. These two quantities correspond roughly to the 'ideal' levels of inventory and production used in the linear decision rule.

To simplify the remainder of the calculation it is best to reduce the minimum value to zero by subtracting $V(P^*, I^*)$ from all the values obtained in one itera-tion. This does not disturb the dynamic programming calculations or the practical use of the value function, which will be discussed later. The relative value func-tion can be considered as the relative merit of any state at time i.

Figure 74 shows the structure of the decision rules in detail, as also the iso-value lines, or lines of equal relative value, for the numerical example previously given; these results were obtained after eighteen iterations. Further iterations did not produce any different results. The 'ideal' state lies at a production level of 100 000 products per period and an inventory level around 40 000 products, which is fairly close to the results of the linear decision rule. On the other hand, the expected total costs per period show an improvement of about 10% compared to those of a 'continuous' linear rule.

The expected costs per period are

inventory costs	£957
backlog costs	£214
production changeover costs	£305
total costs per period	£1476

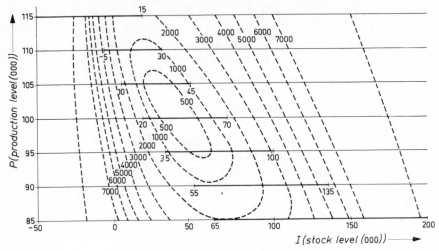

Fig. 74 Optimal strategy and isovalue lines.

Fig. 75 shows the relative value function in tabular form. This permits the evaluation of the relative long-term merit of any state and will prove extremely valuable in adjusting the optimum production levels of a number of different articles in one factory, where the total number of assembly groups available is limited.

Game results

The planning problem relating to one type was rephrased as a 'planning game' and 'played' with numerous members of the planning department. Two reasons account for this.

a. To make the human planners more aware of the delicate balance of costs and thus improve their own intuitive ability to choose the production levels.
b. To obtain a comparison of the performance of human planners with that of systematic planning rules.

The planning game was played in several forms with a number of groups. Some typical results are shown in Figs 76a and 76b, which give the results of the decision rules (linear and DP) and of the players for each of two 48-period games. Each result (or performance) is shown as a point on a graph, with the sum of the inventory and backlog costs plotted along the horizontal, and the changeover costs along the vertical, axis. The dotted lines indicate the locus of points with fixed total costs.

	Production rate (000)						
	85	90	95	100	105	110	115
−70	69638	68638	67638	66638	65638	64638	63638
−65	61249	60249	59249	58249	57249	56249	55249
−60	53402	52402	51402	50402	49402	48402	47402
−55	46122	45122	44122	43122	42122	41122	40122
−50	39456	38456	37456	36456	35456	34456	33456
−45	33421	32421	31421	30421	29421	28421	27421
−40	28024	27024	26024	25024	24024	23024	22024
−35	23290	22290	21290	20290	19290	18290	17290
−30	19217	18217	17217	16217	15217	14217	13217
−25	15810	14810	13810	12810	11810	10810	9810
−20	13053	12053	11053	10053	9053	8053	7053
−15	10918	9918	8918	7918	6918	5918	4918
−10	9425	8425	7425	6425	5425	4425	3425
−5	8372	7372	6372	5372	4372	3372	2429
0	7153	6153	5153	4153	3153	2153	1839
5	6364	5364	4364	3364	2364	1364	1560
10	5392	4392	3392	2392	1392	923	1510
15	4726	3726	2726	1726	726	748	1629
20	4178	3178	2178	1178	346	779	1779
25	3598	2598	1598	598	200	936	1936
30	3239	2239	1239	239	219	1192	2192
35	2966	1966	966	45	374	1374	2374
40	2646	1646	646	0	634	1634	2634
45	2443	1443	443	85	952	1952	2952
50	2346	1346	346	260	1260	2260	3260
55	2208	1208	327	531	1531	2531	3531
60	2118	1118	400	867	1867	2867	3867
65	2089	1094	545	1257	2257	3257	4257
70	2045	1120	763	1689	2689	3689	4689
75	2042	1196	1048	2048	3048	4048	5048
80	2078	1323	1392	2392	3392	4392	5392
85	2149	1498	1791	2791	3791	4791	5791
90	2253	1720	2236	3236	4236	5236	6236
95	2390	1992	2717	3717	4717	5717	6717
100	2562	2309	3229	4229	5229	6229	7229
105	2766	2672	3672	4672	5672	6672	7672
110	3003	3079	4079	5079	6079	7079	8079
115	3274	3527	4527	5527	6527	7527	8527
120	3578	4013	5013	6013	7013	8013	9013
125	3915	4533	5533	6533	7533	8533	9533
130	4286	5082	6082	7082	8082	9082	10082
135	4690	5655	6655	7655	8655	9655	10655
140	5127	6127	7127	8127	9127	10127	11127
145	5596	6596	7596	8596	9596	10596	11596
150	6101	7101	8101	9101	10101	11101	12101

Fig. 75 The value function $V(P, I)$ (related to minimum).

Detailed analysis of the game results pointed quite clearly to a number of conclusions.

a. The players tend to improve for a while, but without ever reaching a stable and consistent strategy (consistent in the sense of Fig. 73).

b. *A posteriori*, that is with full knowledge of the demand figures for a concrete example of the game, it is usually possible to achieve a much better performance

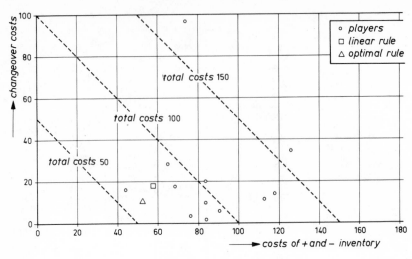

Fig. 76a First game results.

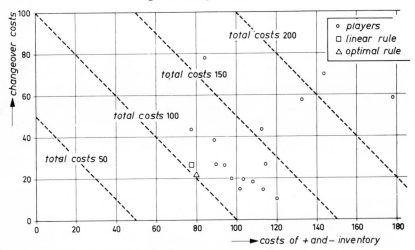

Fig. 76b Second game results.

than that of the DP decision rule, which is the best *a priori* strategy. In particular, for the two games shown in Figs 76a and 76b, the best *a posteriori* strategies attain total costs of £3570 and £4480, respectively, which is about half the total costs of the DP rule. In planning situations of this kind, the effect of uncertainty in demand is very great.

c. The spread of the players' performance is enormous, amounting usually to a factor of two or three in total costs between the best and worst players. In the games played, the best player usually approached the DP strategy costs; these games varied in length from 10 to 48 periods and were played with from 10 to 200 players. Analysis of the results obtained by the best player generally showed that they were at least partially achieved by luck, which is possibly due to the wide margin between the best *a priori* and the best *a posteriori* strategy and results.

To sum up; in the long run, the best human planners cannot be expected to do nearly as well as the dynamic programming rule.

29.3 Applications

Plant scheduling

The preceding sections were confined to the simple model of one type isolated from all others. This simple model was made possible by the artificial introduction of a labour reserve. As pointed out at the time, however, such a reserve can be introduced only if the production level of each of the types is finally so established as to utilise the exact number of assembly teams available, so that by the end of the calculations the reserve is zero. The object of the present section is to show how such calculations can be carried out with the aid of the value function.

The basic idea is as follows. Suppose that we have carried out a dynamic programming calculation in the manner of paragraph 29.2 for each of the types separately. At the beginning of the period we can then establish an optimum production level for each type separately. If the requisite number of teams equals the number available, there is no need for further adjustment and the problem is solved, for the particular period at any rate. If the number of teams required exceeds the number available, however, then some of the types will have to be produced at less than the optimum level originally calculated (for each type separately); conversely, some of the types will be produced at a higher than optimum level in order to keep the labour force working continuously. Clearly, it will be up to us to choose those adjustments of production level, in both cases, which will be least costly in the long run. This is where the value function comes in.

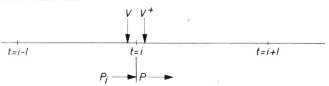

Fig. 77 The distinction between V and V^+.

The value function needed for this purpose is slightly different from that discussed earlier, as will be seen from Fig. 77; this shows the distinction between the value function V just before changing over to a new production level and the value function V^+ immediately after this change. More precisely:

a. Suppose we arrive at time $t = i$ in the state (P_i, I_i) and are about to consider possible changes in the production level. $V(P_i, I_i)$ then represents the total expected costs if the game is played until $t = T$, including the decision to be taken directly at $t = i$.

b. Suppose we are about to leave time $t = i$, having just made the decision (which may *not* be optimal) to change P_i to P. The function $V^+(P, I_i)$ then represents the total expected costs up to $t = T$, if we start at time $t = i^+$ in the state (P, I_i) and continue with the optimum strategy from time $t = i + 1$. The value function V^+ corresponding to the function V of Fig. 75 is shown in Fig. 78. From it we see that $V^+ = V$ for every 'no-change' state and that otherwise $V^+ > V$, which is to be expected. Whenever adjustment of the optimum levels per team takes place and produces non-optimum levels, V^+ will yield the remaining total costs to be expected, provided that the game is played according to the optimum strategy for the remainder of the time. Assuming that it is rarely necessary to deviate from the optimum strategy per team, V^+ will be a very good approximation to the costs we may actually expect to incur.

The following example illustrates the use of this technique. A plant manufacturing five types and operating 98 teams is left at the end of a period with the stocks shown in column 2 of Table 48. To simplify matters it is assumed that the cost structure and demand pattern of all five types are identical and that the value function V^+ of Fig. 78 applies to all of them. The third column of Table 48 shows the old production levels and the fourth column shows the optimum levels per team, which do not take into account the restriction on the total labour force of 98 teams. The suggested new levels require a total of 99 teams, so that one of the types will have to be produced below the optimum level. The next column shows the associated long-term costs, obtained from V^+, of working one team below the optimum. The next column shows the immediate cost of getting to one shift below optimum; type no. 5 saves a changeover by staying below optimum. The last column but one shows the sum of the two preceding columns, or in other words the total costs of one-below-optimum for each of the five types. Type 2 proves to cost least and is therefore chosen. Note that operating type 5 one-below-optimum would have cost very little more than type 2 and would have saved a changeover, so that if the retraining of a second team were particularly inconvenient, the slightly more expensive choice of operating type 5 below optimum might nevertheless have been preferred.

	Production rate (000)						
	85	90	95	100	105	110	115
−70	127553	116359	105294	94415	83789	73506	63638
−65	117359	106294	95415	84789	74506	64638	55249
−60	107294	96415	85789	75506	65638	55246	47402
−55	97415	86789	76506	66638	57246	48395	40122
−50	87789	77506	67638	58246	49395	41106	33456
−45	78506	68638	59246	50395	42103	34423	27421
−40	69638	60246	51395	43103	35418	28361	22024
−35	61246	52395	44103	36418	29349	22917	17290
−30	53395	45103	37418	30348	23890	18110	13217
−25	46103	38418	31348	24887	19060	13933	9810
−20	39418	32348	25887	20053	14842	10386	7053
−15	33348	26887	21053	15827	11231	7453	4918
−10	27887	22053	16827	12201	8205	5095	3425
−5	23053	17827	13199	9149	5720	3372	2429
0	18827	14199	10145	6621	3834	2153	1839
5	15199	11145	7612	4670	2406	1364	1560
10	12145	8612	5650	3147	1392	923	1510
15	9612	6650	4110	2006	726	748	1629
20	7650	5109	2941	1178	346	779	1848
25	6109	3937	2066	598	200	936	2144
30	4937	3058	1418	239	219	1192	2497
35	4058	2403	966	45	374	1523	2877
40	3402	1937	646	0	634	1889	3288
45	2935	1595	443	85	952	2293	3721
50	2591	1356	346	260	1328	2723	4174
55	2348	1208	327	531	1740	3174	4644
60	2192	1118	400	867	2182	3644	5125
65	2089	1094	545	1257	2647	4125	5621
70	2045	1120	763	1689	3127	4621	6133
75	2042	1196	1048	2149	3622	5133	6658
80	2078	1323	1392	2632	4133	5658	7197
85	2149	1498	1791	3137	4658	6197	7747
90	2253	1720	2236	3660	5197	6747	8303
95	2390	1992	2717	4197	5747	7303	8868
100	2562	2309	3229	4747	6303	7868	9444
105	2766	2672	3763	5303	6868	8444	10030
110	3003	3079	4311	5868	7444	9030	10626
115	3274	3527	4872	6444	8030	9626	11231
120	3578	4013	5445	7030	8626	10231	11846
125	3915	4533	6030	7627	9231	10846	12465
130	4286	5082	6626	8231	9846	11465	13094
135	4690	5655	7231	8846	10465	12094	13736
140	5127	6246	7846	9465	11094	12736	14394
145	5598	6853	8465	10094	11736	13394	15071
150	6101	6468	9094	10736	12394	14071	15766

Inventory (000)

Fig. 78 The value function $V^+(P, I)$ (related to minimum).

If the individually optimum levels required several groups more than are available, the procedure of Table 48 is repeated to save a second and if necessary a third team. Increases in the production levels are achieved through similar reasoning.

Production in several factories

Assume that production of the particular components is spread over a number of factories throughout Europe and that tariff barriers and national requirements are such that local demand is best satisfied by local production. With an eye to the future, a policy has been adopted of encouraging the immediate inception of integrated projects for all these factories wherever this is possible and serves a useful purpose. For example, consideration may be given to cross-shipments from one factory to another as a means of avoiding changes in production levels.

Here, costs are balanced by employing the original value function V, shown in Fig. 75. As before, the method is best demonstrated by means of a simple example.

Suppose that there are two factories A and B both producing the same type and both within the scope of Fig. 75. Both factories are currently producing the particular type with 20 teams, but factory A has a stock of 80 000 and factory B a stock of 20 000. Without cross-shipment, A would have to lower, whilst B could only just avoid having to raise, its production level. Table 49 summarizes the changes in the two value functions of A and B resulting from the shipment of successive batches of 5000 products from A to B. Note that the first six

TABLE 48

LEAVE PLANNING FOR A PLANT WITH 98 TEAMS

1	2	3	4	5	6	7	8
1	25 000	21	21	398	1000	1398	21
2	95 000	20	19	−725	1000	275	18
3	50 000	20	20	86	1000	1086	20
4	65 000	18	18	995	1000	1995	18
5	15 000	19	21	1280	−1000	280	21

column 1 = type
     2 = stock
     3 = old production level (teams)
     4 = new production level (teams)
     5 = relative value of the situation: one below optimum
     6 = extra costs due to changing to situation: 1 below optimum
     7 = sum of columns (5) and (6)
     8 = final level

batches of 5000 produce a net saving in terms of the sum of the two value functions; however, the saving becomes smaller with each subsequent batch shipped. If shipping and duty costs are £300 per 5000 products it is advantageous to ship the first four batches, totalling 20 000 products. The resulting long-term savings expected from the cross-shipment are easily seen to be £1503 (after deduction of the £1200 shipping expenses).

The general problem of cross-shipment could be formulated as a simple linear programming problem, but in practice the number of factories involved is so small that a solution obtained by seeking one or two alternatives to the method described here will suffice. The essential step is to use the value function to measure the long-term effects of any change of state.

TABLE 49

VALUE FUNCTIONS OBTAINED BY CROSS SHIPMENT

Batches shipped	Remaining stock A	Remaining stock B	Value for A	Value for B	Total	Successive savings
0	80 000	20 000	2392	1178	3570	–
5 000	75 000	25 000	2048	598	2646	924
10 000	70 000	30 000	1689	239	1928	718
15 000	65 000	35 000	1257	45	1302	626
20 000	60 000	40 000	867	0	867	435
25 000	55 000	45 000	531	85	616	251
30 000	50 000	50 000	260	160	520	96
35 000	45 000	55 000	85	531	616	−96

Extension of the model

The greatly simplified model employed so far is not realistic enough for the above applications. However, the required degree of realism may be imparted to the model without adding unduly to the difficulty of the DP calculation. calculation.

Forecast structure

The forecasts of usage of the components are not stationary. Instead, forecasts are made to cover several periods ahead and a general long-term forecast to describe the level of demand thereafter. Fig. 79 shows a typical series of forecasts. For each period a forecast is given of the average demand and of the standard deviation about this. Because of the nature of the DP calculation, the detailed series of forecasts can be incorporated simply by adding a few iterations to the steady-state long-term value function table. Van Dobben de Bruyn and

Muyen [Do 1] studied the relationship between forecast control and production planning, based upon the foregoing study.

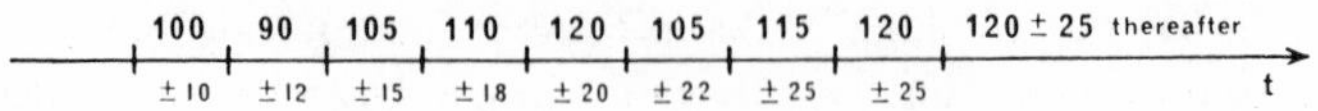

Fig. 79 Detailed forecast structure.

The effect of training (or schooling) time and of production losses

In practice the retraining of a team of workers takes time and causes production losses. The new component is not produced in the planned quantities until several weeks after the decision to retrain a team has been taken. During this period production is lost, which affects not only current costs (an effect already accounted for in the simple model by means of production changeover cost A), but also the inventory level, and therefore the state, of the particular component.

The effect of the training time can be taken into account in the DP solution by redefining the value function explicitly on the assumption that a decision made now will not begin to affect the stock of the new component until a certain training time has elapsed. The training time for downward adjustments of the production level may well remain zero, and only upward adjustments necessarily require a finite training time. However, this does not go very far towards reducing the complexity of the DP solution.

Thus the loss of production is taken into account automatically, albeit subject to a certain amount of rounding to specific periods. Here also, there is scope for further refinement if desired.

Production alternatives

Usually, a number of temporary expedients exist which must be considered as alternatives to the complete retraining of an assembly team. The most important of them are:

a. some teams can work overtime;
b. some teams can make two components alternately at short notice, but with reduced efficiency;
c. there may be a permanent possibility of purchasing from an external source.

All these alternatives can be treated as providing intermediate production levels, which create no changeover costs but have higher running production costs than the 'ordinary' production levels.

Discounting

The time scale in the production of components is rather fine: reasonable level-decisions taken today affect the costs for only a few months ahead. The effect of discounting the value of future cash flows is therefore very minor. In some other planning problems, however, the time scale may be coarse enough to necessitate discounting. This does not add in any way to the difficulty of the DP solution.

29.4 Tables

The DP calculations needed to establish the exact critical stock levels associated with each production level are usually so wide-ranging as to call for a computer.

However, Tables 50 and 51 can be used as an approximate guide. They are the outcome of numerous calculations carried out by means of an electronic computer and enable the left-hand and right-hand end points of the lines in Fig. 73 to be calculated.

Table 50 assumes a fixed ratio of carrying costs to costs of being behind schedule namely $R = 20r$. This limitation does not apply to Table 51.

The tables can be used subject to the following conditions.

a. The forecast of demand per period must be constant.
b. The standard deviation σ of the forecast error is likewise assumed to be constant.
c. The difference between two successive production levels must not exceed $0.3\,\sigma$. Even where the difference is larger the calculated limits will probably not deviate very much from the optimal ones.
d. The costs associated with a change in the production capacity devoted to a particular type are assumed to be proportional to the change.
e. The carrying costs and costs of being behind schedule are considered to be proportional to the quantity and the time involved.
f. The running-in time must not exceed 3 periods.

The symbols employed are defined as follows:

A = the cost of lowering the production level by one product per period (see paragraph 29.2, point c).
R = the stock-out costs of one product during one period.
r = the costs of carrying one product in stock for one period.
α = the service level = $R/(R + r)$†
T = the running-in time expressed in periods; that is, the average interval between a decision to change the production level and the effective implementation of this decision (reaction time).

† In practice the value of R is often established rather arbitrarily.

$L(P_i)$ = the lowest level to which the stock can fall without necessitating a rise in the production level. At the peak production level $L(P_i) = -\infty$.

$R(P_i)$ = the highest level the stock can attain without the production level having to be reduced. At the minimum production level $R(P_i) = +\infty$.

d = a parameter defined by the formulae given in the headings of Tables 50 and 51.

Guide to the proper use of Tables 50 and 51

- To use Table 51 the value of $Z(R/r)$ must be established beforehand by means of the table heading, from the chosen costs ratio R/r or from the service level. A fixed value has been used in Table 50, namely $Z(R/r)$.
- Next calculate the value of d for each jump from P_1 to P_2 by means of the formula provided.
- Find the associated values of x, (d) and $x(d)$ or y, (d) and $y(d)$ in the table.
- Then calculate the values of $L(P_1)$ and $R(P_2)$ by means of the formulae provided.

TABLE 50

CRITICAL STOCK LEVEL APPROXIMATION FORMULAE FOR

$R = 20r$ $(Z(R/r) = 1\cdot67)$ and $T \leqslant 3$

$L(P_1) = \sigma \left[-d + 1\cdot67\sqrt{(T+1)} + x_1(d)\sqrt{(A/r)}\right]$
$R(P_2) = \sigma \left[-d + 1\cdot67\sqrt{(T+1)} + x_2(d)\sqrt{(A/r)}\right]$

$$d = \frac{1}{\sigma}\left[(P_1 + P_2)/2 - F\right]$$

d	$x_1(d)$	$x_2(d)$
$<-1\cdot2$	$+0\cdot30 - 0\cdot2d$	$+0\cdot21 - 2\cdot0d$
$-1\cdot2$	$+0\cdot54$	$+0\cdot61$
$-1\cdot0$	$+0\cdot49$	$+2\cdot22$
$-0\cdot8$	$+0\cdot45$	$+1\cdot84$
$-0\cdot6$	$+0\cdot36$	$+1\cdot48$
$-0\cdot4$	$+0\cdot23$	$+1\cdot13$
$-0\cdot2$	$+0\cdot06$	$+0\cdot79$
0	$-0\cdot08$	$+0\cdot52$
$+0\cdot2$	$-0\cdot18$	$+0\cdot33$
$+0\cdot4$	$-0\cdot28$	$+0\cdot16$
$+0\cdot6$	$-0\cdot37$	$+0\cdot02$
$+0\cdot8$	$-0\cdot46$	$-0\cdot04$
$+1\cdot0$	$-0\cdot54$	$-0\cdot08$
$+1\cdot2$	$-0\cdot63$	$-0\cdot10$
$>+1\cdot2$	$-0\cdot09 - 0\cdot45d$	$+0\cdot02 - 0\cdot1d$

Example

The optimum strategy for two different values of the standard deviation of the forecast error has been calculated with the aid of Table 50. The other parameters are taken to be the same in both cases. The calculations are reproduced in Tables 52a and 52b.

It will be seen that when σ is reduced the zones, within which a production level once chosen remains unchanged, contract and also shift to the left.

As a general rule a decrease in the standard deviation of the forecast error leads to smaller stocks.

For information on how to use Fig. 80 see Fig. 73 on page 254 together with the relevant explanatory notes.

TABLE 51

CRITICAL STOCK LEVEL APPROXIMATION FORMULAE FOR $T \leqslant 3$

AND FOR ONE OR TWO RATIOS FÒR R/r

$$d = \frac{1}{\sigma}[(P_1 + P_2)/2 - F]$$

Costs ratio R/r	1	2	5	10	20	50	100
Service level $\alpha = R/(R + r)$	0·500	0·667	0·833	0·909	0·952	0·980	0·990
Eccentricity $Z(R/r)$	0·00	0·43	0·97	1·34	1·67	2·06	2·33

$$L(P_1) = \sigma\,[-d + Z(R/r)\,\sqrt{(T+1)} + y_1(-d)\,\sqrt{(A/r)} - y_2(+d)\,\sqrt{(A/R)}]$$
$$R(P_2) = \sigma\,[-d + Z(R/r)\,\sqrt{(T+1)} + y_2(-d)\,\sqrt{(A/r)} - y_1(+d)\,\sqrt{(A/R)}]$$

d	$y_1(d)$	$y_2(d)$
$< -1\cdot2$	$-0\cdot05$	$+0\cdot09 + 0\cdot06\,d$
$-1\cdot2$	$-0\cdot05$	$+0\cdot02$
$-1\cdot0$	$-0\cdot05$	$+0\cdot03$
$-0\cdot8$	$-0\cdot05$	$+0\cdot06$
$-0\cdot6$	$-0\cdot04$	$+0\cdot11$
$-0\cdot4$	$-0\cdot03$	$+0\cdot22$
$-0\cdot2$	$-0\cdot01$	$+0\cdot36$
0	$+0\cdot04$	$+0\cdot53$
$+0\cdot2$	$+0\cdot14$	$+0\cdot79$
$+0\cdot4$	$+0\cdot28$	$+1\cdot12$
$+0\cdot6$	$+0\cdot39$	$+1\cdot47$
$+0\cdot8$	$+0\cdot46$	$+1\cdot83$
$+1\cdot0$	$+0\cdot50$	$+2\cdot21$
$+1\cdot2$	$+0\cdot54$	$+2\cdot60$
$> +1\cdot2$	$+0\cdot32 + 0\cdot19\,d$	$+0\cdot20 + 2\cdot00\,d$

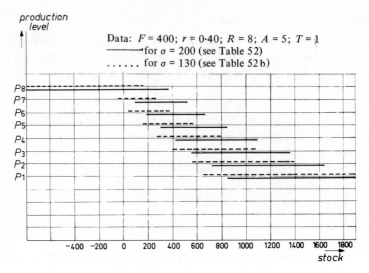

Fig. 80 Graphical representation of the optimum strategy.

TABLE 52a

I	F = 400 units/period r = £0·4 per unit per period R = £8 per unit per period σ = 200 units/period A = £5 per unit per period T = 1 period					

i	P_i	d	x_1	x_2	$L(P_i)$	$R(P_i)$
1	260				850	$+\infty$
		−0·6	+0·36	+1·48		
2	300				720	1640
		−0·4	+0·23	+1·13		
3	340				550	1350
		−0·2	+0·06	+0·79		
4	380				420	1070
		0	−0·08	+0·52		
5	420				300	840
		+0·2	−0·18	+0·33		
6	460				190	670
		+0·4	−0·28	+0·16		
7	500				90	510
		+0·6	−0·37	+0·02		
8	540				$-\infty$	370

TABLE 52b

II	F = 400 units/period r = £0·4 per unit per period R = £8 per unit per period σ = 130 units/period A = £5 per unit per period T = 1 period					

i	P_i	d	x_1	x_2	$L(P_i)$	$R(P_i)$
1	260				650	$+\infty$
		−0·92	+0·48	+2·06		
2	300				560	1380
		−0·62	+0·37	+1·52		
3	340				410	1050
		−0·31	+0·14	+0·98		
4	380				270	800
		0	−0·08	+0·52		
5	420				160	550
		+0·31	−0·34	+0·24		
6	460				40	380
		+0·62	−0·38	+0·02		
7	500				−50	240
		+0·92	−0·51	−0·06		
8	540				$-\infty$	160

Section VI: Calculation of Capacity

30 Calculation of capacity

30.1 Starting point

To calculate a capacity it is necessary to know the total amount of work involved per product or per unit product. Work measurement has already been under review in the work-study sector for some decades. Originally this was merely for the purpose of establishing norms and calculating wages; in many cases work study and wage calculation were virtually synonymous.

Subsequent social developments created a need for greater income stability and in consequence the short-term relationship between performance and earnings is now rather less immediate in its effect.

However, this state of affairs, fully in keeping with our times, involves a risk that the old familiar 'rate' will receive less, and perhaps insufficient attention. The rate may be defined as 'the normative measure of the labour factor in a quantity of work performed according to a prescribed method and with due regard to the desired quality'. As a result of the present evolution in industry the rate is assuming a very much wider role; its present uses may be summarized as follows:

— task rating, performance measurement and wage calculation;
— job allocation;
— improvement of work methods;
— calculation of potential profitability;
— cost price calculation and calculations for decision making
— planning and capacity calculation.

Work measurement will therefore continue to play an important part as one of the starting points for calculations of capacity. It will have to be applied not only to direct but also to indirect labour since this is assuming greater relative importance in modern technological development and will therefore have to feature more prominently in capacity calculations.

30.2 Short-term capacity calculations

Given full specification of the product to be manufactured the capacity can in theory be calculated in as much as the production method and the number of man and machine hours required for the purpose can be deduced from the specification. In principle the capacity calculation is merely a matter of multiplying the time per product by the number of products, but in fact it involves some other practical points as well.

Delays occurring during the process cause the actual output to fall short of that calculated from theory. Such delays result amongst other things from products or components being rejected as failing to satisfy the quality requirements, or from the performance of man or machine being restricted by internal or external factors limiting production. They should be anticipated in an allowance on the necessary man and machine hours and the material required.

Given $p\%$ defective per production phase and n successive phases, the gross quantity of products with which to start corresponds to

$$N\,(\text{gross}) = V\,(\text{nett}) \left(\frac{100}{100-p_1}\right) \left(\frac{100}{100-p_2}\right) \left(\frac{100}{100-p_n}\right)$$

or with $p_1 = p_2 = \ldots p_n$

$$N\,(\text{gross}) = N\,(\text{nett}) \left(\frac{100}{100-p}\right)^n$$

If the allowance factor (f) per production phase (to compensate the restricting factors) is likewise known, then the gross number of hours $[U\,(\text{gross})]$ for each phase can also be calculated, as follows.

In nth phase $\qquad U\,(\text{gross}) = U_n\, f_n \left(\frac{100}{100-p}\right)^n N\,(\text{nett})$

The total number of hours for the entire process is then

$$\text{total } U\,(\text{gross}) = \sum_1^n N U_n\, f_n \left(\frac{100}{100-p}\right)^n \quad \text{(for all the phases)}$$

The results of such calculations can be expressed in very practical terms, for example the so-called 'production figure', indicating how many direct workers are needed for an output of, say, 1000 products per week.

When once such a calculation has been carried out, the 'production figure' can thereafter be used to calculate on the spot how much manpower is needed in the different situations.

30.3 Long-term capacity calculations

The characteristic difference between the problems of short-term and long-term capacity calculation is that the product specification is known in the one case and not known, or at any rate only partly so, in the other.

Consequently the lack of knowledge concerning the essential features of product and components has to be made good by extrapolation or through a forecast.

The planners will be compelled to forecast the work content; this can be done in various ways, for instance by:

— extrapolation of the total manpower required, that is extrapolation of the total work content multiplied by the number of products forecast;
— extrapolation of the ratio of total cost price to total labour costs per product, whereupon manhours can be deduced from the labour costs thus established;
— forecasting the probable technological development together with the resultant work content per product.

Where the calculations are not confined to the total product but have to cover components or assemblies as well, however, this adds to the difficulties considerably, in as much as it is then quite impracticable to institute a separate calculation for each component. Product classification is then *essential.* Such a classification will have to be oriented upon and consistent with the production methods and processes to be used in making the product.

This classification is only feasible provided that the components concerned have been standardized.

Numerous attempts to classify products for the purpose of capacity calculations are described in the literature, but often with disappointing results, and certainly in those cases where the aspect of product standardization does not come fully into its own.

Such standardization will have to be based upon the ultimate function of the component as well as the method of making this. Possible attempts to standardize in only one of these respects may well account for the above failures. The problem can be presented graphically as follows.

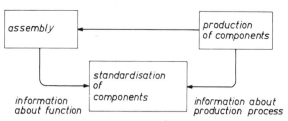

Fig. 81 Effect of product and production process upon standardization.

Standardization thus accomplished enables the end product to be used as a source of information for the classification of components best suited to the process used to make these. Through this classification, then, the relationship between end product and component can be established. Given the characteristic quantities of those types of end products covered by a long-term plan, the supply of components required can be calculated from these quantities via the aforesaid relationship. Because the standardization concerned was also based partly upon the process used to make the components, the number and nature of the production hours needed for the component assortment can then be calculated as well.

Finally it is worth mentioning that increased productivity is an essential feature of long-term capacity calculation. Annual output increases of 5 to 10% are quite normal nowadays and are likely to become considerably larger through progressive technological development.

Where periods of four or more years are concerned, omission of this productivity rise from the capacity calculation has disastrous effects.

Section VII: Some Examples

31 Spares inventory control

31.1 Introduction

Controlling a stock of spare parts very often presents a problem, various solutions to which have already been evolved and introduced. One of these will be discussed in some detail in the present chapter.

The example immediately following (paragraph 31.2) refers to components held in stock as spares for machines constituting part of the production plant.

To deal with this problem an official manual† establishing standards for the prescribed method, tables, information cards and stock cards has been issued within the Philips organization. This manual also contains a brief review of the theoretical principles. The main points of its application will now be discussed.

31.2 The (B, Q) system for spares

Establishing the factors of the system

Taken in proper order these factors are: the average demand per year, usually deducible from records of past demand; the lead time, mainly dependent on the number of operations involved in making the particular part; the re-order level, which can be read from a table; the optimum order quantity, likewise tabulated.

The administrative procedure, also of major importance in our opinion, will be examined in some detail. For problems of this kind it can even be said that carefully thought out procedures are more important than precisely calculated tables of re-order levels and batch or lot sizes.

This applies particularly to cases involving very large stocks of spares. The manual also establishes norms for the average inventory level.

It ends with some remarks on the subject of 'trade cycle policy', including measures for coping with long-term fluctuations on the part of the spares

† (B, Q) system. 'Spares inventory control system for Production Equipment Department', MFT 3–0800–1, September 1964; issued by the T.E.O. Department and Consultative Committee of the Production Equipment Department, N. V. Philips Gloeilampenfabrieken.

supplier or the manufacturer using the production plant (for example, operating two shifts for a long period).

Some of these points merit closer study.

Determination of the lead time

Rules are given for determining the lead time for components ordered from the mechanical engineering works. The relevant text will now be quoted literally.

Regarding the manufacture of machine parts in the mechanical engineering works, a number of agreements have been made to ensure that the lead time is calculated with reference to factors which affect this time. These factors are the number of process equivalents and the material.

The number of process equivalents is determined as follows:

— operations shorter than 15 hours: one process equivalent;
— operations longer than 15 hours: one process equivalent for the first 15 hours, plus one more for every 35 hours or portion of 35 hours that the operation takes over and above 15 hours.

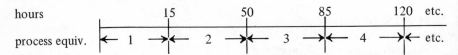

Certain operations are listed below, together with the associated number of equivalents on the right.

marking out	0
annealing, hardening, blasting	1
metal spraying, painting	2
forging, straightening (hot), impregnating	3
plating, polishing, rubberizing, plastic cladding (facing?)	4

For the material a distinction is made between material in stock and material to be ordered. Materials in stock are included in the blue file 'Inventory and Design data' held by the mechanical engineering works. By and large, all the other materials have to be ordered.

Calculation in terms of these process equivalents produces the following analysis of the lead time L for machine parts ordered from the mechanical engineering works.

TABLE 53

ANALYSIS OF THE TOTAL LEAD TIME L (in periods)

Number of process equivalents	Material in stock		Material to be ordered	
	Lead time L $L = l + r$	Analysis $(x + y + z + r)$	Lead time L $L = l + r$	Analysis $(x + y + z + r)$
1–3	$6 + r$	$(4 + 1 + 1 + r)$	$8 + r$	$(6 + 1 + 1 + r)$
4–6	$7 + r$	$(4 + 2 + 1 + r)$	$9 + r$	$(6 + 2 + 1 + r)$
7–9	$8 + r$	$(4 + 3 + 1 + r)$	$10 + r$	$(6 + 3 + 1 + r)$
10–12	$9 + r$	$(4 + 4 + 1 + r)$	$11 + r$	$(6 + 4 + 1 + r)$
13–15	$10 + r$	$(4 + 5 + 1 + r)$	$12 + r$	$(6 + 5 + 1 + r)$

x = time for methods study and provision of materials;
y = time for manufacture;
z = time for run-out;
$l = x + y + z$ = lead time stipulated by the mechanical engineering works (receipt of order to dispatch from M.E.W.);
r = time required by customer to prepare and later receive the order (drawing office, dispatch inspection and spread in the lead time owing to periodic orders and/or deliveries).

Example of an L-calculation

Given

A (B, Q) order for 150 socket nuts, to be made of free-cutting steel 0122016 00069 (N100AH/50), involves the following operations:

	set-up time	cycle time
turning on capstan lathe	1·5 hours	0·1 hour
turning to small diameter	1 hour	0·1 hour
drilling	0·5 hour	0·05 hour
bench work	0·1 hour	0·05 hour

Solution

The material is listed in the blue file and therefore in stock.
The number of process equivalents is:

turning on capstan lathe	$1·5 + (150 \times 0·1) = 16·5$ hours
turning to small diameter	$1 + (150 \times 0·1) = 16$ hours
drilling	$0·5 + (150 \times 0·05) = 8$ hours
bench work	$0·1 + (150 \times 0·05) = 7·6$ hours

These equivalents are 2–2–1–1 respectively, making a total of 6 process equivalents.

In the 'material in stock' column of the table, opposite 6 process equivalents, we find $L = 7 + r$ periods.

If $r = 1$ period, the total lead time $L = 7 + 1 = 8$ periods.

Checking the lead time L

The appendix contains what may be called a tick-off or cross card to give warning of any deviations from the established lead times. In this way the statistical distribution of the lead times and any adjustments which may be necessary can be determined per supplier and per lead time group. Any variation of the lead time is likewise readily detected.

Determination of the re-order level

Two tables for determining the re-order level are included, one for normal circumstances and the other for components any stock-out of which would cause considerable loss of production (the so-called 'emergency table'). The emergency table is based upon a stock-out risk of 5% per order as compared with 15% for the normal table. Considerably abridged versions of the two are reproduced here as Tables 54 and 55 respectively.

TABLE 54

TABLE FOR DETERMINING THE RE-ORDER LEVEL B **IN NORMAL CIRCUMSTANCES**
(B, Q) system

Average demand per		Re-order level for a lead time L of						
year	month							
$\overline{D}$	$\overline{d}$	1 w	2 w	1 m	2 m	4 m	8 m	12 m
1		0	0	0	0	1	1	2
2		0	0	0	1	1	2	3
4		0	0	1	1	3	5	6
8		0	1	1	3	5	9	12
16	1	1	1	3	5	9	16	23
32	3	1	3	5	10	17	31	44
100	9	4	8	15	27	49	89	130
300	25	12	22	42	75	140	250	360
1 200	100	44	79	150	270	500	950	1 400
4 200	350	140	250	480	890	1 700	3 200	4 700
12 000	1 000	370	660	1 300	2 400	4 600	8 800	13 000

This table has been compiled for a 'stock-out risk' $z = 15\%$.

Numerical example: $\overline{d} = 9$, or $\overline{D} = 100$; $L = 4$ months. According to the table B is then 49.
Note: if $L = 13$ months, take B for one year plus the average monthly demand d.

TABLE 55

TABLE FOR DETERMINING THE RE-ORDER LEVEL *B* IN AN 'EMERGENCY'
(*B, Q*) system

Average demand per		Re-order level for a lead time *L* of						
year	month							
$\overline{D}$	$\overline{d}$	1 w	2 w	1 m	2 m	4 m	8 m	12 m
1		0	0	0	1	1	2	3
2		0	0	1	1	2	4	5
4		0	1	1	3	4	7	10
8		1	1	3	5	7	12	16
16	1	1	2	5	8	13	21	29
32	3	2	5	9	15	23	39	53
100	9	8	15	24	38	63	110	150
300	25	22	36	60	98	170	290	410
1 200	100	72	110	200	330	580	1 000	1 500
4 200	350	200	330	590	1 000	1 900	3 400	5 000
12 000	1 000	490	820	1 500	2 700	5 000	9 400	13 700

This table has been compiled for a 'stock-out risk' $z = 5\%$.

Numerical example: $\overline{d} = 9$, or $\overline{D} = 100$; $L = 4$ months. According to the table B is then 63.
Note: if $L = 13$ months, take B for 12 months plus the average monthly demand d.

Determination of the order quantity

The order quantity is established with the aid of a caculation chart as shown in Chapter 20.

Here the carrying costs percentage is put at 25. The ordering costs are calculated as the sum of the administrative ordering costs of customer and manufacturer, plus the tooling costs of the mechanical engineering works.

31.3 Review of alternatives and refinements

The system described in the previous paragraph is a rough and ready one involving several approximations. Variants and occasional refinements are conceivable in other situations and at later stages of introduction. Some aspects of certain existing systems will now be examined, after which two of these systems (Unilever and National Coal Board) will be discussed in more detail under separate headings.

Choice of re-order system

Almost all the cases referred to involve a (B, Q) system. In other words an order is **made out** as soon as the stock card reveals that a particular withdrawal has brought the stock below level B. On the other hand, it often happens that orders are **sent out** periodically, for instance once a month (National Coal Board) or once a fortnight (Philips), so that orders to one and the same supplier can to some extent be combined.

Boothroyd and Tomlinson [Bo 1] (1963; hereinafter called B and T) report that a periodic system with a re-order interval of 6 months was frequently encountered in transactions with the National Coal Board, and demonstrate that a (B, Q) method with a 'call period' of one month costs less overall.

The model employed

In the previous paragraph the approximate order quantity was calculated by means of Camp's formula; the re-order level is established on the basis of a given probability of stock-out per replenishment order. Bosch [Bo 3] (1961) describes the Unilever tables, whence it emerges that the total controllable costs are considered as a function of lot size and re-order level. The calculation is a form of mathematical approximation. The following are regarded as controllable annual costs:

— the ordering costs;
— the carrying (inventory) costs;
— the stock-out costs, presumed to be directly proportional to the number of items per year not supplied direct from stock.

B and T employ the same model; their colleagues, Lampkin and Flowerdew [La 1], describe an exact calculation for the evaluation of this model. They maintain that an approximate calculation is too rudimentary for a widely varying assortment. In some cases they also add stock-out costs directly proportional to the average of orders outstanding. Both Bosch and B and T thus arrive at an acceptable stock-out risk which differs considerably between the individual stock items (B and T stock-out probability ranges from 0·01 to 50% per replenishment order); they also arrive at lot sizes considerably larger than prescribed by Camp. In some cases an optimum lot size three times the Camp batch is found, because the expected stock-out costs per lot may range up to ten times the ordering costs.

In a situation where:

— the demand follows a Poisson distribution;
— annual demand is 30 units;

– carrying costs are £1–50 per unit per year;
– stock-out costs are £1 per unit;
– ordering costs 50p;
– lead time 2 months.

Lampkin's solution is $B = Q = 6$ units as compared with $Q = 4$ according to Camp. Given $Q = 4$ as a basis on which to calculate an optimum B, this would cost 5% more than in the real optimum situation.

Determining the stock-out costs

Karr [Ka 1] describes in detail a method of obtaining a reliable assessment of stock-out costs from estimates made by several qualified individuals. He showed a number of aircraft components to each member of a group of experienced aircraft fitters to whom he then put two questions.

a. The component shown is needed for an aircraft, but out of stock. The aircraft concerned is required next day for a mission. Can the aircraft nevertheless be made serviceable in time? Some of the possible replies are:

– no;
– yes, but only by cannibalizing (removing the part from another grounded aircraft);
– yes, we can repair the component ourselves;
– yes, the aircraft is battleworthy even without the component.

b. The component shown has failed in an aircraft; it is out of stock and there is no possibility of replacing it. What then is the state of the aircraft concerned? Two of the possible replies are:

– the aircraft cannot take off; if it should be necessary to evacuate the airfield then the aircraft would have to be destroyed;
– the aircraft can take off on missions, but its fighting capabilities are somewhat impaired.

A final evaluation is then extracted from these expert opinions by methods of processing customary in psychology, after which an attempt can be made to assess the harm caused by a single shortage of the particular component. If the component is irreplaceable and the aircraft thereby rendered unserviceable, then the consequences are disastrous, but little harm is done if the component is readily replaceable and/or its absence does not affect the battleworthiness of the aircraft appreciably. Where the harm resulting from such a deficiency is considerable the term 'essentiality' is used. For components with a high 'essentiality' rating but a low cost price, a large stock will of course be built up to minimize the risk of stock-out. The cost-estimates thus obtained are still rather rough, but:

'since only reasonable approximations are needed for most inventory control purposes, such an estimate would be adequate . . . Once the items have been sorted out from high to low essentiality and a reasonable set of penalty factors have been attached, most of the benefit of considering essentiality will have been achieved'.

Bosch uses the following analysis to estimate the costs of shortages:

a. The article can be replaced by a different one if necessary;
b. The article is obtainable at a few hours' notice if required;
c. The article can be made in the local workshop if need be;
d. The article is so essential as a component part that a production machine lacking it (for instance one of twenty working in parallel) has to be taken out of service for a few days;
e. The article has a very long lead time and is part of a machine operating virtually continuously throughout the year as an indispensible link in the chain of production.

He establishes a lower limit of £2·50 for the costs of delay to avoid involving too many minor shortages; in one case the losses are quoted at £1000.

   B and T recognize only four classes of stock-out costs, each of which can be tabulated separately. Lawrence and associates (1961) give detailed descriptions of methods of estimating stock-out costs.

The frequency distribution of demand per period

The Philips table is based on the relationship detected between demand and variability of demand (see Fig. 82). The Poisson distribution proved suitable where the offtake is relatively small. Where this is large the variability very soon exceeds that of a Poisson distribution; starting from a given mean and variability, a gamma distribution invariably matches reasonably well in these circumstances.

   The Unilever table is based entirely on a Poisson distribution: 'this is found to suit very well provided that the average amount deducted for a repair is chosen as the unit of quantity'. It is noted in all the studies that the annual demand for a high proportion of the inventory items involved is very small indeed (less than two per year).

   If serial chains of stock items occur it becomes extremely important to know *where* the demand has been measured (see Chapter 26). B and T use the Poisson distribution for annual demands of up to 12 units, beyond which the variability is greater than Poisson suggest. It emerged that for a large group of stock items, $\sigma = 0.9\mu$, whilst a normal distribution (cut off at the origin and at $\mu + 30$) could be used to represent the demand over a period of several months.

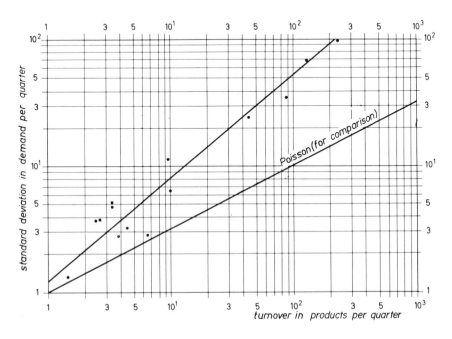

Fig. 82 Relationship between demand and variability of demand.

According to Peterson and Geisler [Pe 1]:

It was decided that we could accept the Poisson distribution as a reasonable characterization of the demand function for a typical aircraft spare part. We did find, however, that the variability of demand for many parts, particularly low priced parts, was greater than is indicated by a Poisson distribution. (Apparently the demand for many low valued items comes in clusters, probably related to the demand for high valued major components. This makes the combined demand for such items even more unstable than would be indicated by a Poisson distribution.)

Note once again that the above only applies to the **spares** usage pattern.

Forecasting the demand

A good forecast is the foundation of the system. The solution mostly adopted is that also described by B and T: no mechanical extrapolation rules have been introduced. It is recommended that the demand figures used as a starting point for the forecast be taken from records extending as far into the past as possible and that due consideration be given to technical modifications, conversion programmes and so forth. The forecast is made by a company engineer.

Shaunty and Van Court Hare [Sh 1] (1960) describe a system used to order spares for aircraft on an airfield. In forecasting the demand they utilize the correlation discovered between the number of landings a given type of aircraft makes (possibly: certain types), and the usage of a given component, per period; only expensive (high valued) components are taken into account.

Recent reports from the RAND corporation describe the so-called METRIC-system recommending a $(S - 1, S)$ system for 'high value, low usage items' and employing calculations based upon a compound Poisson distribution of demand.

Waiting time formulae for a stock problem

In special circumstances the conventional waiting time formulae can be applied to a stock problem. Such a situation is described by Shaunty and Van Court Hare:

— it concerns a stock of high-value components;
— the order quantity is put at 1, or in other words a unit is ordered whenever another is used;
— the economic (control) stock is therefore always constant, for instance 4.

This can be regarded as a queuing problem; there are four serving positions or hatches. A customer coming in corresponds to a demand; the service time (lead time) starts with the placing and ends with the filling of the order. Each hatch occupied means the withdrawal of one unit from the physical stock; when all four hatches are engaged the next customer has to queue.

Lead time and lead time control

This was discussed in some detail in paragraph 31.2; similar comments are to be found in other studies of the subject.

Tables or charts? Layout

General experience has shown that tables are more convenient for ordering systems implemented 'by hand'. The information required for the system (for

instance *B* and *Q*) is read from the table as a function of certain parameters:
Input data are:

— the expected annual usage in terms of the number of units;
— the price per unit;
— the lead time in weeks;
— the costs per unit shortage;
— the acceptable stock-out risk;
— the ordering costs;
— the carrying costs.

The number of parameters chosen in any given case should be kept within reasonable bounds. That is the main reason for trying to establish a fixed correlation between mean annual usage and variability of demand. What usually happens is that two parameters (for instance annual usage and price) are employed on each page of the book of tables whilst each complete page refers only to one specific value of the other variables.

A special problem

Aeronautical publications give the solution to the problem of the 'flyaway kit'; if only a limited weight of spares can be carried, what kit assortment will contribute the most to the fighting effectiveness of the particular aircraft squadron (see for instance Karr and Geisler [Ge 1] (1956)).

Future developments

We may certainly expect to see further progress towards more effective preventive maintenance and standardization of components; type limitation as applied to the plant or vehicle fleet for which the parts are intended also reduces costs in many cases.

31.4 The Unilever tables

The Unilever tables are based on the following suppositions:

— the usage, expressed in units, conforms to a Poisson distribution;
— ordering costs and carrying costs are the same for all the inventory items and are fixed per factory (in the example given 18p and 18% of the investment value);
— stock-out costs a given amount per unit, that is per product deficient.

Table 56 is taken from the article by Bosch [Bo 3], in which the following instructions are also given.

TABLE 56.

Optimum order-size and re-order level for spares and other technical articles
(re-order costs per article per order 18p annual carrying costs 18% of average value)

Start here ↓

Price per unit in £s. Optimum order size (bold figures)											Annual usage	Lead time in weeks								
0·001 / **1000**	0·013 / **400**	0·050 / **200**	0·20 / **100**	1·10 / **44**	4·00 / **24**						1000								1	2
0·001 / **1000**	0·009 / **400**	0·035 / **200**	0·15 / **100**	0·80 / **44**	3·00 / **24**						700							1	2	
0·001 / **1000**	0·006 / **400**	0·025 / **200**	0·10 / **100**	0·60 / **44**	2·00 / **24**	4·00 / **18**					500						1	2	4	
0·001 / **700**	0·004 / **400**	0·018 / **200**	0·07 / **100**	0·40 / **44**	1·50 / **24**	2·70 / **18**	4·50 / **14**				350					1	2	4	6	
0·003 / **400**	0·013 / **200**	0·05 / **100**	0·28 / **44**	1·00 / **24**	2·00 / **18**	3·50 / **14**	6·30 / **11**				250				1	2	4	6	8	
0·002 / **400**	0·01 / **200**	0·04 / **100**	0·21 / **43**	0·80 / **23**	1·60 / **17**	3·00 / **13**	5·50 / **10**	14·0 / **7**			180			1	2	4	6	8	12	
0·006 / **200**	0·024 / **100**	0·14 / **43**	0·52 / **23**	1·00 / **17**	1·80 / **13**	3·60 / **10**	8·50 / **7**	24·0 / **5**			120		1	2	4	6	8	12	16	
0·006 / **160**	0·018 / **100**	0·10 / **43**	0·39 / **23**	0·80 / **17**	1·40 / **13**	2·70 / **10**	6·50 / **7**	18·0 / **5**			90	1	2	4	6	8	12	16	24	
0·012 / **100**	0·07 / **43**	0·25 / **23**	0·50 / **17**	0·90 / **13**	1·70 / **10**	4·00 / **7**	11·0 / **5**	25·0 / **4**			60	1	2	4	6	8	12	16	24	
0·011 / **80**	0·05 / **43**	0·20 / **23**	0·40 / **17**	0·70 / **13**	1·40 / **10**	3·20 / **7**	9·00 / **5**	22·0 / **4**			45	1	2	4	6	8	12	16	24	
0·01 / **60**	0·036 / **42**	0·14 / **22**	0·27 / **16**	0·50 / **12**	1·00 / **9**	2·70 / **6**	10·0 / **4**	30·0 / **3**	50·0 / **3**		30	1	2	4	6	8	12	16	24	
0·027 / **40**	0·09 / **22**	0·18 / **16**	0·35 / **12**	0·70 / **9**	1·80 / **6**	6·00 / **4**	20·0 / **3**	50·0 / **3**			20	1	2	4	6	8	12	16	24	
0·036 / **30**	0·07 / **22**	0·14 / **16**	0·25 / **12**	0·50 / **9**	1·40 / **6**	4·50 / **4**	10·0 / **3**	25·0 / **3**	50·0 / **3**		15	1	2	4	6	8	12	16	24	
0·055 / **20**	0·09 / **16**	0·17 / **12**	0·33 / **9**	0·90 / **6**	3·00 / **4**	10·0 / **3**	20·0 / **3**	40·0 / **3**			10	1	2	4	6	8	12	16	24	
0·07 / **16**	0·14 / **12**	0·26 / **9**	0·70 / **6**	2·40 / **4**	8·00 / **3**	15·0 / **3**	32·0 / **3**				8	1	2	4	6	8	12	16	24	
0·10 / **12**	0·25 / **8**	0·50 / **6**	1·60 / **4**	5·00 / **3**	14·0 / **3**	14·1 / **3**	50·0 / **2**				6	1	2 4 / 6	8	12	16	24			
0·17 / **8**	0·35 / **6**	1·10 / **4**	3·30 / **3**	9·00 / **3**	9·10 / **2**	50·0 / **2**					4	1	2 4 / 6	8	12	16	24			
0·26 / **6**	0·80 / **4**	2·40 / **3**	7·00 / **3**	7·10 / **2**	50·0 / **2**						3	1	2 6 / 4 8	12	16	24				
0·50 / **4**	1·50 / **3**	3·80 / **3**	3·90 / **2**	40·0 / **2**							2	1	2 4 / 8 12	16	24					
1·90 / **2**	40·0 / **2**										1	1 4 / 2 6	8 12 / 16	24						

Check: order size must be at least:

	3	4	5	7	10	14	20	30	40
0 0 0 1	1	2	2	3	3	5	6	9 12 17	24 33 45
0 0 1 1	2	2	3	4	4	6	8	10 14 19	26 35 48
0 1 1 2	3	3	5	5	7	9	11	15 20 28	37 51
1 1 1 2	3	4	4	6	6	8	10	13 18 23	31 41 55
1 2 2 3	4	4	6	7	8	10	12	16 21 27	35 45 61
2 2 3 4	5	5	6	8	9	11	14	18 24 30	40 48 65

Bottom rows (estimated costs owing to a shortage):

1·00	2·00	5·00	8·00	40·0						
1·0	2·00	4·0	10·0	15·0	80·0					
1·20	2·0	4·0	8·0	20·0	30·0	160·0				
1·00	2·00	2·50	4·0	6·00	10·0	20·0	40·0	100·0	150·0	800·0
1·00	2·00	4·00	10·0	20·0	40·0	60·0	100·0	200·0	400·0	
4·00	10·0	20·0	40·0	100·0	200·0	250·0	400·0	600·0		

Estimated costs owing to a shortage (production hold-up costs) — Optimum re-order level in units

Note: The thin lines correspond to the explanation given in the text

To find the order quantity and re-order level in Table 56, proceed as follows: Find the annual usage, expressed in units, on the positive Y-axis (45 in the example).

Then search to the left for the value nearest the actual price in £ per unit, for instance £3·20. Immediately under this you will find a value printed in bold characters denoting the optimum order quantity in units (7 in this case). Therefore, if the unit is 2 kg it is necessary to order 14 kg at a time. To verify that this order quantity is not so small as to involve placing more than one order at a time within a delivery period, consult the figures along the positive X-axis. The optimum order quantity found (7) must equal or exceed the figure read in searching the X-axis, as will be explained shortly. If no figure is given, there, no check is needed. Practical experience has shown that verification is hardly ever necessary.

Starting from the quadrant at the top left-hand side given as an example (32/7) search downwards for the amount corresponding to the estimated costs of delay in the event of a shortage (for instance £10). Then begin again from the annual usage on the Y-axis and trace to the right as far as the estimated lead time, in weeks (2 in the example). In tracing downwards from this point cross the X-axis to check the validity of the order quantity found. The fact that no figure is given in the example shows that no check is needed.

Next proceed downwards as far as the line indicating the costs of delay and read from the appropriate square the bold figure representing the optimum re-order level (6). Therefore, if the unit is 2 kg, then 7 X 2 = 14 kg should be ordered when the stock has fallen to 6 X 2 = 12 kg.

32 Fixing parts for assembly [†]

32.1 Description of the situation

A plant produces domestic consumer goods. The production process involves the assembly of parts and subassemblies. The parts are either obtained from sources within the company or purchased from outside suppliers. Parts in the latter category include fixing parts such as screws, nuts and washers. The fixing parts store contains about 500 different articles, varying in price from 0·005p to 0·05p each. The total monthly turnover is about £20 000. Despite the fact that the fixing materials are obtained from many different suppliers, there is no appreciable difference in the lead times of the various articles.

The fixing parts store not only supplies parts for the assembly, but also serves as the central store for fixing parts for the company as a whole. This means that parts are also drawn from the stores by service workshops, maintenance departments and so on. The number of 'customers' per part varies from 3 to 15. Only the expected demand of the assembly department can be deduced, by explosion from the schedules for the end product. Information as to the expected demand of the other users is very unreliable, inadequate and completely lacking in uniformity. Accordingly, the person responsible for ordering the fixing material was faced with difficult problems. He did his best to estimate the future demand per article, but this involved maintaining a complex record of schedules, orders, reserves and tentative forecasts.

As a rule he placed an order for each article with one of his suppliers once a month or once every two months.

To cope with this situation, a re-order system was developed with the object of:

— introducing a measure of control into the replenishment of stock;
— replacing the 'book-keeping' system of assessing the expected demand by a method of extrapolation.

The re-ordering system was intended to be the prototype of similar systems for all the articles within the company and for this reason was required to be suitable for processing by means of an electronic computer. Such processing was possible at a frequency of once a month.

† This chapter has been written by C. J. G. J. van Ham.

32.2 Analysis of past records of demand

A sample of 50 was taken at random from the overall assortment of 500 articles and past records of demand for these 50 articles were consulted. It then emerged that the existing records only covered the demand for the past eighteen months; previous records had been destroyed. Fig. 83 gives the historical demand series of a number of articles. Although these time series were useful as a means of acquiring an insight into the situation, they did not contribute materially to the dis-

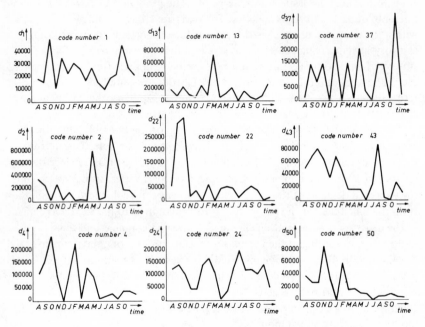

Fig. 83 Historic demand size of some articles from the
assortment of fixing parts.

covery of any systematic element in the demand. A calculation of average demand and spread in the demand for each time series proved very much more valuable in this respect.

Fig. 84 is the result of the investigation into the relationship between average demand ($\bar{d}$) and standard deviation of the demand (σ). Each point in this diagram corresponds to the demand time series of one article (see also paragraph 20.3).

It emerged that there is a relationship between $\bar{d}$ and σ for the assortment of fixing parts, of the form

$$\sigma = c\bar{d}^p \qquad (1)$$

where c and p had values of 1·13 and 0·98, respectively. The high degree of correlation found warranted the assumption that the same relationship applies to

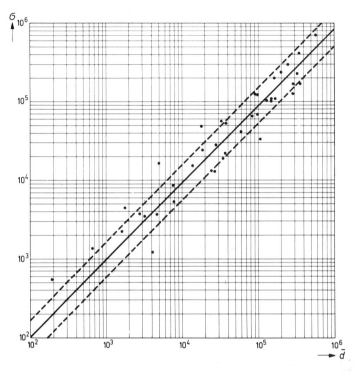

Fig. 84 Relationship between average demand ($\bar{d}$) and standard deviation of demand (σ)

— line of regression; $\sigma = c\bar{d}^p$; $c = 1\cdot13$; $p = 0\cdot98$.

all 500 articles. For a given value of the average demand, it was then possible to calculate the standard deviation of the demand for each article by means of formula (1). Moreover, the values of c and p found were so close to unity that it seemed safe to assume that the demand figures constituted 'draws' from a negative exponential distribution (see also Chapter 5.1).

An χ^2 test confirmed this with a high degree of probability.

32.3 Forecasting the demand

To determine the expected demand in the future, the existing 'book-keeping' had to be replaced by an extrapolation method, which had to be suitable for processing by means of an electronic computer. Accordingly, such techniques as that of the 'moving average' did not come into consideration.

For these reasons, a method on the lines of 'single and double smoothing' was sought. The enquiry as to the 'best' method was wholly empirical in its execution. Forecasts for the above 50 historical series of demand figures were calculated with the aid of single and double smoothing. The advantage of this simulation was that it enabled the forecasts to be compared with the real demand data so as to give an idea of the value of the methods tested. An essential condition was that the same method of forecasting had to be employed for all 500 articles of the assortment. This precluded the possibility of choosing the best method for each article, given the nature of the demand time series. In view of the difference in the time series (Fig. 83) and given the different characteristics of the methods of forecasting, it will be evident that the ultimate choice of a forecasting system was bound to be a compromise.

The enquiry revealed that neither method could strictly be called the 'best', considered in relation to all the time series tested. Finally, the choice fell upon single smoothing,† because this is the simplest in the whole arsenal of exponential smoothing methods and for that reason would present fewest problems when the re-ordering system was introduced (see paragraph 32.8).

The choice of the smoothing constant α was likewise made empirically. Of course, the choice of α invariably constitutes a compromise between prompt reaction to significant changes in the time series (high α) and a minimum of 'interference' in the forecast (low α). On the basis of a number of tests, the value of α was fixed at 0·2.

A forecasting system is invariably linked with a system of signals, since it is necessary to ascertain whether the forecast error (difference between forecast and real demand), or more precisely the cumulation of forecast errors, exceeds acceptable limits.

To determine whether the cumulation of forecast errors has reached an abnormal level, what is called a 'tracking signal' is used. The tracking signal (ts) may be defined as follows

$$ts_i = \frac{\sum\limits_{j=1}^{i} \Delta_j}{\Delta_i} \tag{2}$$

† See for instance Brown (1959) [Br 2].

As explained earlier, there is a relationship between the average absolute deviation ($\overline{\Delta}_i$) and the standard deviation of the demand. The tracking signal therefore denotes the ratio of the cumulation of deviations to the 'spread' in the demand. If the absolute value of the tracking signal exceeds a given limit, then a discrepancy between forecast and real demand can be deduced with a known degree of confidence. The wider the signal limits chosen, the greater the reliability of the 'discrepancy' signal, but the longer the time interval before the signal is given.

Obviously, the choice of the signal limit will also be a compromise between speed of response and reliability of the signalling system.

The value 4 was chosen as the limit on the basis of theoretical considerations and the results of an investigation with the aid of simulation. As soon as the absolute value of the cumulation of deviations exceeded four times the average absolute deviation, then, a significant difference between forecast and real demand was signalled.

Given the methods of forecasting and signalling, the next question was: 'What action is to be taken in response to a signal indicating a significant difference between forecast and real demand?'.

Such a difference could be corrected either inside or outside the system (by the customer). The first alternative was chosen, amongst other reasons for the following:

— a correcting procedure within the system is under control and does not vary;
— the customer would have to maintain his own system of 'book-keeping' in order to be able to correct the situation.

As we have seen, a high value of the smoothing constant (α) ensures prompt reaction of the forecast. The obvious method of correcting the forecast was therefore to raise the value of α. There is a definite relationship between the value of α and the number of operations (one operation per month) necessary to ensure that the forecast will follow a step-by-step change in the demand accurately to within 10%. Having regard to this relationship, the following correction procedure was chosen: 'After the signal has been received, the value of α is raised during three operations to 0·4'. By means of this procedure, a jump in demand after the correcting procedure has been completed is reflected accurately to within 10% by the forecast.

The overall forecasting, signalling and correcting procedure is illustrated in Fig. 85, where it should be noted that the signalling system starts with a clean slate from the beginning of the corrective procedure. This is accomplished by resetting the cumulation of deviations to zero as soon as the first of the corrective operations takes place.

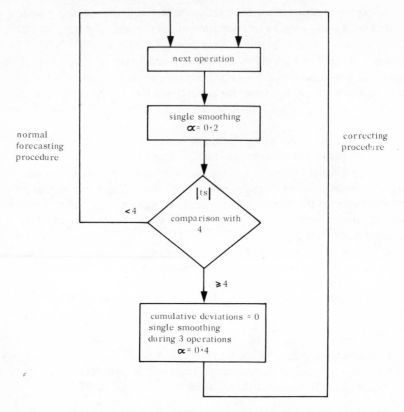

Fig. 85 Forecasting, signalling and correcting procedure.

32.4 The re-ordering system

Facilities were available for an operation to be carried out once a month on an electronic computer. Thus the opportunity to assess the need for replenishing the stock of each article likewise occurred once a month.

The re-ordering system belongs to the category of (s, S) systems.

32.4.1 The lowest level s

The principle for the lowest level s is similar in principle to that for the re-order level B, the only difference being that a correction has to be made for a delay, on average, in the detection of the need for replenishment, owing to the periodic processing. The lowest level s is calculated according to the formula

$$s = \hat{d}\,(t + 0\cdot7) + b \tag{3}$$

where $\hat{d}$ is the forecast of the demand per month;
  t is the lead time, in months;
  b is the buffer stock.

The factor $0\cdot7$ is the above correcting factor, the value of which is determined on the basis of experience.

To determine the buffer stock b, it is necessary to plot the frequency distribution of the deviation as between forecast and real demand. The frequency distribution of the real demand is a negative exponential distribution (see paragraph 32.2). For low values of the smoothing constant ($\alpha < 0\cdot3$), the forecast is a 'draw' from a normal distribution. The frequency distribution of the deviations must then be equivalent to the convolution of a negative exponential, and a normal, distribution. This hypothesis has been tested and confirmed by simulation.

Often, however, the frequency distribution of demand is used instead of the frequency distribution of the deviations to calculate the buffer stock. This practice is correct if the forecast of demand is constant and equal to the average demand, since in these circumstances we have

$$z = P[(d(t) - \overline{d}(t)) > b] = P[d(t) > b + d(t)] \tag{4}$$

where b is the buffer stock and z is equal to the probability that the stock will be negative when the replenishment order arrives.

Even if equation (4) does not apply exactly, it is often possible to use the frequency distribution of the demand to calculate the buffer stock, without introducing any serious error. In the case of the fixing parts, this error proved to amount to only a few per cent for chances of excess smaller than 25%. This fact was again established through a combination of theory and simulation (Fig. 86).

The formula for the lowest level s can now be written as follows

$$s = \hat{d}\,(t + 0\cdot7) + a(z)\,\sigma\,\sqrt{(t + 0\cdot7)} \tag{5}$$

where $a(z)$ is a safety factor, and
  σ is the standard deviation of the demand per month.

Formula (1) could be used to determine σ, provided that the value of d, instead of $\overline{d}$, per article is known. However, a relationship is also known to exist between σ and the average absolute deviation. This average (or mean) absolute

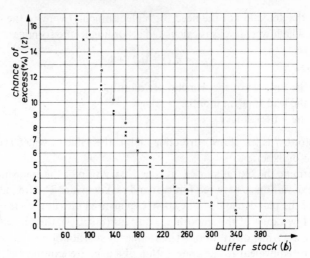

Buffer stock calculated on the basis of:
x frequency distribution of the demand;
· frequency distribution of the deviations, $\alpha = 0\cdot1$;
o frequency distribution of the distributions, $\alpha = 0\cdot4$.

Fig. 86 Chance of excess (z) plotted against the buffer stock (b).

deviation ($\overline{\Delta}$) is already calculated as part of the forecasting procedure for determining the tracking signal. The obvious course was to use ($\overline{\Delta}$) also as a means of determining the buffer stock, by means of the formula

$$\sigma = \frac{e}{2}\,\overline{\Delta} \tag{6}$$

32.4.2 The highest level S

The replenishment batch Q is calculated by means of the formula

$$Q = S - e \tag{7}$$

where e is the effective stock.

The highest level S follows from the formula

$$S = Q^* + s - \tfrac{1}{2}\hat{d} \tag{8}$$

On average, owing to the correcting factor $\hat{d}/2$, the replenishment batch (Q) will equal the optimum batch size (Q^*).

The optimum batch size is calculated by means of the general formula of Camp, in which the annual demand (D) is superseded by 12 x the forecast of the demand per month $(12 \times \hat{d})$. Therefore

$$Q^* = \sqrt{\left(\frac{24\hat{d}F}{C_i}\right)} \tag{9}$$

where F is the fixed costs per batch;

C_i is the cost of carrying product i for one year.

The costs C_i are taken equal to a fixed percentage of the purchase price of article i.

$$C_i = \beta K_i \tag{10}$$

where β is a fixed percentage;

K_i is the purchase price of article i.

32.5 Overall survey

Fig. 87 is the general block diagram of the forecasting and ordering procedure for fixing parts, which clearly illustrates the relationship between the contents of paragraphs 32.3 and 32.4. This block diagram is checked through every month for each of the 500 articles. The result of the process is an order list (Fig. 88) with one line per article. This order list gives:

— the orderer the information he requires to place orders with the different suppliers and chase outstanding orders;
— other information required for the 'maintenance' of the system.

32.6 Results and parameters

The principal parameter in the system is z, the probability that the stock will be negative by the time a replenishment arrives. A relationship exists between z and the capital invested in the inventory.

The total stock of fixing parts is made up of two components

$$I = \frac{1}{2} \sum_{i=1}^{n} Q_i^* + a(z) \frac{e}{2} \sqrt{(t + 0 \cdot 7)} \sum_{i=1}^{n} \bar{\Delta}_i \tag{11}$$

where n is the total number of articles.

To put it in another way: the total average stock is equal to half the sum of all the optimum batch sizes plus the sum of all the buffer stocks. The capital invested in stock is calculated by means of the formula

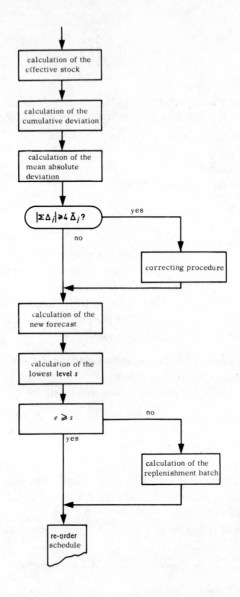

Fig. 87 Forecasting and re-ordering procedure for the fixing parts.

Auxiliary code	Code number	Replenishment batch	C$_1$	C$_2$	Urgency of order	Urgency of delivery	Stock on hand	Effective stock	On order	Demand last month	Forecast for next month	Tracking signal	Mean absolute deviation
017020670050	8020ED/2		0	6	2·07	4·15	4 229	8 229	4 000	606	1 019	0·39	633
017020670050	8020ED/6	4 800	0	6	−1·17	1·23	2 600	9 500	7 000	3 319	2 022	3·24	1 134
017020680081	8020EE/3		1	6	5·35	0·36	559	15 559	15 000	1 608	1 516	1·00	152
017049070120	8049AH/6	8 500	0	6	−1·14	2·91	6 389	10 389	4 000	3 281	2 192	1·12	1 235

Fig. 88 Order schedule for fixing parts.

Explanation:

C$_1$, C$_2$: numerators, necessary in the forecasting procedure;

urgency of order: aid to determining the sequence in which the replenishment batches should be ordered;

urgency of delivery: aid to chasing outstanding orders.

$$I(\pounds) = \frac{1}{2}\sqrt{\left(\frac{24F}{\beta}\right)} \sum_{i=1}^{n} \sqrt{(\hat{d}_i K_i)} + a(z)\frac{e}{2}\sqrt{(t+0\cdot7)} \sum_{i=1}^{n} \overline{\Delta}_i K_i \qquad (12)$$

The problem now consists in finding the value of the expressions

$$\sum_{i=1}^{n} \hat{d}_i K_i \qquad \text{and} \qquad \sum_{i=1}^{n} \overline{\Delta}_i K_i$$

A possible solution is to add $d_i K_i$ and $\overline{\Delta}_i K_i$ for all the code numbers. However, the problem can be solved more neatly by means of the lognormal distribution. The variables $\hat{d}_i K_i$ and $\overline{\Delta}_i K_i$ were found to follow a lognormal distribution.

Fig. 89 shows the result of the calculation, bearing in mind that the quantity

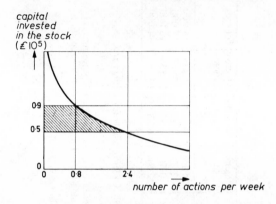

Fig. 89   Relationship between the capital invested in the stock
of fixing parts and the number of actions required per week
to avoid stock-out.

plotted on the horizontal axis is not z, but the number of actions necessary per week for the entire assortment of articles in order to avoid stockout.

This number of actions can be deduced from z by means of

$$\text{number of actions} = z \sum_{i=1}^{n} \frac{D_i}{Q_i^*} \qquad (13)$$

D_i is estimated as $12d_i$. By substituting the formula for Q_i^*, we transform formula (13) into

$$\text{number of actions} = z \sqrt{\left(\frac{\beta}{2F}\right)} \sum_{i=1}^{n} \hat{d}_i K_i \qquad (14)$$

The lognormal distribution of $(d_i K_i)$ was used again to calculate the number of actions.

Next, the value of the parameter z was established by means of Fig. 89, taking into account on the one hand the results upon the capital invested in stock and on the other hand the number of actions required per week to avoid stock-out.

Fig. 90 clearly illustrates the result of introducing optimum batch sizes; this diagram shows the frequency histograms of the value of the orders $(Q_i K_i)$. The

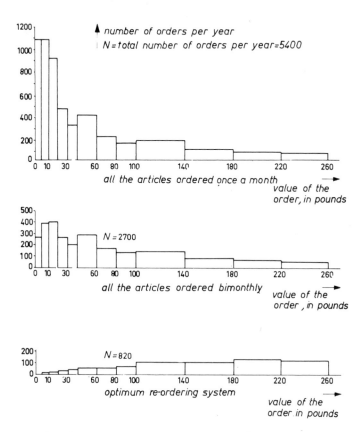

Fig. 90 Relationship between the number of orders per year and the value of the order, for different ordering systems.

difference between periodic re-ordering (once a month; once every two months) of all the articles and re-ordering in optimum batch sizes emerges clearly from this illustration. The difference relates to the total number of orders per year (N) as well as to the distribution of the value of the orders.

32.7 Stock norms

Given the value of the parameter z, the norm for the total stock can be read from Fig. 89.

If the total expected average turnover per month of the assortment of fixing parts is also known, a norm for the average turnover rate of the total stock can be derived from the norm for the financial stock level. This is an important factor in the signalling of significant changes within a company (see also Section IV, Chapter 28).

The orderer also needs to have some idea of the maximum stock to be expected per article. This norm for the stock per article can be deduced from a combination of formulae (5) and (9). The contribution made by the buffer stock will be independent of the average turnover per month, whereas that made by the batch size stock is directly dependent upon this turnover. Fig. 91 shows the range within

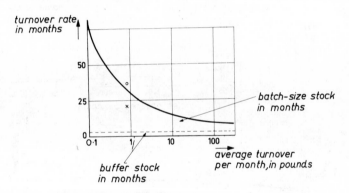

Fig. 91 Relationship between turnover rate per article, in months, and average turnover per article per month.

$$\text{turnover rate} = \frac{\text{stock on hand}}{\text{average expected demand per month}}$$

Example: x normal
          o abnormal, action necessary

which the turnover rate per article will normally lie. If a particular article proves to have a turnover rate outside this range, then the orderer will have to ascertain the cause of this and if necessary intervene in the system.

32.8 Introduction and evaluation

The introduction of the system had the following aspects:

— co-ordination with an existing stock administration;
— communication of basic information on the subject of ordering and forecasting to the person responsible for ordering fixing parts and to others concerned in the planning and purchasing departments;
— acquainting the buyer with the new system; input control, interpretation of the order schedule, etc.;
— guidance of the buyer for a few months.

The utmost attention was given to the task of imparting basic and detailed information to the buyer, in view of the fact that such re-ordering systems were hitherto unknown in the planning and purchasing departments.

The guidance given to the buyer was thorough and continued for several months. It was assumed, without very much in the way of investigation, that the existing stock administration would be capable of supplying the necessary data. Of course, problems arose. The sudden change from 'book-keeping' linked with ordering once a month or bimonthly, to 'relying upon an order schedule' proved too great and formed an obstacle to the acceptance of the system.

In future, such abrupt changes will certainly have to be avoided and instead an attempt will be made to introduce the system step-by-step. This can be accomplished, say, by first showing the buyer the results of a forecasting procedure instead of his 'book-keeping' and letting him decide for himself, with the aid of re-order level and batch size tables, when to order and what size the order should be.

Another advantage of this approach is that it facilitates the communication of information.

The second, and more serious problem arose out of the link-up with an existing stock administration. This was organized for financial accounting and fulfilled that task admirably. However, it proved to be a mistake to assume that the data from the stock administration (stock and demand data) would also constitute a sound basis for controlling the flow of goods. The causes were manifold. Once a month without fail, the buyer had to recheck all the information from the stock administration and correct it where necessary before proceeding to use the order schedule for his work. This need for repeated correction naturally created antipathy which could only be overcome when a new, quantitatively sound system of stock administration had been established as a basis for the re-ordering system.

33 Planning and inventory control in a woodworking factory

33.1 Introduction

The present chapter deals with the situation in a woodworking factory manufacturing mainly cabinets. A brief account of the organization and successive phase of the production process is followed by a description of the system of scheduling and accepting incoming orders and planning the components required.

The factory concerned is one of several owned by a company making products for the furniture trade. It receives orders from other factories in the group ('the demand') and delivers direct to these factories and to warehouses located mainly in the Benelux countries and one or two other major European countries.

The production process has the following phases:

a. Chip-boards previously sawn to roughly the right size are veneered on both sides in the plywood department.
b. The premachining department makes supports such as fillets and profiled slats.
c. The task of the machining department is to saw the boards previously veneered, make holes, slots and so forth and work up the profiled slats from the premachining department into components, which are then stored in a warehouse.
d. The 'assembly I and II' department is responsible for assembling the required end products from the components by gluing, sanding and staining.
e. The paint shop applies the varnish.
f. 'Drying' involves drying the end product to a high-gloss or semi-matt finish.
g. 'Packing'; the semi-matt cabinets are finished and packed immediately after being varnished.
h. 'Sanding and polishing'; after being allowed to dry for a time the high-gloss cabinets are sanded and polished to the desired finish and then packed.
i. Storage of end product; the end products are stored in a warehouse pending dispatch to the customers.

These phases are represented graphically in Fig. 92.

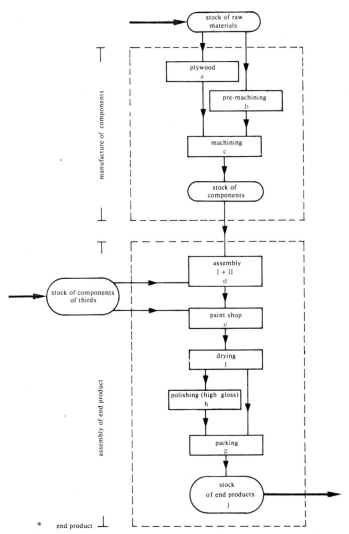

Layout of production process

manufacture of components

stock of raw materials

plywood
a

pre-machining
b

machining
c

stock of components

assembly of end product

stock of components of thirds

assembly
I + II
d

paint shop
e

drying
f

polishing (high gloss)
h

packing
g

stock of end products
j

end product

Fig. 92 Flowchart of the production process.

33.2 Problems

Capacity planning is one of the principal tasks of the planning department. It involves calculating the capacity required, determining the capacity actually available and reconciling the two. The reliability of deliveries, the stock level and the profitability of the concern depend very largely upon these two quantities being correctly balanced.

If the balance is disturbed by changes in demand, a new capacity utilization plan will have to be prepared as quickly as possible.

Quick reaction to changes in demand is vital in as much as it enables the possible consequences to be perceived and absorbed without delay. The different planning method used before made for slower reaction:

— owing to the information on changes being collected by a central agency within the concern and processed in various places before being presented to the production-planning department of the cabinet-making factory;
— because the component production process was linked directly to the assembly of end products. Whenever the production level was raised the component production process had to be adjusted before the output of the assembly department could be increased. The stock of components was not so constituted as to be capable of absorbing a (large) part of the increment in the assembly planning;
— owing to the time spent on administrative processing in the planning office; this processing involved calculating the capacity and the components required as well as preparing a production schedule for components, assembly and material.

33.3 The capacity calculation

Information as to the effect of every change in demand upon the capacity is vital to the cabinet-making factory to enable them to decide whether the modifications asked of them can be accepted and implemented.

The assembly, painting, drying and polishing departments account for almost 80% of the total factory capacity (in man hours); the first step is to ascertain whether the distribution of capacity planned for these departments will have to be altered and if so how much.

In principle new cabinet schedules are prepared monthly, in accordance with current information as to the state of the order book. Such recent data may well necessitate an immediate re-appraisal of the factory planning.

The horizon of the demand forecast is from eight to twelve months ahead.
The capacity required by the above departments for each type of cabinet is deduced from:

— the production rate to be established in order to implement the forecast;
— the ratio of high-gloss to matt-finish required per type; this ratio has a marked effect upon the capacity needed for finishing, in as much as the high-gloss production groups require considerably more capacity than the semi-matt groups. Hence any disturbance of the high-gloss/semi-matt ratio usually entails considerable alteration of the finishing capacity required overall.

The number of man hours needed for the various phases of the production process is usually known for each type of cabinet.

Assuming a fixed labour force in, and planning for full utilization of the assembly department automatically puts a ceiling on the factory output.

The labour force is distributed amongst the different types of cabinet (fifteen to twenty main types); each type is assigned a group of employees as its line team.

Although their individual sizes can be varied, these groups together constitute the total labour force of the particular department, which is supposed to be more or less permanent. This total labour force is the criterion for deciding whether or not to accept a new batch of orders.

Because in this case just *one* department is regarded as the criterion of capacity the question of whether or not to accept an order can be decided very quickly.

The finishing capacity is planned so as to present no problems when the departmental labour force is at full strength, except at extreme ratios of high-gloss to semi-matt.

The production of components is given an over-capacity capable of:

— absorbing any sudden upsurge of component usage;
— being assigned to cope with any incidental call for additional capacity in the finishing or assembly departments.

This policy with regard to capacity has made the factory more flexible.

So that any changes needed in the existing plan can be quickly evaluated, certain rules are followed in establishing the weekly output per type and the ratio of high-gloss to semi-matt. The cumulative output and the stock level are plotted in, and read from charts.

Similar information used to be obtained by much complicated arithmetic; the process (= reaction) time required for this purpose was far too long (5 to 10 days), particularly in the case of short-term changes.

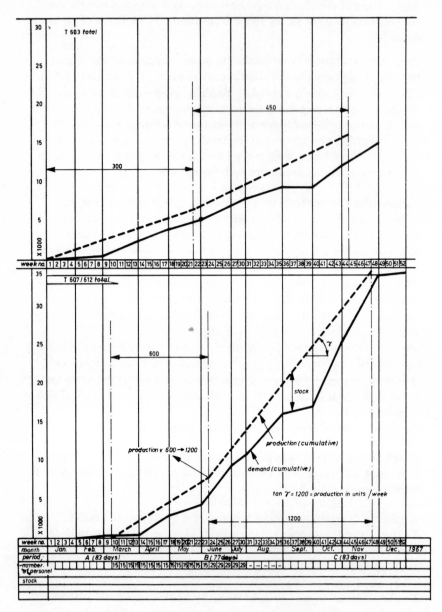

Fig. 93 Production planning with cumulative charts.

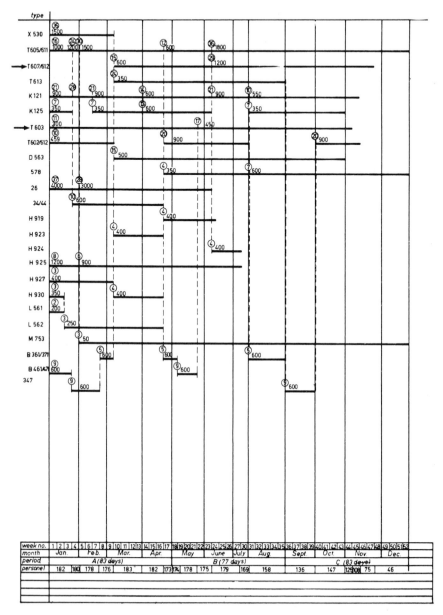

Fig. 94.

33.4 Production planning with the aid of cumulative charts

The current cumulative demand per cabinet and the associated high-gloss/semi-matt ratio are recorded graphically. The related (= planned) output is marked in these charts by a dotted line. The charts display the current situation more clearly than figures (see Fig. 93).

The quantities produced are plotted vertically, 1 cm representing 1000 cabinets; along the horizontal axis there is a scale of working days with the normal calendar for a year projected on to it so as to make a distinction between weeks of five and of four working days (for example, Easter) and allow for the fact that, for instance, the summer holiday month spans eleven working days.

The cumulative demand or output can thus be represented by lines at certain angles to the horizontal (or time) axis.

Due to the scale employed on the time axis, like angles invariably represent like quantities of cabinets on demand or scheduled for production. The line labour requirements for a wide range of production rates were established to enable the number of operators required on the assembly line to be calculated from the production rate represented by the angle shown in the chart.

This information together with the stock of cabinets (planned output less demand) is expressed quantitatively in the charts, constructed for all the principal types of cabinet (fifteen to twenty of them).

As an extension of the above procedure the basic production schedule is compiled, showing the period scheduled for production together with the production rate for each main type on a horizontal line. Particulars of all the types are brought together on one sheet, showing when production has been switched from one type to another and how many people are involved (Fig. 94). This schedule is submitted to the local factory management and, if approved, adopted as a basis for planning the assembly and finishing processes of the various models or code numbers of each type. The administrative tasks of procurement and calculation involved take about 1 man-week (when done by hand).

The procedure for dealing with changes in demand is as follows:

— the quantities requisitioned are totalled per period. Totals are obtained for all the different versions of a given type of cabinet;
— these data are recorded on prints of the charts for the previous period. A new cumulative demand line is then drawn and compared with that used hitherto;
— if necessary new production lines are plotted on these charts, after which the new production rate can be calculated by measuring the angles with a protractor. The line labour requirement then follows from this new rate.

Whilst these charts are being brought up to date the planner can already discern any difficult periods which may appear imminent. This involves only a moderate amount of work and, what is more, it can be done very quickly.

In this way the above delay of from five to ten days has been reduced to one or two, with the result that information can now be fed back to the users far more quickly.

The change procedure ends with the completion of the new line plan, after which the charts are again put into a form suitable for reproduction.

The present method has the following advantages as compared with that mentioned earlier:

— the effect of changes in demand upon capacity is soon established;
— reliable information from which to decide whether to augment the capacity for a given type or product is made available at a very much earlier stage;
— when the demand exceeds the peak production level an immediate decision can be taken as to what types should be transferred to another supplier;
— the demand for cabinets stems directly from the flow of customers' orders; omitting the intermediate phase in a central office enables the total stock of cabinets to be reduced.

Note

It will be seen from the charts that the stock level is influenced by the number of switches in production.

Each set in the dotted line (= cumulative production) represents a change of production level. Chapter 29 explained how to find the proper balance between changeover costs and inventory (carrying) costs in continuous production.

The calculation described there could be carried out for each type individually as a matter of routine, but this would involve a great deal of arithmetic. Detailed calculations carried out in a number of cases suggest a rise or fall of at least 50% as a reasonable norm for a change of production level in this particular case.

33.5 Calculation of materials and components required

The above assembly and finishing plan in which the numbers of cabinets to be produced are reviewed per type and per week provides the initial data for the calculation of material requirements. Information as to what components and materials are required for each type is also available (parts list). This calculation determines when and in what quantities all the different components and materials to be used in the cabinets will be needed (= requirement, or demand function).

On completion of the calculation these data are compared with the inventory and order data, after which decisions are made as to the placing of new orders with component suppliers and any associated call-off schedule.

This calculation of requirements (= parts list quantities multiplied by planned output of end products) is carried out for about 120 end-product type numbers distributed amongst fifteen to twenty main types. Each cabinet involves on average twenty different components and materials, although some of the components are more or less common to all.

The horizon of the calculation is three months (13 weeks) ahead.

Since it is so comprehensive and time consuming this calculation of requirements is an obvious candidate for automation by the use of a computer. In the present case the documentation of parts lists has, in fact, been automated and the calculation resulting from any change in the assembly planning is carried out with the aid of a computer.

At present the updating of the assembly schedules with the cumulative charts is still being done by hand, partly as a matter of policy towards the overall factory labour force. As we have seen, however, this manual processing is reinforced by decision rules. Next, the assembly schedule is put into machine language and recorded. The first phase of this automation covers documentation and the calculation of requirements; the second is a logical extension of this: the automated recording of orders and a call-off schedule for materials and components from thirds, followed by the preparation of a production plan for the manufacture of components.

The principal advantages of automation in the first phase are faster and more accurate calculation giving scope for adequate response to change. It also provides a starting point for better inventory control of materials and components. The next step is the planning of components.

33.6 Components planning by means of a modified (B, Q) system

At one time the aim was to fit the component planning exactly to the assembly planning. This involved producing ('running') much of the overall range of components once a week to once a fortnight, with the result that the production of components was frequently interrupted due to changes in the assembly planning. Also, much time and money was wasted in retooling machines for the production of components.

The present system has three main aspects:

— the production runs are based on optimum lot sizes;

- the timing of each run is deduced from the through-put time (per product) and the desired buffer stock of components;
- the optimum batch per run is used as a basis for deciding whether the batch of cabinet 'runs' covers a sufficient time ahead ('isn't the horizon too close?'). Too near a horizon adds to the overall changeover costs.

Experience with the calculation of optimum lot sizes for the production of components has shown that although none are identical, there are whole groups which differ only slightly.

Hence all the components are divided into three categories:

a. specific, high-cost components (group 1);
b. specific, low-cost components (group 2);
c. universal components (group 3).

An exact calculation of optimum lot size for a large batch of components gives some indication of the merits of this rather crude classification. There is one lot size formula for each group and the calculation involves only one variable, namely 'the usage in the assembly department'.

Careful analysis of the consequences of this method reveals that in the present case the following formulae may be employed for each article in the groups concerned:

group 1: $Q_I^* = 90\sqrt{Y}$
group 2: $Q_{II}^* = 350\sqrt{Y}$ Y = weekly usage in the assembly department.
group 3:   No special formula applies here; all the runs are long, or in other words cover at least two to three months' usage. This group can also be used to level out the capacity required for the total assortment of components.

To simplify the calculation two curves representing the relationship between the optimum lot sizes Q_1^*, Q_2^* and the weekly usage Y are plotted in a chart.

In practice this method also involves two summaries, one showing in which cabinet each component occurs, the number of 'man-minutes' it takes in the plywood and machining departments, and the size of the buffer stock expressed quantitatively in terms of individual units.

The horizon of this survey is four months, divided into individual weeks; the size of the inventory, the requirement and the throughput time are also given.

The optimum lot size (formulated as above) is also specified together with particulars of when to run the batch and the period this must 'cover'.

The other summary is issued weekly to the plywood and machining departments and is a kind of job form listing all the batches of components to be run and delivered in the particular week.

33.7 Calculation

In conclusion a graphic review (Fig. 95) of the necessary activities and data is presented.

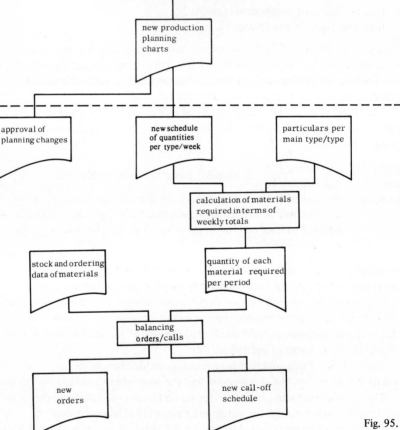

Fig. 95.

The activities below the dotted line are suitable for mechanical data processing which, as we have seen, has already been implemented.

34 Example: the production of simple parts for electronic components

The product

The department concerned produces small, invidual products.

The assortment

The number of different types (code numbers) manufactured is in the region of 350. All of them are made of the same basic material. The 35 types having the largest turnover together constitute about 90% of the total turnover.

The production process

The production process (see Fig. 96) comprises:

— a simple roughing operation (by hand);
— a press operation (blanking), which is the essence of the process;
— inspection;
— a simple surface treatment.

The production plant

The press shop, containing about 50 presses of much the same type, is of primary interest in this paragraph. This department operates partly in two shifts. To enable a given code number to be blanked on a press, the latter must first be fitted with the appropriate blanking tool (punch). The life of these tools is very uncertain and tool breakage sometimes presents a problem. For code numbers having a large turnover it is necessary to have more than one punch available. The exact number of tools required is another problem, which will not be discussed here, nor will the problem of the stock of spare parts required for tool repairs.

Customer

The parts are made for a number of assembly plants in the Netherlands as well as for others in the Benelux countries and some factories abroad, some of them outside Europe. All these factories, supplier and consumers alike, belong to the same concern (see Fig. 96).

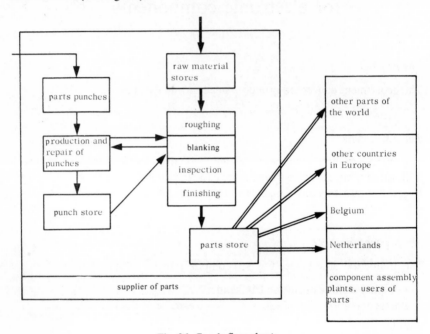

Fig. 96 Goods flow chart.

34.1 Original system

The system of production and inventory control originally employed for the parts concerned was very similar to the 'periodic system' of Burbidge – Gigli, described in 'An Introduction to Production and Inventory Control', paragraph 11.2. For the benefit of supplier and consumers, a central planning bureau (CPB) produced a forecast of the expected turnover per code number once every four months. This forecast was based on the assembly programme for end products, established in consultation with the commercial department. For each period of four months, the CPB sent a batch of production orders to the production department well in advance. This department also received a distribution schedule for each code number, showing how many parts had to be dispatched from the manufacturer's stores to the different customers each week. The production orders and distribution schedules alike were based on the expected demand in the assembly plants using the parts concerned. For various reasons the real demand differed from the expected demand, so that extra shipments became necessary; these were made on the basis of the observed stock levels, as follows.

A neighbouring customer received each week the number of parts given in the distribution schedule. However, this schedule did not provide exact delivery instructions, but merely indicated the number to be shipped at the end of each week. If everything went according to plan, one week's stock of each code number should be on hand at the end of each week. The customer reviewed his stock carefully once a month. If the stock of a certain code number showed an appreciable upward deviation, the customer was entitled to ask the supplier to 'hold back' the surplus next month, from the quantities given in the distribution schedule.

In compiling the production orders, about two months before the start of the production period, the CPB collected reports of the stock levels per code number from the supplier and the customers. Any stock surplus was then subtracted from the production orders. It will be evident that although this system does involve feedback, the response is very slow indeed. Any sudden fall-off in demand leads to a corresponding rise in the stock level, first on the part of the customer and afterwards (owing to the 'hold-back') on the part of the supplier.

In the most unfavourable case it will be three months before a stock surplus is disposed of through a cut-back in production.

If the opposite occurs, that is if demand somewhat exceeds expectation, a rapid increase in the quantities to be shipped is likewise difficult to realize. As a result, the customers involved in such a system tend to cover themselves, say, by systematically 'boosting' the forecast of demand.

Accordingly, the original system exhibited the drawbacks mentioned in 'An Introduction to Production and Inventory Control', paragraph 11.2:

- the same frequency of production batches is chosen for all the parts, despite recurrent major differences in annual demand, changeover costs and cost price, and in some cases in storage costs as well;
- as already mentioned, the lead time for the end product is long;
- the system operates with delivery data established a long time beforehand. Consequently, detailed schedules are prepared which are no longer valid by the time the appropriate delivery dates arrive. This tends to destroy all confidence in deliveries, while on the other hand there is a constant flow of information concerning parts required sooner than originally expected;

— an organization is set up which is subject to central control covering a vast amount of detail;
— all the orders for a given period have the same delivery date, but in practice they will be completed one after another. Most orders are then ready too soon.

All this leads to high stock levels, a tardy response and many instances of 'chasing' in order to avoid stockout. The original system was sometimes called 'theoretical' by the ordering bureaux of the customer and the supplier, because it was based too much upon the 'theoretical' demand for parts.

It should be borne in mind that in this system the instructions to the manufacturer were clear enough; the production orders must be delivered to the stores once a month. The inconsequence of this system is, however, that it may create shortages of some code numbers and surpluses of others precisely if the manufacturer keeps strictly to his instructions (prepared two months in advance).

34.2 The new system

In view of the simplicity of the production system and the frequent shipments between the different factories, it was possible to introduce a (B, Q) system for the orders from the users to the factory stores and for the orders from the factory stores to the production departments.

The forecast, prepared once every four months by the CPB, is also now very necessary, namely:

— to enable the required capacity to be determined (that is, the utilization of the plant);
— to enable the necessary tools to be ordered;
— to enable batch sizes and re-order levels to be established.

According to this system, however, the CPB does not place monthly orders or circulate distribution schedules in the old sense; thus it does not give any instructions concerning shipment or production. The CPB merely fixes the procedure whereby the local ordering offices (PB) should formulate instructions. The instruction for shipment to user X is made out by the PB of customer X himself and sent to the factory stores; the same applies to the production order given when the economic stock in the factory store falls below level B. The principles of the (B, Q) method are discussed in 'An Introduction to Production and Inventory Control'.

A few words on the subject of the division of labour are of relevance here (see Fig. 97):

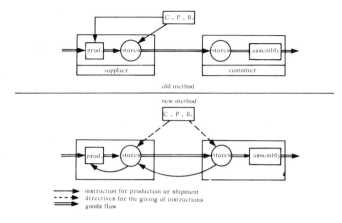

Fig. 97 Information flow chart for old and new methods,
relating to only one customer.

— CPB gives directives concerning ordering by issuing series of B and Q values every four months;
— the PB's control the stocks and usually place orders in accordance with the directives given them.

The PB of the parts manufacturer has under its control: the stores, the stores administration, the stock administration, the order administration. The stock is reviewed daily and an order is sent if necessary.

Fig. 98 is an example of the stock chart as employed in the suppliers stores according to the new system. The stock chart also incorporates a kind of 'distribution schedule', but the actual signal to ship comes from the goods-inwards store of the customer. By noting the shipment to each customer, the factory stores staff can use the information on the distribution schedule to ascertain whether the customers (or one of them) have (has) fallen too far short of, or gone too far beyond, their (his) forecast demand.

If desired, these charts can be placed in a Si Extra file with bottom margin display indicating, amongst other things, the stock position in relation to the re-order level.

If the department cannot keep to the agreed delivery time owing to capacity problems, lower Q values are adopted temporarily; it is also necessary to keep a check on the control of the total demand and the total production to see that this is functioning properly. In the event of any difficulties with the tools, the customer(s) must be warned in case of emergency.

At the same time that they are booked on the stock chart, which is done on an accounting machine, the data are also recorded on a punched tape for the computer which keeps the financial accounts.

The customers within the Benelux zone also check their stock once a day and send a replenishment order to the factory stores if necessary.

The following is worth noting concerning the calculation of B and Q for production orders.

As regards the lead time it has been established that the interval between the date of placing the order and the date of the first delivery of a portion of that order should not be more than eight working days. After the first day's output has been delivered, a full day's production continues to pass to the stores daily

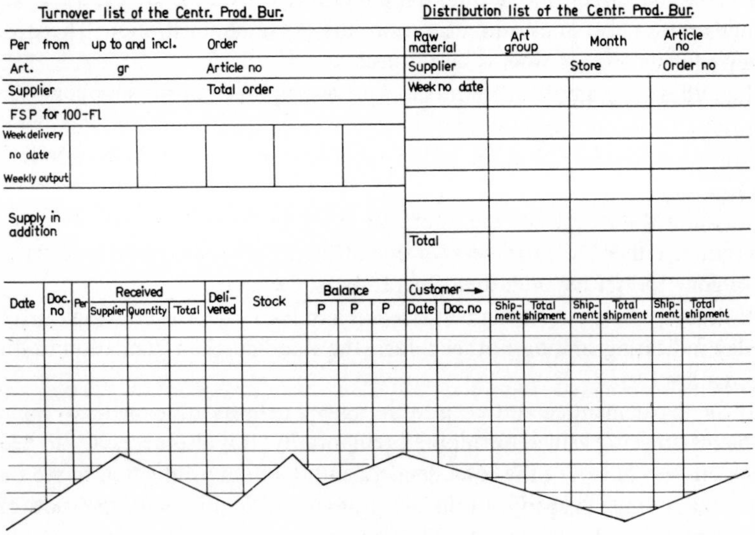

Fig. 98 Example of a stock chart

until the order has been completed; the entire order must be delivered within eighteen days of the order date.

The stipulation that the first delivery must take place after eight days means in practice that the press shop must never have more than four days' work on hand, in view of the throughput time required for the other operations; these other operations never constitute a bottleneck.

B can now be determined on the basis of the agreed lead time. Accordingly, B is determined separately for each code number as follows:

B = (forecast average demand during the lead time of 8 days) x safety factor. The safety factor is recalculated once a year by the staff bureau of the CPB. To facilitate this, all the articles have been divided into three turnover groups, as follows:
1. turnover 0 to 50 000 per four months;
2. turnover 50 000 to 150 000 per four months;
3. turnover more than 150 000 per four months.

For each group, a cumulative frequency distribution is constructed of the quotient $\dfrac{\text{real demand}}{\text{forecast demand}}$ per eight days (see Fig. 45). The 5% risk point of this distribution is adopted as the safety factor for the particular turnover group.

The batch size is determined in the first instance according to Camp's formula. A correction for the effect of the production rate is then made in the major turnovers. Batches representing more than four months turnover are reduced to four months.

The following applies to the calculation of B and Q for shipment orders. Adopting the slogan: 'Manageability comes first; optimality comes second', they took for all the code numbers:

$B = Q = 1$ week's turnover, after which the shipment batches were rounded to the nearest number of packing units. It proved necessary to compare the real stock regularly with the stock as shown on the stock chart in order to make sure that the two agreed reasonably well.

The following points relating to the detailed planning in the production department are worth noting. The production department has undertaken:

— to deliver, each period, as total output whatever the replenishment orders call for, as long as this does not exceed, or fall short of, the forecast level of demand by more than 5%. At a later stage this was changed to: not more than 10% above or below the level;
— to deliver all the code numbers to the factory store according to the agreed

lead time, provided that the demand per code number does not deviate by more than 50% from the forecast, taken over the period as a whole (otherwise there would be too few tools available).

When the new system was introduced, the production department adopted an ordinary strip planning board for detail planning and work allocation. At first, a strip of the correct length was cut for each production order. This was placed on the board after a particular machine. The stipulated first delivery date was noted on the strip. The different orders were monitored individually on the board according to the method usual with Gantt charts [Cl 2]. After a time, the function of the planning board was restricted to that of a work allocation board. It proved unduly laborious, and pointless, to keep all these data up to date on the planning board. In fact, information is required for certain decisions only.

These decisions will now be summarized:

— if there is a temporary shortage of capacity, all the production orders from a given date are fixed at $\frac{2}{3}Q$ instead of Q. In anticipation of this eventuality, the reduced batch size is already noted on each stock chart. The signal for this decision is: the number of production orders on the books of the department (including the quantities still outstanding in respect of orders partly completed). A point to remember in this connection is the agreement that a production order is regarded as complete if the tool breaks after more than $\frac{3}{4}Q$ has been produced. To be able to ascertain whether a capacity shortage is in fact temporary, it is necessary to have regular access to information concerning total stock, total output, total demand;
— if there is a temporary shortage of production orders, higher values of B are adopted temporarily. They are also indicated beforehand on the charts. The nature of the information required has already been discussed;
— when an order is in production, the quantity produced so far must be ascertainable at any time in order to discover whether the order has been completed yet or (if the tool breaks) whether more than $\frac{3}{4}$ of the order has been completed. To provide this information, the department keeps a simple record of the deliveries to date on the order form;
— if a machine runs out of work, it should be possible to ascertain from the order book which order is next in line. The new production orders are dealt with in order of arrival. Orders already in production, but interrupted owing to tool failure (where no spare tool was immediately available), have priority. If the order date and/or first delivery date are noted on the order form, there can be no misunderstandings;
— if a tool to be used for an interrupted production order is returned from the repair shop and there is no prospect of a machine becoming available for some

time, then another order in production at the time may be interrupted if necessary in order to meet an urgent demand.

The later version of the planning board shows at a glance what the next order is for each machine and which orders have been interrupted owing to tool failure.

To ensure that the orders also pass through the inspection and finishing operations in the correct sequence, a work-allocation tray is employed in which the work vouchers are inserted in the sequence of the order dates. For a production order involving more than one day's work in the press shop, more than one work voucher is required; these vouchers are then placed in order of arrival in the press shop.

It will be more or less evident from what has been said so far, that the following information is required to keep the overall situation under control:

— total numbers produced per week;
— total demand per week;
— total stock at the end of the week;
— number of code numbers for which deliveries are in arrears at the end of the week.

These data are plotted against time in a graph. Every week, a revised graph is prepared for the departmental head and the head of the PB. If desired, a survey showing the percentage of all the factory orders completed within the agreed lead time can also be constructed. All these graphs can only be plotted accurately if water-tight definitions are established for the different terms so that the exact measuring points are known.

As we have seen, the four-monthly forecast is another important source of information. Changes in these forecasts (and therefore also in B and Q values) may only be made in consultation with PB and the production department, after ascertaining whether the necessary capacity and tools are available.

In conclusion, there are one or two individual points worth mentioning. Some Some code numbers are not made for, and delivered from, stock, but are made as a single order.

The production department, in turn, must reach clear agreements with the repair shop as to the lead time for tool repairs.

An obvious point, which is nevertheless often overlooked, is that such factors as rejects, scrap, illness and so on have to be taken into account in calculating the capacity required. Equally obvious, but even more frequently ignored, is the need for a reliable system of stock administration; therefore we make no excuse for repeating it once again.

If a certain code number has to be superseded for technical reasons by a more or less modified design, then the time for introducing this depends amongst other things upon two factors:

— when will the new tool be ready?
— is it desirable to use up the old stock first?

34.3 The introduction of the new system

The change from the old to the new system could not be made in one step. A gradual transition was necessary, mainly for the following reasons:

— everyone concerned had to assimilate new ideas and procedures and acquire confidence in them;
— gradual introduction gave scope for the discovery and elimination of certain minor flaws in the system, before they attained serious proportions;
— a change from one ordering system to another usually involves adapting the stock level. It is seldom either possible or advisable to do this quickly.

For these reasons, a step-by-step transition was accomplished by transferring one or two groups of code numbers successively to the new system. In the mean time, staff at different levels were given courses, varying in the amount of detail they contained, to familiarize them with the background and operation of the new system; ordering 'games' played an important part in this. In other respects also, the change took place step-by-step.

At the outset, the importance of monitoring the total stock, total production and total demand was underestimated, as also was the importance of the tools (punches). Again, it only became evident later that the method of assigning projects to the production department had changed.

In conclusion it is worth mentioning that from yet another point of view the system did not cover every aspect of the problem as a whole; the part discussed here is only one of several required in the component assembly plants.

34.4 Advantages of the change

The advantages of introducing the new system proved to lie in the following points:

— a useful organization has been established, which made the task of the management easier and the system more flexible. For example, a removal to other premises which took place later and led to temporary loss of capacity was absorbed smoothly and without very much extra effort;

— the number of cases in which chasing became necessary diminished;
— the stock level fell, in the factory stores as well as in the customer's stores; partly as a result of this, the orders to the factory stores acquired a more regular pattern;
— there were fewer changeovers in the production; one result of this was found to be that the tool life increased.

Section VIII: Approach to a Problem

Section VIII. Approach to a Problem

35 Approach to a project

35.1 How important is a proper approach?

The right approach is vital to the success of all activities connected with production and inventory control. Alas, there are all too many examples of investigations which bring no real improvement but merely result in a more expensive system. This is either abandoned as soon as the investigators have gone or simply falls apart in course of time. All such cases constitute a sad waste of time, money, effort and misplaced enthusiasm.

Example 1

The plant spares inventory of a factory engaged in mass production was considered by the management to be excessive. Following a thorough analysis of demand pattern, costs figures, lead times and so forth a system of inventory control was introduced, which was expected to reduce the inventory substantially.
Although this did fall originally, however, it was soon back to the original level. The reason was that the forecast of usage per inventory item was made by the technical supervisors, relying on their own judgement and experience. They had no faith in the new system and soon realized that this could be circumvented by making an exaggerated forecast to bring the inventory back to what they considered an adequate (high) level.

Example 2

The stock of components on an assembly belt for major appliances was considered by the management to be too high from the point of view of finance. A new ordering system was therefore planned to involve a temporarily decreased procurement followed by control at a lower inventory level. But in the event there was virtually no appreciable curtailment of orders. It emerged that the assembly line operators considered the new stocks far too small and therefore found ways and means (for instance the official rejection of useable components) to keep the stock (including concealed 'hoards') of most components at the old level.

All this again goes to show that: the right approach is just as essential to the successful conclusion of a project as a sound knowledge of analysis and arithmetic. Although equally necessary, expert knowledge in the narrower sense is in itself no guarantee of success.

An investigation into systems of production and inventory control usually leads to changes involving reorganization. That being so it should be borne in mind that mastering the different methods of reorganization is an art in itself. Although much has already been written on the subject we feel that a whole chapter of this book is required to discuss the approach to the problem. Our reasons are:
— that any book on production and inventory control which failed to mention the approach would lack one of its most essential elements;
— that we would not feel justified in merely referring the reader to other sources.

At the same time we have attempted to summarize the views of some other writers together with our own experience of these matters in the present chapter.

35.2 What is really meant by 'the right approach'?

The phrase 'the right approach' may seem self-explanatory at first glance, but what are in fact the essential features of such an approach? Can we make do with a simple list of things to be done, in chronological order? Or should we be more concerned with the methods the investigator is to employ than with precisely what he should measure, analyse or calculate? Is it not more important for the investigator to have the full support of the management than the best possible information as to costs? As we have seen the actual investigation often involves some form of reorganization. Not only the literature but also our own experience and that of others lead to the conclusion that the right approach is a matter of complying with certain fundamental conditions. Failing this all other directives as to the technical aspects of planning are pointless. The prime conditions are discussed in paragraph 35.4. Particulars of the technical aspects of the approach, of importance only in the secondary phase, follow in paragraph 35.5. In anticipation of paragraph 35.4 it can already be said that the most important of the fundamental conditions for success must be: genuine interest, support and drive on the part of the factory management. Therefore we can refer to the right approach in two different senses, namely:

— in the sense that those concerned are inspired to offer positive co-operation;
— in the sense of a sound approach to the technical aspects of the planning problem.

The following example may serve to illustrate how relative the concept of 'the right approach' can sometimes be, particularly in the latter sense. In the course of a lecture given in 1965, Leavitt [Le 1] conjured up a convincing image of a manager who invited three different firms of consultants to carry out a preliminary investigation in a factory whose financial results in the past year had been

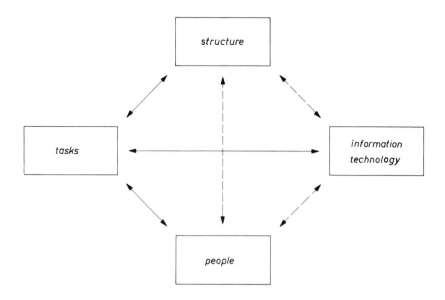

Fig. 99 Interaction postulated by Leavitt.

disappointing. It happened that each of these firms specialized in a particular approach, that is a specific way of looking at a problem.

The first of these consultancies, having recruited most of its staff from big companies, talked mainly in terms of structure and was mainly concerned with changing this; it spoke of organization per product rather than per operation, of increasing decentralization, better job description and so on.

The second firm, employing mainly psychologists, wanted to start indoctrinating and training the factory staff at a conference centre.

The third, whose people were mainly quantitatively inclined, talked mostly about control systems and information processing techniques and wanted to introduce different methods of calculation involving computers.

Leavitt then used the diagram reproduced in Fig. 99 to demonstrate that the concept of separate specialisms is false and that, in fact, modern large-scale organizations generally involve four highly interdependent subelements, namely:

— the tasks of the organization;
— its structure;
— its people;
— its 'information technology'.

The moral of this story is that premature and overenthusiastic commitment to any one aspect of a problem (for instance methods of production and inventory control) should be avoided and that instead the relationship between the above elements should be borne in mind not only at the outset but throughout the remainder of the investigation as well.

As we said earlier various authors have dealt with the actual processes of analysis and reorganization, but the difference in their technical background sometimes causes them to lay stress on different aspects of the matter.

For instance Magee (1958) includes a chapter on 'Design of a production control system' in his book 'Production planning and inventory control', Ackoff and Sasieni [Ac 2] devote more than one chapter to the approach to the problem, and Morse and Kimball deal with the same subject in the first and last chapters of 'Methods of operations research' (1950). Part III of Verburg's 'Organisation and organisation research' [Ve 3] is devoted exclusively to the planning and imple-mentation of organizational research and includes a section on 'The introduction of changes'; see also for instance, Oldendorff's 'Co-operation in the factory' [Ol 1]. Last but not least a summary of particular interest from our point of view was given by Marx [Ma 4], the following discussion is based entirely on what he had to say in his lecture.

Reorganization can be approached in different ways, that is referring to 'the right approach' in the first sense of leading to positive co-operation. Marx begins by finding out the conditions best suited to each approach and what effect each may be expected to have. In the main he adopts Leavitt's classification and terminology and subscribes to the views of Bakke and McGregor.

An organization may be defined as a combination of people and physical resources for a specific purpose. It therefore embraces what may be called the 'human element' (people individually and in groups large or small) and the '(physical) resources element' (resources including plant and production methods covering the whole range of organizational procedures).

These two elements interact. Summed up very briefly, Marx has the follow-ing to say.

An organization involves two distinct processes:

a. an attempt to so influence people individually and in groups that they behave in accordance with the aims of the organization;

b. efforts by the people individually and in groups to realize their own personal aims, that is to achieve self-realization in the widest sense.

With the organization actually at work these two processes merge into a new one, namely the 'fusion process'. Marx attempts to distinguish between the different methods of reorganization according to their effects upon the process of fusion, as follows.

The structural approach is directed towards changing the social structure of the organization through task redistribution, by defining hierarchical relationships, establishing channels of communication and so on.

The technological approach aims to restructure the technical aspects of processes requiring reorganization, by introducing aids which are predominantly technical in themselves, for example methods engineering and computers. A common feature of the technological and structural approaches is that both propose to alter the 'resources element'. This does not necessarily mean that the 'human element' is ignored, but does imply that no active or creative contribution by the staff is envisaged beforehand. The object of the 'human element' type of approach is to transform the organization by modifying the behaviour and attitudes of the people in it. Within this particular category a further distinction can be made between:

— training methods, that is training according to the conference system, designed to change the bias, or attitudes of people; here success depends amongst other things on there being no matters in any way difficult to grasp which have to be carried over to the resources sector.

— process methods ('clinical methods') aimed at both elements (human and resources) and therefore at the 'fusion process' itself. Training is through active participation in changing the resources element and therefore fosters the most intensive co-operation between all concerned throughout all phases of the project.

The following passage is quoted literally:

'The secondary effects or aims in view, pursued by specific methods, are often formulated in terms of the elimination or avoidance of certain obstacles or shortcomings contrary to the fulfilment of the task which the organisation has set itself. Here the goal of the re-organisation may perhaps be described as presenting a task of a certain size, or having a certain "task dimension".

A given impasse can still be approached by a variety of methods, at any rate provided that the only real distinction between these lies in their primary effect. For example, an executive in an organisation proves absentminded from time to time, with various ill effects upon the organisation. He can perhaps remedy this by using a notebook, which represents the technological approach. However, a possible alternative solution is for him to engage a secretary, who may or may not keep a register of appointments; so much for the structural approach.

A third alternative is to discuss more thoroughly with the executive just what matters of business he tends to be absentminded about. It may then emerge that he forgets some things and not others, also perhaps that what he forgets are those tasks which he cannot readily accept as part of his duties. Given a fresh view of the matter he could conceivably adopt a different attitude towards the work he has found oppressive and so reduce his forgetfulness, possibly by using a notebook or engaging a secretary as well (process method).

This example therefore illustrates the fact that despite the appreciable difference in their primary effects all the various methods of reorganization are alternatives for the elimination of the same impasse. To put this more generally: the mere formulation of reorganisational aims in terms of the task dimension is not in itself an adequate basis for deciding between the different methods of reorganisation judged by their primary effects.

Before a valid choice can be made the secondary effects envisaged will have to be defined in terms of another dimension. Having called our first the task dimension, we shall call the second the $X-Y$, or integrative dimension for reasons which will shortly be apparent'.

The X-point on line XY denotes a minor, and the Y-point a major degree of integration between the processes earlier designated a and b. If the fusion process involves inherent change, this can be represented by displacement along the XY line.

The actual scope of the different approaches can now be defined as follows:

— the process approach tends mainly to change the nature of the fusion process, namely towards the Y-point, as also does the training method;
— the structural and technological approaches are more appropriate where the only change considered necessary is in the resources component;
— but a note of warning: the further an organization proceeds towards Y, the more risk there is that the staff will become frustrated by a unilateral structural and technological approach after having expected to play an active part in the reorganization.

The conclusions to be drawn from all this are that:

— the initial phase of the investigation, during which the actual method of reorganization has to be decided, should be fairly broadly based so that the situation existing in the factory concerned can be properly defined;

— if a typical 'human approach' proves necessary the planning consultant concerned should not hesitate to seek the advice of a colleague trained in the social sciences if need be.

35.3 Project analysis in terms of decision levels

Building on Marx's terminology we can now classify the projects in terms of the task dimension. These then fall into two distinct categories, albeit that the second one must at once be subdivided as between two different cases.

Category one embraces: the permanent (once-and-for-all) solution of an isolated problem, usually as a result of a unique decision taken at a high managerial level. (Note: this decision is unique only to the person making it, since the consultant may well be accustomed to studying similar decisions as a matter of routine.)

The following examples are worth mentioning:

— deciding the optimum number and/or location of factories;
— calculating the profit-earning capacity of high-cost production plant;
— deciding whether or not to deliver from stock.

Projects of this kind will be mainly a matter for the specialists themselves. They will try to bring their combined knowledge to bear upon the problem, using complex tools such as computers where necessary. Certain phases of the final solution will only be fully understood by the specialists. Intricate relationships can be integrated in the mathematical model employed. At the same time the information supplied and the answer obtained must be clear and explicit. The client is usually more interested in the actual result and in the starting points selected than in the methods of arriving at a solution, although in most cases he will require to be told in simple terms just what these methods involve.

Yet it is essential for the client to have confidence in quantitative methods generally and in the consultant in particular, even though he often has to make the final decision himself. As a final comment on projects of this kind it is worth mentioning that quantitative analysis is intended to assist the decision maker and to improve on the existing procedure without in any way superseding this. Much of the information employed will have to be collected by the specialists themselves.

The second of our two categories covers the formulation of decision rules for subsequent large-scale implementation at subordinate levels, for instance:

— ordering instructions;
— rules for establishing stock norms;
— priority rules in job shops;
— planning throughput schedule for production orders;
— forecasting short-term usage.

A basic distinction must also be made between those cases in which the decision rules have to be wielded so to speak 'manually' and those in which these rules are embodied in a computer programme.

Here it is rarely the client himself who has to apply the new decision rules and procedures but his personnel, and here also, rather than in the first category, the new rules do tend to supersede those previously employed.

The less accustomed the client has been to system, to mathematical approximation and to computers, the more necessary it will be to adopt some form of 'process approach', whilst the future user will have to be involved from the outset in all such cases. Only with his active co-operation from the beginning can there be any reasonable hope of his acquiring enough confidence in the established decision rules to adopt and employ them in due course in place of the old familiar procedures. It is typical of the specialist in this situation that although of course giving full rein to his own insight and vision he exercises a good deal of self-discipline regarding the methods of calculation and the aids he employs. Because new rules often have to be introduced by stages the specialist tends to feel that time is being wasted.

In fact as the first step it is often necessary for the particular executive body to put its existing affairs in order without, at this stage, any sign of optimalization. Specialists often overlook the fact that proper control of the flow of goods cannot be achieved without reliable measurements. A well-organized initial (goods inwards) inspection, accurate stock administration, a thorough grasp of costs coupled with a knowledge of the plant idiosyncracies and the skills of the labour force are more important in the initial stages of an investigation than familiarity with difficult calculation techniques from operational research. Deliberate analysis and complete mastery of these apparently simple aspects is an essential but alas often neglected step and one which the future user ultimately has to take for himself, albeit with the encouragement and assistance of the specialist.

This again goes to show that although the general approach to problems can be suggested, the type of project often has to be established first.

35.4 Recommendations

Let us begin by discussing a few points of a more general nature, all the more important in as much as the investigation itself is bound to change the form of co-operation between people in the company concerned. For the most part these points are more crucial in cases belonging to the second than to those in the first of the above categories.

Active interest and support on the part of the company management

Unless the company management is genuinely convinced of the need for investigation and the possible introduction of a new system, the project will probably fail or at best produce some rather illusory short-term benefits. To the planning specialist this means two things:

— that in the absence of managerial support his first concern must be to try to secure it. With this in view he may have to begin, for instance, with those problems in which the management *are* interested in order to create the necessary confidence. Having done so he may be able to carry out a small-scale test in some section of the company or department where he is assured of at least local co-operation;

— that if he fails to secure genuine support from the management even after repeated attempts he should not put any more time or thought into the project since this would be mere waste of effort.

Initiating the future users

Those who will shortly be called upon to implement the new system will have to be drawn into the work at an early stage. They can assist with the analysis and in designing the new system by helping to decide such matters as the layout of forms and so forth. This alone will enable them to become accustomed to and acquire confidence in the new procedures.

Taking the abilities of the administrative staff into account

The system should be planned with due regard to the capabilities of the administrative staff who will ultimately be available. A relatively uncomplicated ordering rule actually enforced is always vastly preferable to one which, although shrewdly framed, is either misapplied or ignored altogether (see for instance the lot-size instruction in paragraph 31.2); this point cannot be overstressed. Hence the need to ensure above all that the staff receive the necessary information regularly and understand this fully.

Nature of the project

Because the exact nature of the project has so important a bearing on the approach to this, it should be determined as soon as possible. Is the company already accustomed to a particular system and merely seeking to refine this? Or is the idea of systematic procedures still entirely foreign to most of the staff? In the latter event very much more attention will have to be given to initiating and training not only the future administrative staff, but everyone else concerned as well.

Understanding the existing system

Unless the existing system is fully understood any transfer from this to a new system inevitably involves a considerable risk. Without such understanding it becomes impossible to explain in terms of the current situation just how the new one is to be achieved. Moreover we need to know whether the existing situation involves any disturbing influences which may cause the proposed new system to fail.

35.5 Recommendations concerning the technical aspects of the approach

35.5.1 Phases of an investigation

An investigation can be phased in various ways; see for instance Marx, Verburg, Van der Burg and Ackoff. The following arrangement seems best suited to this book:

a. introduction and orientation;
b. formulation of the problem;
c. construction of a (mathematical) model and systematic collection of data required for this;
d. deciding upon a solution, that is deciding the most suitable form of organization, ordering system and associated procedures, together with the information flow;
e. testing the solution;
f. introducing the new work method;
g. monitoring the system introduced.

Although inherently distinct, these phases are not always chronologically so, since it is often necessary to switch back and forth between them. For instance it may emerge in constructing the model that the original formulation was not strictly correct. As mentioned earlier, phase *ii* sometimes has to be followed by another, perhaps most aptly described as: 'putting existing affairs in order'. Putting the solution to the test may reveal errors which necessitate partial repetition of an earlier phase, and so on.

Finally, as we have seen, the ultimate objective of all the earlier stages must be the introduction of the proposed new system.

35.5.2 Step-by-step approach

If the project concerns a company with several departments, some parallel and others so to speak in series, and making many different products it is always difficult to know precisely how and where to begin.

The initial stage of introduction and orientation should usually be planned on a fairly broad basis. That being so, however, the terms of reference are best limited as soon as possible, in the initial phase as well as later. The first essential of many company problems is not so much optimum efficiency as manageability, sometimes coupled with stability. To draw a parallel: there is not much point in discussing the m.p.g. of a car as long as its brakes remain faulty, its steering loose and its windscreen clouded.

In the first instance company problems are often seen as a matter of learning to understand the process, defining measuring points and establishing simple controls. Only after all this has been accomplished is it possible to arouse any interest in aiming at the optimum (see also paragraph 28.1 'Control'). A perennially difficult question in defining the problem is: how far is this susceptible to examination as a complete picture? Our ultimate objective is of course to optimize the entire system. Failing any direct route to this target we must begin by studying, optimalizing and establishing control over a fraction of the whole and while doing so, we must keep this target in mind.

In any case it is advisable to begin with a part of the problem simply because:

i. to grasp the whole we must first understand the function of its parts;
ii. the whole is often impossible to control without knowing how to guide the individual links;
iii. in so doing some results emerge relatively soon (most important to the introduction of new techniques);
iv. any other course frequently involves being passed from pillar to post in as much as every member of an organization invariably sees errors introduced by others before or after him.

Not until the system does finally come to be studied as a whole do the essential problems of the company management begin to emerge, for instance the 'Forrester effect'.

The following questions now remain: what and approximately how large a part should be selected for initial study? The size depends mainly upon:

— how accustomed to system the company already is;
— the accumulated experience of the investigator(s).

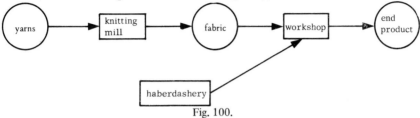

Fig. 100.

Suppose for instance that the project is to design a production and inventory control system for a clothing company comprising a knitting mill and a ready-made clothing workshop. There are intermediate stocks of yarns, knitted fabrics, haberdashery and end products (Fig. 100).

It will probably be best to study the stock of end products only taking into consideration the production control of the workshop. Moreover if the stock items are also divided on the ABC principle a specific system can first be introduced for group B alone if so desired. The root problems of capacity balancing and manufacture of knitted fabrics do not come into this.

In many cases it is logical to work from back (end product) to front (raw material). System and order are then imposed retrogressively beginning with the ultimate demand.

If the existing situation is too unreliable it will still be necessary to remedy matters by working forward first.

Another situation in which it is advisable to begin at the beginning is where the process is based on just a few raw materials subject to inadequate inventory control.

However, it may also be that, for instance, a department midway along the chain of operations constitutes a serious bottleneck owing to its capacity being both expensive and limited. That being so it may be best to begin at the trouble spot (for example a stoving process in a large oven) provided that the operations beyond this do not present any major problems.

Experience has shown that it is seldom possible to consider all the products and departments collectively and then introduce not only a new system, but a new organization structure and new procedures as well. On the other hand we must repeat our earlier maxim to the effect that: despite beginning with a part, one must never lose sight of the very much larger picture as a whole.

Nor should it be forgotten that production and inventory control is only one aspect of the activities in a department, albeit usually closely linked with others such as cost-price calculation, wages, etc. It should therefore be borne in mind that the information flow, for example, not only activates planning, but has one or two other functions as well; hence one cannot with impunity discontinue or modify this flow without knowing precisely what those other functions are. A general idea of them can be obtained from an input—output analysis of information per department; this need only cover the main flows, since detailed analysis is unnecessary.

Again it is almost impossible to say how much time will be required to complete a particular project. The governing factors are: the flexibility of the existing organization and its staff, the number of stock items, the number of closed groups of operations and the quality of the existing system.

35.5.3 *Appointment of steering committee and work group*

A useful version of the 'process approach' is the setting up of a steering committee and a work group. The work group should include those people who will have to perform the tasks involved in the various phases, as well as at least one person who will continue to bear responsibility for the success of the new system after the investigation is completed. The membership of a work group often ranges from two to six, with the possible assistance of specialists in analysis and processing. A steering committee meeting jointly with the work group, for instance once a month, advises the latter on policy matters, receives progress reports and sees that the group is supplied with whatever information and capacity it needs. Magee rightly warns against any undue formality in arranging such meetings since this would take up too much of the work group's time. The steering committee membership should of course include the heads of the company departments concerned; it must not be allowed to become a consortium of super-specialists.

35.5.4 *Preliminary research; introduction and orientation*

An initial introduction, designed to make the investigators acquainted with the personnel, is followed by a tentative preliminary investigation. This is planned on a fairly broad basis, but without going into any detail whatever. For instance although the investigator will ask whether any conversion costs have been incurred, and if so whether particulars of them are available, he will not attempt to analyse the data during this phase. Instead he will simply try to get some idea of the order of size of these costs, say, by asking whether the process of resetting a particular oven to a different temperature takes a matter of minutes, hours, days or weeks.

The object of the preliminary research may be summarized as being: to analyse the processes with a view to the provisional objective of the investigation.

This involves the following activities:

— define the form of organization and the membership of the group, make a rough estimate of the job distribution;
— describe the existing production and distribution system ('hardware' and 'software';
— describe the demand for the products;
— define the principal types of costs involved and establish their order of size;
— describe the effect of the existing system in terms of one or two characteristic quantities.

To obtain the information needed to describe the 'hardware' (products and production equipment) certain questions have to be posed, for instance:

— what products are sold or delivered? Prepare a provisional ABC analysis of the assortment from a few different points of view (turnover, capacity involved), for instance by taking a small sample;
— how is the plant constituted?
— what is the process layout of the products?
— what is purchased, and where?
— where are the stocks located?

Questions which need answering in order to describe the 'software' (information flow, decision rules) are:

— who decides when to order, how much to order and the production level. On the basis of what information? How often?
— are there any specific contracts with suppliers?
— is there a formal forecast of demand? If so who prepares this, how often and on what information?

Bear in mind that there is often a considerable difference between allegation and fact. The investigator must try to compensate for such discrepancies through personal observation and deduction. This sometimes tends to make the investigation rather like something out of a detective story. For example: At first glance the flow of goods from initial inspection to the materials store seems inexplicably irregular, but subsequent investigation reveals that because the inventory is taken at the end of the month the chief storekeeper is wont to hold down his total stock towards this time by informal contacts with the inspection department; the arrangement is that the goods are retained for inspection rather longer than usual so that they are not booked in until the first of next month.

Again it is sometimes found that orders actually received, for instance on the third of September, have been booked in as of the last day of August, the reason being that sales during the latter month fell short of the quota and the sales force were nevertheless anxious to show the management 'good' figures in the monthly review.

The following anecdote is also typical.

The existing situation in a large firm of manufacturing chemists was investigated. During interviews the company management and the chief planners claimed to employ the following system. At quarterly meetings attended by the production manager and the different district sales managers a list was produced showing the quantities of each item to be made and sold. These figures were then used to calculate re-order levels and lot sizes after which production was controlled according to a kind of (B, Q) system. But after a superficial examination of the figures the investigators came to the conclusion that the total storage tank capacity available could not possibly accommodate the stock which would have had to be maintained according to the alleged system. Brief conversations with the personnel directly concerned then revealed the explanation. The actual production orders were issued by the charge-hand, who invariably disposed of the official orders by putting them in his desk drawer with the comment 'all that is just head office theory'. His system was to ride past all the storage tanks on his bicycle every morning, note any that were nearly empty and order whatever product they contained to be made the same day!

Precise information as to the real demand is difficult to obtain. In this phase a small sample can be used to define the demand for specific items. It is important to understand the nature of the clientele. Are there many customers or few? Are these manufacturers, retailers, wholesalers or consumers? Is the demand liable to fall off abruptly? Is there a good deal of stock in the pipeline from the end stock of the company investigated to the ultimate consumer? In the main, stocks can be classified as those which are and those which are not affected by decisions within the realm of production and inventory control.

In order to express the results of the existing system in terms of just a few characteristic quantities the investigator will have to ask such questions as:

— how much money is invested in inventory?
— are the stocks properly balanced? In some stores for example a frequency distribution of the quantity

$$\frac{\text{existing stock (or backlog, if any)}}{\text{average monthly usage}}$$

can be sketched for a sample covering all the stock items. Again the observed values of this ratio can be plotted against the average monthly usage.

— what are the throughput times of the production process (mean and variability)?
— what are the lead times for the consumers of the end product?
— how many items are out of stock?
— how many part-deliveries have been sent to customers?
— how much output has been lost owing to lack of materials or components?

One can always enquire into the purpose of the existing stock. Or in other words what would the consequences be if there were no such stock? Try to find out how serious these consequences already are.

The preliminary enquiries must be searching enough to give the team a thorough grasp of the existing system and enable them to evaluate throughput times, lead time and stocks quantitatively, at any rate as to order of size.

Inexperienced investigators tend to make the mistake of seeking a solution before they fully understand the existing situation. As Magee very rightly says:

'Until the team does understand the existing system, it is not in a good position to suggest modifications, since lack of understanding of the existing system and of its impact on operations may imply either that the team has not spotted certain essential characteristics of the operations or that there are decisions being made in some hidden way which they have not yet ferreted out. These decisions may continue to be made under a new system in a way which might wreck its effectiveness.'

Moreover the company staff will be more inclined to trust someone who knows and fully understands their existing problems.

To sum up, what is needed is a deliberate choice of strategy as regards the depth of the investigation.

Aspects revealed by the ideal approach are:

i. aims;
ii. problems;
iii. facts;
iv. programme for improvement;
v. results.

Improvement programmes are all too often begun without full knowledge of the facts or even of the problems, let alone adequate understanding of the objectives in view within the group concerned. Small wonder, then, that a strategy covering points *iv* and *v* alone would be virtually pointless.

35.5.5 Defining the problem

The very first thing to ascertain is whether the existing system is or is not under proper control. If not, a number of measuring points will have to be established with which to bring the system under control. This bringing under control is often more difficult and time consuming than the subsequent process of optimalization. With one already accomplished we can begin to think about the other. The question then is: how to define the aims and boundary conditions of the system? This definition must provide an unambiguous basis for the subsequent formulation of decision rules for use at various levels and might be worded for instance as follows: 98% of all customer orders must be filled within fourteen days; subject to this stipulation the total costs must be kept to a minimum, but without any staff dismissals. Or alternatively: the capital investment in stock must be reduced by 10% at the least possible extra cost and without altering the times of delivery to the customer.

It is really a matter of ascertaining managerial policy, aims and limiting conditions. The question is what precisely does the particular company have in view?

Does it want to minimize costs or perhaps aim for maximum safety? Is it trying to achieve a certain 'standing' or in other words to create a specific reputation or 'image' of reliability? These last factors, inherently subjective and difficult to evaluate, often dictate the final solution.

35.5.6 Constructing the model and collecting data

Our earlier warning against making the system either too unwieldy or too complicated is particularly apt in this phase. Young investigators are somewhat prone to flaunt their knowledge unduly, for instance by planning courses for the ultimate implementors of the system to include attempted explanations of far too much difficult theoretical background material. Because the inherent risks of such behaviour have already been strikingly illustrated by other writers, we feel that two particularly apt quotations will suffice: referring to operational research activities during the Second World War, Rivett [Ri 1] says that:

It is probably true that had the work not been carried out by leading scientists with the whole weight and status of their experience behind them, the consumer would have received the advice with scepticism. It takes a great deal of courage to produce a short simple solution to a management problem. More important, had this early work been carried out by more junior scientists I doubt very much whether they would have arrived at the simple sweeping solutions which were derived by the Blacketts and Williams; and even had they done so, I am quite sure that they would never have been listened to.

And in 1960 Hurni [Hu 1] then manager of General Electric's 'Operations Research and Synthesis Consulting Service', wrote that:

... for the foreseeable future, most industrial businesses will be pretty much constituted as they are now. They will be loosely coupled systems in which many people will continue to play a major role in sensing, deciding, regulating, adjusting and innovating. They will, moreover, have legitimate authority and responsibility for doing so.

My point is that if business research is to have real and growing impact in such businesses, it must be by and through these people. It must be shown to aid them in *their* reasoning processes. Developing the use of applied business research is *not merely doing research*, but it involves a peculiar form of teaching since people are involved. This teaching takes the form of doing research on the gross or fundamental situations first, so that people can reason more effectively about them. More detailed research work may come later.

The actual construction of the mathematical model will have to be based upon the aims and limiting conditions discussed in 35.5e. There will probably be a number of possible alternative solutions, each with its own mathematical model. Optimum values can be established for the parameters within the particular model. As we have seen it may emerge from the calculation just how accurate the necessary cost data will have to be. Given the most suitable solution we also know what decisions this will involve and what information (namely, what forecasts) will be needed for them.

35.5.7 Testing the solution

The points of departure will have to be tested or, failing this, at least the solution itself. The methods of doing so are:

a. Recapitulation. What would have happened had a different method been employed?
b. Monte Carlo; what might have happened instead.
c. Shadow system; in other words the old system is retained in the company but operated side by side with a new system feigning the same course of events.

   The advantages of this method are that it enables:

   i. the superiority of the new system to be demonstrated to the staff in order to convince them;
   ii. possible rough edges to be detected and removed;
   iii. the staff to be trained simultaneously for the new system.

   On the other hand the drawback is that it is a long time before a valid comparison can be made. Also such comparison is often made more difficult by major discrepancies occurring very soon between the real and shadow situations. For instance: a machine breaks down owing to component failure. Would this failure also have occurred had the shadow planning been real?

d. Partial implementation. The danger of this is that it involves actually using two systems side by side with the likelihood that the staff through preferring the old system will give no chance to the new. Moreover the situation does not always permit both systems to be used simultaneously. When the Swedes went over to left-hand drive this could not be introduced gradually by shifting transport vehicles to the right-hand side of the road first and private cars a week later!

36 Simulation as a method of investigation and training

The term simulation as employed in this book means: the step-by-step imitation of an inventory and/or production pattern such as might be encountered in reality.

Simulation can be used as a method of exploratory calculation. In certain situations where no effective analytical method is available for calculating the optimum combination of values of s and Q, this optimum can be established by simulation.

Another form of investigation worth mentioning is: simulation as applied to the phase 'testing' of a project to ascertain whether a predetermined solution will produce satisfactory results. Alternatively simulation can also be used as a training technique, in which case the decisions are taken by a person without the aid of fixed rules, instead of by a computer. This is what is called an inventory game or an ordering game, the two constituting a special category of business game (see for instance Greene and Sisson [Gr 1], Prins [Pr 1] (1966)).

How the games used in training are actually played depends on whether the training is intended to be general (for instance a general planning course) or specific, as part of the programme for introducing a given ordering system in a particular company.

Space does not permit us to go any further into the different methods of simulation, which is already beginning to emerge as a subject in itself with its own specialized literature; see for instance Tocher [To 1] and Kosten [Ko 1] (1963).

36 Simulation as a method of investigation and training

Appendices

Appendix 1
THE NORMAL DISTRIBUTION

$\dfrac{x-\mu}{\sigma}$ (a)	Ordinate (y')	Area between μ and $\mu + a\sigma$ or μ and $\mu - a\sigma$	$\dfrac{x-\mu}{\sigma}$ (a)	Ordinate (y')	Area between μ and $\mu + a\sigma$ or μ and $\mu - a\sigma$
0·00	0·399	0·000	1·60	0·111	0·445
0·05	0·398	0·020	1·65	0·102	0·450
0·10	0·397	0·040	1·70	0·094	0·455
0·15	0·394	0·060	1·75	0·086	0·460
0·20	0·391	0·079	1·80	0·079	0·464
0·25	0·387	0·099	1·85	0·072	0·468
0·30	0·381	0·118	1·90	0·066	0·471
0·35	0·375	0·137	1·95	0·060	0·474
0·40	0·368	0·155	2·00	0·054	0·477
0·45	0·361	0·174	2·05	0·049	0·480
0·50	0·352	0·191	2·10	0·044	0·482
0·55	0·343	0·209	2·15	0·040	0·484
0·60	0·333	0·226	2·20	0·036	0·486
0·65	0·323	0·242	2·25	0·032	0·488
0·70	0·312	0·258	2·30	0·028	0·489
0·75	0·301	0·273	2·35	0·025	0·491
0·80	0·290	0·288	2·40	0·022	0·492
0·85	0·278	0·302	2·45	0·020	0·493
0·90	0·266	0·316	2·50	0·018	0·494
0·95	0·254	0·329	2·55	0·015	0·495
1·00	0·242	0·341	2·60	0·014	0·495
1·05	0·230	0·353	2·65	0·012	0·496
1·10	0·218	0·364	2·70	0·010	0·496
1·15	0·206	0·375	2·75	0·009	0·497
1·20	0·194	0·385	2·80	0·008	0·497
1·25	0·183	0·394	2·85	0·007	0·498
1·30	0·171	0·403	2·90	0·006	0·498
1·35	0·160	0·411	2·95	0·005	0·498
1·40	0·150	0·419	3·00	0·004	0·4986
1·45	0·139	0·426	3·25	0·003	0·4994
1·50	0·130	0·433	3·50	0·002	0·4998
1·55	0·120	0·439			

Appendix 2
POISSON DISTRIBUTION $P(x \leqslant k)$

m \ k	0	1	2	3	4	5	6	7	8	9	10	11	12	13	14	15	16	17	18	19	20	21	22
0·05	0·951	0·999	1·000																				
0·10	0·905	0·995	1·000																				
0·15	0·861	0·990	0·999	1·000																			
0·20	0·819	0·982	0·999	1·000																			
0·25	0·779	0·974	0·998	1·000																			
0·30	0·741	0·963	0·996	1·000																			
0·35	0·705	0·951	0·994	1·000																			
0·40	0·670	0·938	0·992	0·999	1·000																		
0·45	0·638	0·925	0·989	0·999	1·000																		
0·50	0·607	0·910	0·986	0·998	1·000																		
0·55	0·577	0·894	0·982	0·998	1·000																		
0·60	0·549	0·878	0·977	0·997	1·000																		
0·65	0·522	0·861	0·972	0·996	0·999	1·000																	
0·70	0·497	0·844	0·966	0·994	0·999	1·000																	
0·75	0·472	0·827	0·959	0·993	0·999	1·000																	
0·80	0·449	0·809	0·953	0·991	0·999	1·000																	
0·85	0·427	0·791	0·945	0·989	0·998	1·000																	
0·90	0·407	0·772	0·937	0·987	0·998	1·000																	
0·95	0·387	0·754	0·929	0·984	0·997	1·000																	
1·00	0·368	0·736	0·920	0·981	0·996	0·999	1·000																
1·1	0·333	0·699	0·900	0·974	0·995	0·999	1·000																
1·2	0·301	0·663	0·879	0·966	0·992	0·998	1·000																
1·3	0·273	0·627	0·857	0·957	0·989	0·998	1·000																
1·4	0·247	0·592	0·833	0·946	0·986	0·997	0·999	1·000															
1·5	0·223	0·558	0·809	0·934	0·981	0·996	0·999	1·000															
1·6	0·202	0·525	0·783	0·921	0·976	0·994	0·999	1·000															
1·7	0·183	0·493	0·757	0·907	0·970	0·992	0·998	1·000															
1·8	0·165	0·463	0·731	0·891	0·964	0·990	0·997	0·999	1·000														
1·9	0·150	0·434	0·704	0·875	0·956	0·987	0·997	0·999	1·000														
2·0	0·135	0·406	0·677	0·857	0·947	0·983	0·995	0·999	1·000														
2·2	0·111	0·355	0·623	0·819	0·928	0·975	0·993	0·998	1·000														
2·4	0·091	0·308	0·570	0·779	0·904	0·964	0·988	0·997	0·999	1·000													
2·6	0·074	0·267	0·518	0·736	0·877	0·951	0·983	0·995	0·999	1·000													
2·8	0·061	0·231	0·469	0·692	0·848	0·935	0·976	0·992	0·998	0·999	1·000												
3·0	0·050	0·199	0·423	0·647	0·815	0·916	0·966	0·988	0·996	0·999	1·000												
3·2	0·041	0·171	0·380	0·603	0·781	0·895	0·955	0·983	0·994	0·998	1·000												
3·4	0·033	0·147	0·340	0·558	0·744	0·871	0·942	0·977	0·992	0·997	0·999	1·000											
3·6	0·027	0·126	0·303	0·515	0·706	0·844	0·927	0·969	0·988	0·996	0·999	1·000											
3·8	0·022	0·107	0·269	0·473	0·668	0·816	0·909	0·960	0·984	0·994	0·998	0·999	1·000										
4·0	0·018	0·092	0·238	0·433	0·629	0·785	0·889	0·949	0·979	0·992	0·997	0·999	1·000										
4·5	0·011	0·061	0·174	0·342	0·532	0·703	0·831	0·913	0·960	0·983	0·993	0·998	0·999	1·000									
5·0	0·007	0·040	0·125	0·265	0·440	0·616	0·762	0·867	0·932	0·968	0·986	0·995	0·998	0·999	1·000								
5·5	0·004	0·027	0·088	0·201	0·358	0·529	0·686	0·810	0·894	0·946	0·975	0·989	0·996	0·998	0·999	1·000							
6·0	0·002	0·017	0·062	0·151	0·285	0·446	0·606	0·744	0·847	0·916	0·957	0·980	0·991	0·996	0·999	0·999	1·000						
6·5	0·002	0·011	0·043	0·112	0·224	0·370	0·527	0·673	0·792	0·877	0·933	0·966	0·984	0·993	0·997	0·999	1·000						
7·0	0·001	0·007	0·030	0·082	0·173	0·301	0·450	0·599	0·729	0·830	0·901	0·947	0·973	0·987	0·994	0·998	0·999	1·000					
7·5	0·001	0·005	0·020	0·059	0·133	0·242	0·379	0·525	0·662	0·777	0·863	0·921	0·958	0·978	0·990	0·996	0·998	0·999	1·000				
8·0	0·000	0·003	0·014	0·042	0·100	0·191	0·313	0·453	0·593	0·717	0·816	0·888	0·936	0·966	0·983	0·992	0·996	0·998	0·999	1·000			
8·5	0·000	0·002	0·009	0·030	0·074	0·150	0·256	0·386	0·523	0·653	0·763	0·849	0·909	0·949	0·973	0·986	0·993	0·997	0·999	0·999	1·000		
9·0	0·000	0·001	0·006	0·021	0·055	0·116	0·207	0·324	0·456	0·587	0·706	0·803	0·876	0·926	0·959	0·978	0·989	0·995	0·998	0·999	1·000		
9·5	0·000	0·001	0·004	0·015	0·040	0·089	0·165	0·269	0·392	0·522	0·645	0·752	0·836	0·898	0·940	0·967	0·982	0·991	0·996	0·998	0·999	1·000	
10·0	0·000	0·000	0·003	0·010	0·029	0·067	0·130	0·220	0·333	0·458	0·583	0·697	0·792	0·864	0·917	0·951	0·973	0·986	0·993	0·997	0·998	0·999	1·000

$$P = \sum_{i=0}^{k} \frac{m^i}{i!} e^{-m}$$

Appendix 3

TABLE OF POWERS OF e

x	e^{-x}	x	e^{-x}	x	e^{-x}
0·00	1·000000				
0·05	0·951229	2·05	0·128735	4·05	0·017422
0·10	0·904837	2·10	0·122456	4·10	0·016573
0·15	0·860708	2·15	0·116484	4·15	0·015764
0·20	0·818731	2·20	0·110803	4·20	0·014996
0·25	0·778801	2·25	0·105399	4·25	0·014264
0·30	0·740818	2·30	0·100259	4·30	0·013569
0·35	0·704688	2·35	0·095369	4·35	0·012907
0·40	0·670320	2·40	0·090718	4·40	0·012277
0·45	0·637628	2·45	0·086294	4·45	0·011679
0·50	0·606531	2·50	0·082085	4·50	0·011109
0·55	0·576950	2·55	0·078082	4·55	0·010567
0·60	0·548812	2·60	0·074274	4·60	0·010052
0·65	0·522046	2·65	0·070651	4·65	0·009562
0·70	0·496585	2·70	0·067206	4·70	0·009095
0·75	0·472367	2·75	0·063928	4·75	0·008652
0·80	0·449329	2·80	0·060810	4·80	0·008230
0·85	0·427415	2·85	0·057844	4·85	0·007828
0·90	0·406570	2·90	0·055023	4·90	0·007447
0·95	0·386741	2·95	0·052340	4·95	0·007083
1·00	0·367879	3·00	0·049787	5·00	0·006738
1·05	0·349938	3·05	0·047359	5·25	0·005248
1·10	0·332871	3·10	0·045049	5·50	0·0040868
1·15	0·316637	3·15	0·042852	5·75	0·0031828
1·20	0·301194	3·20	0·040762	6·00	0·0024788
1·25	0·286505	3·25	0·038774	6·25	0·0019305
1·30	0·272532	3·30	0·036883	6·50	0·0015034
1·35	0·259240	3·35	0·035084	6·75	0·0011709
1·40	0·246597	3·40	0·033373	7·00	0·0009119
1·45	0·234570	3·45	0·031746	7·25	0·0007102
1·50	0·223130	3·50	0·030197	7·50	0·0005531
1·55	0·212248	3·55	0·028726	7·75	0·0004307
1·60	0·201897	3·60	0·027324	8·00	0·0003355
1·65	0·192050	3·65	0·025991	8·25	0·0002613
1·70	0·182684	3·70	0·024724	8·50	0·0002035
1·75	0·173774	3·75	0·023518	8·75	0·0001585
1·80	0·165299	3·80	0·022371	9·00	0·0001234
1·85	0·157237	3·85	0·021280	9·25	0·0000961
1·90	0·149569	3·90	0·020242	9·50	0·0000749
1·95	0·142274	3·95	0·019255	9·75	0·0000583
2·00	0·135335	4·00	0·018316	10·00	0·0000454

Appendix 4

PERCENTAGE POINTS OF THE χ^2-DISTRIBUTION

'Biometric tables for statisticians', Volume I of E. S. Pearson and H. O. Hartley

Q	0·995	0·990	0·975	0·950	0·900	0·750	0·500
v							
1	392704·10⁻¹⁰	157088·10⁻⁹	982069·10⁻⁸	393214·10⁻⁹	0·0157908	0·1015308	0·454937
2	0·0100251	0·0201007	0·0506356	0·102587	0·210720	0·575364	1·38629
3	0·0717212	0·114832	0·215795	0·351846	0·584375	1·212534	2·36597
4	0·206990	0·297110	0·484419	0·710721	10·63623	1·92255	3·35670
5	0·411740	0·554300	0·831211	1·145476	1·61031	2·67460	4·35146
6	0·675727	0·872085	1·23747	1·63539	2·20413	3·45460	5·34812
7	0·989265	1·239043	1·68987	2·16735	2·83311	4·25485	6·34581
8	1·344419	1·646482	2·17973	2·73264	3·48954	5·07064	7·34412
9	1·734926	2·087912	2·70039	3·32511	4·16816	5·89883	8·34283
10	2·15585	2·55821	3·24697	3·94030	4·86518	6·73720	9·34182
11	2·60321	3·05347	3·81575	4·57481	5·57779	7·58412	10·3410
12	3·07382	3·57056	4·40379	5·22603	6·30380	8·43842	11·3403
13	3·56503	4·10691	5·00874	5·89186	7·04150	9·29906	12·3398
14	4·07468	4·66043	5·62872	6·57063	7·78953	10·1653	13·3393
15	4·60094	5·22935	6·26214	7·26094	8·54675	11·0365	14·3389
16	5·14224	5·81221	6·90766	7·96164	9·31223	11·9122	15·3385
17	5·69724	6·40776	7·56418	8·67176	10·0852	12·7919	16·3381
18	6·26481	7·01491	8·23075	9·39046	10·8649	13·6753	17·3379
19	6·84398	7·63273	8·90655	10·1170	11·6509	14·5620	18·3376
20	7·43386	8·26040	9·59083	10·8508	12·4426	15·4518	19·3374
21	8·03366	8·89720	10·28293	11·5913	13·2396	16·3444	20·3372
22	8·64272	9·54249	10·9823	12·3380	14·0415	17·2396	21·3370
23	9·26042	10·19567	11·6885	13·0905	14·8479	18·1373	22·3369
24	9·88623	10·8564	12·4011	13·8484	15·6587	19·0372	23·3367
25	10·5197	11·5240	13·1197	14·6114	16·4734	19·9393	24·3366
26	11·1603	12·1981	13·8439	15·3791	17·2919	20·8434	25·3364
27	11·8076	12·8786	14·5733	16·1513	18·1138	21·7494	26·3363
28	12·4613	13·5648	15·3079	16·9279	18·9392	22·6572	27·3363
29	13·1211	14·2565	16·0471	17·7083	19·7677	23·5666	28·3362
30	13·7867	14·9535	16·7908	18·4926	20·5992	24·4776	29·3360
40	20·7065	22·1643	24·4331	26·5093	29·0505	33·6603	39·3354
50	27·9907	29·7067	32·3574	34·7642	37·6886	42·9421	49·3349
60	35·5346	37·4848	40·4817	43·1879	46·4589	52·2938	59·3347
70	43·2752	45·4418	48·7576	51·7393	55·3290	61·6983	69·3344
80	51·1720	53·5400	57·1532	60·3915	64·2778	71·1445	79·3343
90	59·1963	61·7541	65·6466	69·1260	73·2912	80·6247	89·3342
100	67·3276	70·0648	74·2219	77·9295	82·3581	90·1332	99·3341
X	−2·5758	−2·3263	−1·9600	−1·6449	−1·2816	−0·6745	0·0000

$$Q = Q(\chi^2 / v) = 1 - P(\chi^2 / v) = 2^{-1/2v}\{\Gamma(\tfrac{1}{2}v)\}^{-1} \int_{\chi^2}^{\infty} e^{-1/2x} x^{1/2v-1} \, dx$$

Conversion to the terminology of this book:

$Q = \alpha \qquad v = 2n$

Appendix 4 — continued.

Q	0·250	0·100	0·050	0·025	0·010	0·005	0·001
ν							
1	1·32330	2·70554	3·84146	5·02389	6·63490	7·87944	10·828
2	2·77259	4·60517	5·99147	7·37776	9·21034	10·5966	13·816
3	4·10835	6·25139	7·81473	9·34840	11·3449	12·8381	16·266
4	5·38527	7·77944	9·48773	11·1433	13·2767	14·8602	18·467
5	6·62568	9·23635	11·0705	12·8325	15·0863	16·7496	20·515
6	7·84080	10·6446	12·5916	14·4494	16·8119	18·5476	22·458
7	9·03715	12·0170	14·0671	16·0128	18·4753	20·2777	24·322
8	10·2188	13·3616	15·5073	17·5346	20·0902	21·9550	26·125
9	11·3887	14·6837	16·9190	19·0228	21·6660	23·3893	27·877
10	12·5489	15·9871	18·3070	20·4831	23·2093	25·1882	29·588
11	13·7007	17·2750	19·6751	21·9200	24·7250	26·7569	31·264
12	14·8454	18·5494	21·0261	23·3367	26·2170	28·2995	32·909
13	15·9839	19·8119	22·3621	24·7356	27·6883	29·8194	34·528
14	17·1170	21·0642	23·6848	26·1190	29·1413	31·3193	36·123
15	18·2451	22·3072	24·9958	27·4884	30·5779	32·8013	37·697
16	19·3688	23·5418	26·2962	28·8454	31·9999	34·2672	39·252
17	20·4887	24·7690	27·5871	30·1910	33·4087	35·7185	40·790
18	21·6049	25·9894	28·8693	31·5264	34·8053	37·1564	42·312
19	22·7178	27·2036	30·1435	32·8523	36·1908	38·5822	43·820
20	23·8277	28·4120	31·4104	34·1696	37·5662	39·9968	45·315
21	24·9348	29·6151	32·6705	35·4789	38·9321	41·4010	46·797
22	26·0393	30·8133	33·9244	36·7807	40·2894	42·7956	48·268
23	27·1413	32·0069	35·1725	38·0757	41·6384	44·1813	49·728
24	28·2412	33·1963	36·4151	39·3641	42·9798	45·5585	51·179
25	29·3389	34·3816	37·6525	40·6465	44·3141	46·9278	52·620
26	30·4345	35·5631	38·8852	41·9232	45·6417	48·2899	54·052
27	31·5284	36·7412	40·1133	43·1944	46·9630	49·6449	55·476
28	32·6205	37·9159	41·3372	44·4607	48·2782	50·9933	56·892
29	33·7109	39·0875	42·5569	45·7222	49·5879	52·3356	58·302
30	34·7998	40·2560	43·7729	46·9792	50·8922	53·6720	59·703
40	45·6160	54·8050	55·7585	59·3417	63·6907	66·7659	73·402
50	56·3336	63·1671	67·5048	71·4202	76·1539	79·4900	86·661
60	66·9814	74·3970	79·0819	83·2976	88·3794	91·9517	99·607
70	77·5766	85·5271	90·5312	95·0231	100·425	104·215	112·317
80	88·1303	96·5782	101·879	106·629	112·329	116·321	124·839
90	98·6499	107·565	113·145	118·136	124·116	128·299	137·208
100	109·141	118·498	124·342	129·561	135·807	140·169	149·449
X	+0·6745	+1·2816	+1·6449	+1·9600	+2·3263	+2·5758	+3·0902

For $\nu > 100$ take

$$\chi^2 = \nu\left\{1 - \frac{2}{9\nu} + X\sqrt{\left(\frac{2}{9\nu}\right)}\right\}^3 \quad \text{or} \quad \chi^2 = \tfrac{1}{2}\{N + \sqrt{(2\nu - 1)}\}^2,$$

according to the degree of accuracy required. X is the standardized normal deviate corresponding to $P = 1 - Q$, and is shown in the bottom line of the table.

Appendix 5

DERIVATION OF THE GENERAL EQUATION IN THE QUASI-POISSON PROCESS

(*see page* 36)

Given: the number of orders per period $\underline{A}$ is a draw from the discontinuous probability distribution (μ_A, σ_A).

The size of each individual order $\underline{B}$ is a draw from the probability distribution (considered continuous) (μ_B, σ_B).

The problem is to determine μ_C and σ_C of the probability distribution for the quantity required per period, indicated by $\underline{C}$.

Proof

For the probability distribution of A itself, we have

$$\mu_A = E(A) = \sum_0^\infty AP[\underline{A} = A] \qquad \Big| \qquad P(A) = P[\underline{A} = A]$$

$$E(\underline{A}^2) = \mu_{A^2} + \sigma_{A^2} = \sum_0^\infty A^2 P[\underline{A} = A] \Big|$$

Subject to the condition $P[\underline{A} = A] = 1$, the following would apply

$$\underline{C} = \underline{B} + \underline{B} + \ldots + \underline{B} \text{ (sum of } \underline{A} \text{ draws from } (\mu_B \sigma_B)$$
$$E(\underline{C}) = \mu_C = A\mu_B \text{ (expectation sum = sum of the expectations)}$$
$$\sigma_{C^2} = \sigma_{B^2} A \text{ (square law standard deviation)}$$

Therefore $E(\underline{C}^2) = \mu_{C^2} + \sigma_{C^2} = A\mu_B^2 + A\sigma_B^2$ since expectation of the sum = sum of the (provisional) expectations.

However, A itself is following probability distribution, thus

$$\mu_C = \sum_0^\infty P[\underline{A} = A] A\mu_B = \mu_B \sum_0^\infty AP[\underline{A} = A] = \mu_A \mu_B$$

$$E(\underline{C}^2) = \sum_0^\infty P[\underline{A} = A] (A^2\mu_{B^2} + A\sigma_{B^2}) = \mu_{B^2} \sum_0^\infty A^2 P[\underline{A} = A] + \sigma_{B^2} \sum_0^\infty AP[\underline{A} = A]$$

$$= \mu_{B}^2 (\mu_{A^2} + \sigma_{A^2}) + \sigma_{B^2} \mu_A = \mu_{C^2} + \sigma_{C^2}$$

Thus

$$\sigma_{C^2} = \mu_{B^2} \mu_{A^2} + \mu_{B^2} 0_{A^2} + \sigma_{B^2} \mu_A - \mu_{C^2} = \mu_A \sigma_{B^2} + \mu_{B^2} \sigma_{A^2}$$

Appendix 6

CALCULATION OF $f(e)$

A concise method of calculating the intermediate values of $f(e)$ is given here without proof.

1	2	3	4	5
e				$f(e)$
0	0·064	0·064	−9·296	30
1	0·144	0·208	−7·712	20·704
2	0·204	0·412	−5·468	12·992
3	0·219	0·631	−3·059	7·524
4	0·174	0·805	−1·145	4·465
5	0·111	0·916	0·076	3·320
6	0·056	0·972	0·692	3·396
7	0·021	0·993	0·923	4·088
8	0·006	0·999	0·989	5·011
9	0·001	1·000	1·000	6·000

Those values of e for which $f(e)$ is to be calculated are listed in column 1. It should be possible to calculate $f(e)$ direct for the highest and lowest values in this column (see above).

Column 2 lists the probabilities that $D_3 = e$, whilst in column 3 these probabilities are cumulated to represent the probability that $D_3 \leqslant e$.

In column 4 we have $(10 + 1) \times$ column 3 − 10.

The first value of column 5, $(f(0))$ is known, whilst the formula:
$f(e)$ = column 4 + column 5 (both of the previous line) applies to the other lines in this column.

The last result $(f(9) = 6·000)$ is a check on errors of arithmetic.

Appendix 7

TABLE OF ITERATIONS

e	$V(e)$	iteration 1 $W(e)$	$V(e)$	iteration 2 $W(e)$	$V(e)$	iteration 59 $W(e)$	$V(e)$	iteration 60 $W(e)$	$V(e)$
−10	0·000	130·000	100·000	230·000	100·000	230·000	100·000	230·000	100·000
− 9	0·000	120·000	100·000	220·000	100·000	220·000	100·000	220·000	100·000
− 8	0·000	110·000	100·000	210·000	100·000	210·000	100·000	210·000	100·000
− 7	0·000	100·000	*96·680	198·672	100·000	200·000	100·000	200·000	100·000
− 6	0·000	90·000	86·680	183·676	100·000	190·000	100·000	190·000	100·000
− 5	0·000	80·000	76·680	166·012	100·000	180·000	100·000	180·000	100·000
− 4	0·000	70·000	66·680	146·680	100·000	170·000	100·000	170·000	100·000
− 3	0·000	60·000	56·680	126·680	100·000	160·000	100·000	160·000	100·000
− 2	0·000	50·000	46·680	106·680	100·000	150·000	100·000	150·000	100·000
− 1	0·000	40·000	36·680	86·680	*82·604	140·000	100·000	140·000	100·000
0	0·000	30·000	26·680	66·680	62·604	130·000	100·000	130·000	100·000
1	0·000	20·704	17·384	47·666	43·590	120·704	100·000	120·704	100·000
2	0·000	12·992	9·672	31·080	27·004	112·088	*97·731	112·085	*97·708
3	0·000	7·524	4·204	18·252	14·176	101·838	87·481	101·836	87·460
4	0·000	4·465	1·145	9·857	5·781	90·844	76·488	90·851	76·474
5	0·000	3·320	*0·000	5·471	1·396	79·616	65·260	79·640	65·263
6	0·000	3·396	0·076	4·076	*0·000	68·717	54·360	68·764	54·387
7	0·000	4·088	0·768	4·532	0·457	58·804	44·447	58·875	44·499
8	0·000	5·011	1·691	5·933	1·857	49·842	35·485	49·937	35·561
9	0·000	6·000	2·680	7·740	3·665	41·860	27·504	41·973	27·596
10	0·000	7·000	3·680	9·691	5·615	34·883	20·526	35·003	20·627
11	0·000	8·000	4·680	11·681	7·605	28·910	14·553	29·028	14·652
12	0·000	9·000	5·680	13·680	9·604	23·953	9·596	24·060	9·684
13	0·000	10·000	6·680	15·680	11·604	20·018	5·661	20·106	5·730
14	0·000	11·000	7·680	17·680	13·604	17·108	2·752	17·173	2·797
15	0·000	12·000	8·680	19·680	15·604	15·223	0·866	15·264	0·887
16	0·000	13·000	9·680	21·680	17·604	14·357	*0·000	14·376	*0·000
17	0·000	14·000	10·680	23·680	19·604	14·502	0·145	14·507	0·130
18	0·000	15·000	11·680	25·680	21·604	15·649	1·293	15·647	1·271
19	0·000	16·000	12·680	27·680	23·604	17·789	3·432	17·790	3·413
20	0·000	17·000	13·680	29·680	25·604	20·911	6·554	20·924	6·548

Appendix 8

Optimum batch, with due regard to risk of obsolescence

A. R. W. Muyen gives the following derivation.
Let:

Q = lot size in units;
F = ordering costs per lot;
D = annual usage in units;
K = purchase price per unit;
δK = inventory (carrying) costs per unit per year;
β = average number of modifications per year.

Also suppose that:

a. the variability of demand is negligible;
b. the lead time is constant; in other words the inventory level is the same whenever a replenishment lot arrives;
c. modifications are equally probable in every time interval Δt;
d. whenever a modification occurs all the items in stock at once become wholly unusable.

The expected costs per year can be calculated as the quotient of expected costs per batch and expected period of usage per batch, that is

$$C = \frac{C_Q}{t_Q}$$

Since the probability of modification is the same in every time interval Δt, namely $\beta \Delta t$, the time t from the arrival of a batch to the next modification follows a negative exponential distribution. The probability that this interval will be between t and $t + dt$ is

$$f(t)\, dt = \beta e^{-\beta t}\, dt$$

The time required to consume the entire batch Q is

$$t_0 = \frac{Q}{D}$$

Immediately after the arrival of a replenishment batch there are two possible courses of events: the entire batch may be steadily consumed without interruption $(t > t_0)$ or a modification introduced at some point during the consumption of the batch may render the remainder of the stock unuseable $(t < t_0)$.

Batch used up without modification $(t > t_0)$

The time interval for usage of the batch is $t_0 = Q/D$.

The average stock is $Q/2$. Hence the inventory costs of the batch are

$$\frac{Q}{D} \times \frac{Q}{2} \times \delta K = \frac{Q^2}{2D} \times \delta K$$

Because the ordering costs are F, the overall costs, designated C_0, amount to

$$C_0 = \frac{Q^2}{2D} \times \delta K + F$$

Batch subject to modification $(t \geqslant t_0)$

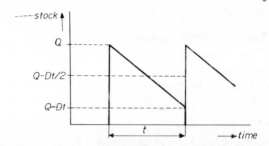

Fig. 101 The stock variation where a modification is introduced after time t.

The time until the modification is t; that is the usage period of the batch. The
stock falls from Q to $Q - Dt$ whereupon it becomes entirely valueless.

The average stock is $Q - Dt/2$. Therefore the inventory costs of the batch are

$$t\left(Q - \frac{Dt}{2}\right)\delta K$$

Added to this are the ordering costs F and the costs of obsolescent stock,
amounting to $(Q - Dt)K$.

Thus the total costs C_t become

$$C_t = QK + tK(\delta Q - D) - \tfrac{1}{2}t^2 \delta QD + F$$

Expected costs per year

To determine C_Q and t_Q we integrate the expressions found in t with respect to
t with weight $f(t)$.

The expected costs per batch are

$$C_Q = \int_0^{t_0} C_t f(t) \, dt + C_0 \int_{t_0}^{\infty} f(t) \, dt$$

The expected period of usage in years per batch is

$$t_Q = \int_0^{t_0} t f(t) \, dt + t_0 \int_{t_0}^{\infty} f(t) \, dt$$

Therefore the expected costs per year are

$$C = \frac{C_Q}{t_Q}$$

Elaboration and substitution of mD/β for Q gives

$$C = \frac{\beta^2 F + KD(e^{-m} - 1 + m)(\delta + \beta)}{\beta(1 - e^{-m})}$$

Quantity m is introduced to simplify the formula and in fact represents the average number of modifications within a time interval t_0.

Optimum lot size

To determine the optimum lot size Q^* let

$$\frac{dC}{dQ} = 0$$

However, we may also write

$$\frac{dC}{dQ} = \frac{dC}{dm} \times \frac{dm}{dQ} = \frac{\beta}{D} \times \frac{dC}{dm}$$

so that there evidently also applies $dC/dm = 0$.
   Finally, from $dC/dm = 0$ we have

$$e^m - 1 - m = \frac{\beta^2 F}{KD(\delta + \beta)}$$

whilst $Q = mD/\beta$.
   From this m^* and Q^* can be determined. A multi-stage method is most convenient for calculating Q^* from the derived formula in practice.
   To find a first approximation of m', substitute $1 + m + \frac{1}{2}m^2$ for e^m.

Thence it follows that

$$m' = \sqrt{\left[\frac{2\beta^2 F}{(\delta + \beta)KD}\right]}$$

Then let $m^* = \lambda m'$.

The specified method of calculation thus becomes

1st step.   Calculate $Q' = \sqrt{\left[\frac{2FD}{(\delta + \beta)K}\right]}$

and $m' = \dfrac{\beta Q}{D}$

This is a first approximation of Q^*.

2nd step.   Read λ from Fig. 102.

This chart shows the relationship between m' and λ.

$$e^{\lambda m'} = 1 + \lambda m' + \tfrac{1}{2}(m')^2$$

3rd step.   Calculate Q^* from $Q^* = \lambda Q'$.

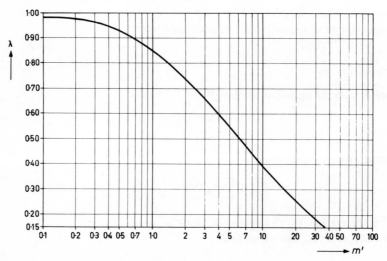

Fig. 102.

Bibliography

page

Ac 1 ACKOFF, R. L., *Production and inventory control in a chemical process,* Operations Research, August 1955.   152

Ac 2 ACKOFF, R. L., and SASIENI, M. W., *Fundamentals of operations research*, Wiley, 1968.

Bl 1 BLUCK, P. M., SMITH, P. G. and THACKRAY, G., *Production planning and inventory control on a chemical plant*, O.R. Quarterly, **11**, No. 4.   152

Bo 1 BOOTHROYD, H. and TOMLINSON, R. C., *The stock control of engineering spares,* Operational Research Quarterly.   284

Bo 2 BORGNANA, R., *Het A.B.C.-voorraadbeheer*, internal report, N.V. Philips' Gloeilampenfabrieken, October 1968.   237

Bo 3 BOSCH, H., *Optimaal voorraadniveau van reserve-onderdelen* (Optimum re-order level of spare parts), Sigma, **7** (1961), No. 1, p. 9.   35, 284, 290

Br 1 BROWN, R. G., *Smoothing, forecasting and prediction of discrete time series*, Prentice-Hall, Englewood Cliffs (N.Y.), 1963.   18, 212, 317

Br 2 BROWN, R. G., *Statistical forecasting for inventory control*, McGraw-Hill, 1959.   39, 48, 236, 294

Bu 1 BURBIDGE, J. L., *The principles of production control*, MacDonald & Evans, London, 1962.   5

Ca 1 CAMP, W. E., *Determining the production order quantity*, Management Engineering, **2**, No. 1.   203

Cl 1 CLARK, A. J. and SCARF, H., *Optimal policies for a multi-echelon inventory problem.* Management Science, **6** (1960), pp. 475–490.   219

Cl 2 CLARK, W., *De Gantt-kaart*, Stenfert Kroese, 1952.   324

Co 1 COX, D. R. and SMITH, W. L., *The superposition of several strictly periodic sequences of events*, Biometrika, **40**, 1 June 1953, pp. 1–11.   36

Do 1 DOBBEN DE BRUIJN, C. S. VAN and MUIJEN, A. R. W., *The effect of information delays in a production control system*, International Journal of Production Research, **3** (1964), No. 3, p. 167.   263

Ei 1 EILON, S., *Dragons in pursuit of the EBQ*, Operational Research Quarterly, **15** (1964), No. 4.   95

Fo 1 FORRESTER, J. W., *Industrial Dynamics*, Wiley, 1961.   18

Fr 1 FRASER, D. J. and VAN WINKEL, E. G. F., *Tijdreeksvoorspellingen en hun bewaking*, Samsom, 1970.   64

Ga 1 GALLIHER, H. P., MORSE, P. M. and SIMOND, M., *Dynamics of two classes of continuous inventory systems*, Operations Research, **7**, p. 362.   203

Ge 1 GEISLER, M. A. and KARR, H. W., *The design of military supply tables for spare parts*, Operations Research, **4** (1956), No. 4, p. 431.   289

Go 1 GOUDRIAAN, J., *Statistische bepaling van de veiligheidstoeslag in het bestelniveau* (Statistical determination of the safety margin in the re-order level), T.E.D., **32** (1962), No. 8.   34, 35, 154

Mo 1   MORONEY, M. J. Facts from figures. Penguin, 1953.
Mo 2   MOONEN, H. J. M., *Het bepalen van bestelniveaus wanneer afname en levertijd gamma-verdeeld resp. normaal-verdeeld zijn* (The determination of re-order levels when the demand and the lead time follow gamma and normal distributions respectively), Statistica Neerlandica, **16**, No. 1, pp. 113–120.   177
Mu 1   MUIJEN, A. R. W., *De 20-80 regel verklaard*, Doelmatig Bedrijfsbeheer, **13** (1961), No. 8, p. 315.   46
Mu 2   MUIJEN, A. R. W., *Optimum lot size policy if tools break down frequently*, Proc. 2nd Intern. Conf., Aix en Provence, 1960.   117

Ol 1   OLDENDORFF, A., Samenwerking in het bedrijf. Utrecht, Bijleveld, 1966.   334

Pe 1   PETERSEN, J. W. and GEISLER, M. A., *The costs of alternative air base stocking and requisitioning policies*, TDCK OR179.   287
Pr 1   PRINS, G., *Voorraadbeheersing*, Stenfert Kroese, 1966.   349
Pr 2   PRINS, H. J., *Transformations for finding probabilities and variate values of a distribution function in tables of a related distribution function*, Statistica Neerlandica, **14** (1960), No. 1, pp. 1–18.   31

Ra 1   RAYMOND, F. E., *Quality and economy in manufacture*, McGraw-Hill, New York, 1931.   110
Ri 1   RIVETT, P., *Measurement and integrated systems – the main areas for O.R. development*, O.R. Quarterly, **15** (1964), No. 1, p. 4.   347

Sc 1   VAN DER SCHROEF, H. J., *Kosten en kostprijs* (Cost and cost price), Amsterdam, 1963.   83
Se 1   SEEBACH, G., *Langfristige Lieferverträge in der Industrie*, Diss, Nuremburg, 1963.   140
Sh 1   SHANTY, J. A. and VAN COURT HAVE, JR., *An airline provisioning problem*, Management Technology, December 1960.   288
Si 1   SIMPSON, K. F., *A theory of allocation of stocks to warehouses*, Operations Research, 8 (1960), pp. 797–805.   206
Si 2   SIMPSON, K. F., *In process inventories*, Operations Research, 7 (1959), pp. 863–873.   220
St 1   STARR, M. K. and MILLER, D. W., *Inventory Control Theory and Practice*, Prentice-Hall, 1962.   133, 136, 235

To 1   TOCHER, K. D., *The Art of Simulation*, London, 1963.   349
To 2   TORN, R. VAN DER, *Planning*, De Haan, 1953.   346

Ve 1   VEEN, B. VAN DER, *Introduction to the theory of operational research*, Philips Technical Library, 1967.   49
Ve 2   VERBURG, P., *Enige aspecten van de organisatie van de vernieuwing*, Stenfert Kroese, 1966.   16
Ve 3   VERBURG, P., *Organiseren en Organisatieonderzoek*, Stenfert Kroese, Leiden, 1959.   334

Wa 1   WALLIS, W. A., and ROBERTS, H. V., *Statistics as a new approach*, Free Press, New York. 1956.   241
Wi 1   WINTERS, P. R., *Multiple triggers and lot sizes*, Operations Research, 9 (1961), pp. 621–634.

SOME OTHER BOOKS ON PRODUCTION AND INVENTORY CONTROL

ARROW, K. J., KARLIN, S. and SCARF, H., *Studies in the mathematical theory of inventory and production*, Stanford, California, Standford University Press, 1958.

BATTERSBY, A., *A guide to stock control*, Pitman, 1962.

BROWN, R. G., *Decision rules for inventory management*, Holt, Rinehard Winston, 1967.

BUCHAN, J. and KOENIGSBERG, E., *Scientific inventory management*, Prentice-Hall, 1963.

BURBIDGE, J. L., *The principles of production control*, McDonald & Evans, London, 1962.

DALLECK, W. C. and FETTER, R. B., *Decision models for inventory management*, Irwin, 1961.

EILON, S., *Elements of production planning and control*, Macmillan, 1962.

ELMAGHRABY, S. E., *The design of production systems*, Reinhold, 1966.

GREEN, J. H. (editor), *Production and inventory control handbook*. Prepared under the supervision of the Handbook Editorial Board of APICS. McGraw-Hill, New York, 1970.

HADLEY, G. and WITHIN, T. M., *Analysis of inventory systems*, Prentice-Hall, 1963.

HANNSMAN, F., *Operations research in production planning and inventory control*, Wiley, 1962.

I.C.I. Monograph nr. 4, editor A. J. H. MORRELL, *Problems of stocks and storage*, 1967.

MAGEE, J. F., *Production planning and inventory control*, McGraw-Hill, 1958.

MAGEE, J. F., *Physical distribution systems*, McGraw-Hill, 1967.

MÉLÈSE, J., *La pratique de la recherche operationelle*, Dunod, 1967.

NADDOR, E., *Inventory systems*, Wiley, 1966.

NILAND, P., *Production planning, scheduling and inventory control*, Macmillan, London, 1970.

PRINS, G., *Voorraadbeheersing*, Stenfert Kroese, 1966.

SCARF, H. E. e.al., *Multistage inventory models and techniques*, Stanford University Press, 1963.

STARR, M. K. and MILLER, D. W., *Inventory control, theory and practice*, Prentice-Hall, 1962.

VAN HAM, C. J. (editor), *Planning en besturing in de praktijk,* Markareeks nr 98, 1969.

WAGNER, H. M., *Statistical management of inventory systems*, New York, Wiley, 1962.

WHITIN, T. M., *The theory of inventory management*, rev. ed., Princeton, N.J., Princeton University Press, 1957.

Index